The
Lottery Lie

Gamblers, Money and Hungry Kids

by Ivan L. Zabilka, Ph.D.

THE LOTTERY LIE: Gamblers, Money and Hungry Kids

Bristol House, Ltd.
P.O. Box 4020
Anderson, Indiana 46013-0020
Phone: 765-644-0856
Fax: 765-622-1045

To order call: 1-800-451-READ (7323)

Table of Contents

Editor's Note

The term "mob" is lowercase in this book because it is used as a generic shorthand term to refer to all types of organized crime. The uppercase version of "Mob" is, in the minds of many people, identified with organized crime from one specific ethnic group. However, organized crime involves individuals from a variety of backgrounds and national origins.

Preface

My motivation for writing this book is very personal. In 1987 I sought to end a nineteen-year career in university administration. The most attractive offer was a middle school mathematics position in Lexington, Kentucky. With trepidation I made the radical career change, searched for extra energy and waded into teaching the "transescent" child (*transescent* is educational jargon to describe a child making the transition through preadolescence to adolescence). During my second year of teaching, Kentucky adopted a lottery amendment.

I had not thought much about lotteries. Missouri had adopted a lottery while I lived there, but it had not affected me directly. I noticed that only a few Baptists fought the lottery vigorously, and I remained indifferent. In Kentucky, however, I taught in a school with a large percentage of economically disadvantaged children. I loved my kids, who wormed their way into my heart. I often became frustrated with my kids' laziness, their lack of foresight and their irresponsible behavior, but I nevertheless loved them, and some of them responded.

Then the lottery came. During the first week of ticket sales, the newspapers were full of stories as the poor state of Kentucky nearly matched Pennsylvania's record first week. Millions of dollars were spent on tickets, enough to build a great school system. There were other stories as well. Northside Lexington stores reported a 17% drop in grocery sales, a decline which eventually leveled off at about a 2% loss. At school I noticed kids falling asleep during the second and third hour of the day. I saw kids break into clammy sweats, totally exhausted after physical education classes. Upon inquiry I found they had eaten nothing since the previous day's school lunch because there was no food at home. The money had been spent on the lottery. For one of the few times in my life I felt outrage. Perhaps there are more significant and complex social and moral issues than the lottery, but I was angry with parents who would let their children go hungry to try for an impossible dream. I was angry with legislators who accepted the lottery as easy revenue without taxes. I was angry with the governor who rode the issue into office, voters who unknowingly voted for the lottery and indifferent Christians who voted against it but didn't do anything else. I was angry because my kids were being hurt.

I am proud of those who picket and peacefully protest the social injustice that gambling represents. In a desire to join their campaign, this book represents my letter to every legislator, my sign in every rally, my crusade against the waste and corruption that permeates gambling and my appeal to the latent moral sense in our society. The cry of "something for nothing" is not in tune with the dignity of whatever vocation to which God has called us. While I have attempted to coolly and dispassionately present facts and historical analysis, my desire to end the foolishness that hurts the children of the poor burns passionately on every page.

In the late nineteenth century, Chief Justice Waite of the U. S. Supreme Court said lotteries prey upon the hard earnings of the poor, and plunder the ignorant and simple. Two centuries earlier, in 1699, the ministers of Boston called the lotteries a cheat and the managers of them "pillagers of the people." More than twenty centuries earlier than that, the writer of Ecclesiastes called greed a "striving after the wind." The truth of these statements has never been more clear than during the current mania to win money by gambling.

I lovingly dedicate this book to three people who give rather than take. One served as controller for the non-profit Appalachian Regional Healthcare System, another as a thirty-year public school teacher. In addition, they have provided food to Eastern Kentucky orphanages, dug wells in Haiti and given freely in time and money to numerous humanitarian and church efforts to alleviate suffering. It is an honor to have them as my sister and brother-in-law, Doris and Robert Hager. The third person serves at Cardinal Hill Rehabilitation Hospital in Lexington, Kentucky, after a career of missionary service to the people of Italy. Carol is precious, adorable, loving and godly. I am privileged to be married to her.

Ivan L. Zabilka, Ph.D.
Wilmore, Kentucky
January, 1998

Note to Those Who Teach from This Book

This book has ten chapters, but can lend itself to a thirteen-week quarterly study if extra time is devoted to chapters five, six and ten. The questions at the end of each chapter are intended to provoke thought, highlight important issues and promote study beyond this book. Selected chapters may be used for shorter studies. The footnotes open the door to extensive resources on the history, literature and impact of gambling. Most of the citations are available in college libraries. The intention of the author and the editors is that you have the means to understand and take action concerning this social and moral problem.

Chapter 1

The Mania for Money

During his adult life George Washington, the first president of the United States, meticulously kept a diary of his wins and losses at cards, raffles and lotteries. The diary shows Washington to be a loser at gambling but does not tell us who the winners were. Then as now the real winners at gambling are seldom known to the public.

The people who get rich from gambling are seldom in the papers. Most Americans believe that the winners are the ones with the right numbers. That is only partly true. This book is intended to untangle the web of deceit surrounding gambling and to reveal those gambling entrepreneurs who destroy their state and country, socially and economically, because of greed.

Gambling is a social illness and an economic disaster—it burdens the states with social services costs and depresses their economies in the same manner that increased taxes do. Gambling is morally reprehensible and calls for opponents who are not afraid to say so. In October 1966 the editors of *The Nation* soberly quoted Anthony Scaduto, who said lotteries are "a plague invented by despots to silence the people."[1]

Most Americans gamble. In the late twentieth century, gambling has become so common that most people assume it is part of human nature, not a learned behavior. For thirty years gambling proponents have claimed that ". . . the urge to gamble is deepseated and irrepressible."[2] Felicia F. Campbell, a former University of Nevada psychologist (most of whose salary was paid by state revenue derived from gambling), conveniently labeled it a "fundamental human activity."[3] Others have called gambling an instinct.[4] Such statements imply that gambling is as important a need as food, shelter and sex—an idea that is obviously false to anyone not blinded by the temporary excitement of gambling. Quite simply, gambling is the payment of money without receiving goods, services or aesthetic value. The winner wins directly at the expense of the loser, whose risk was avoidable. Giving away one's resources does not appear to be a natural instinct, for anthropologist A. L. Kroeber found many non-gambling cultures in isolated areas.[5]

While many Americans reject the extreme view that gambling is fundamental to human existence, most think it is normal. A quarter century ago a writer in *The Economist* said, "If gambling can gradually come to seem so innocuous, the chances are good that it will spread far and wide."[6] Polls demonstrate that public approval of lotteries grew from 48% in 1964 to 72% in 1982.[7] At present, nine of every ten Americans gamble at least occasionally. More than one-third gamble weekly. With regard to lotteries, men and women gamble about equally in numbers. With other forms of gambling, except bingo, men predominate. However, simply because the overwhelming majority participates does not make gambling ethical, just or moral.

Americans are not unique in succumbing to gambling fever. Nearly every major government around the world has a national lottery, usually to augment general revenue. One hundred thirty-five nations allow some form of gambling. In an effort to convince the public to play, more than two-thirds of the countries do not tax winnings. The United States does tax winnings; nevertheless, some of the state lotteries are larger than those of other nations. Some of the largest prizes are offered by the Christmas lottery in Spain, which has been operating since 1763. Australia seems to have the highest percentage of regular gamblers. In the 1930s the former USSR used lotteries to repair and build roads. Iceland supported its university, Sweden its hospitals and cultural events and Turkey the air force with proceeds from gambling. All these countries are filling the public coffers by exploiting the desire to escape poverty.

How serious is gambling in other nations? In 1982 Spaniards spent $9 billion on legal gambling, more than on education, science, defense and public works combined.[8] A 1986 estimate pegged the spending by Spaniards at 15% of their available income, the most of any nation in the world. The amount spent on slot machines alone in a single year equalled the national deficit.[9] This outpaced the Japanese, who had spent $30 billion on both legal and illegal gambling in 1976, more than 7% of their gross national product.[10]

The current generation is also not unique in its taste for gambling. The equivalents of dice have been with us almost since the dawn of recorded history, for they were used in ancient Egypt, Assyria, Greece and Rome. In ancient mythology Mercury "played at tables" to win a share of the Moon's light.[11] Drawing lots has been a common form of decision-making for millennia, as mentioned in passages in both the Old and New Testaments of the Bible. The Roman emperors Nero and Claudius appear to have been pathological gamblers.

Organized lotteries have been with us for over 400 years. Although commodity lotteries had been held on a small scale previously, the first money lottery was held in Florence, Italy in 1530.[12] Francis I of France established a government lottery in 1539. England established a lottery in 1567, but tickets sold very slowly, and the drawing was not held until 1569.[13] The Irish Hospital Sweepstakes was founded in 1750.

Nothing historically, however, has ever matched the magnitude of today's availability and scale of gambling. Lotteries seem to give the poor their only hope for achieving the American dream of going from rags to riches. Meanwhile, casinos lure the middle and upper classes. The media frequently use a variety of psycho-medical metaphors to describe gambling: mania, fever, plague, epidemic, compulsion, spree, obsession. These names seem to fit a society in which betting is organized around events such as the precise moment when the ice will break on Alaska's Tanana River at the village of Nenana.[14] The metaphors seem even more appropriate when we realize that gambling fever is acquired, and for nearly one out of twenty persons it can become pathological.

Have Americans Always Gambled?

Gambling has appealed to Americans since the beginning of our colonial history. Those who came here in colonial times were risk-takers who were comfortable with gambling as a form of risk-taking. The British government authorized a lottery in 1612 to assist the Virginia Company in its efforts to send relief to the first settlement at Jamestown.[15]

Lotteries were fairly common in the early colonial and federal periods of American history. Each colony participated at one time or another, although lotteries were excluded from Pennsylvania in 1682 along with other vices.[16] Roads and bridges were scarce and occasionally financed by lottery. George Washington ran a lottery to finance the Mountain (Cumberland) Road in 1768. Ben Franklin promoted a lottery to finance a battery of cannon to protect Philadelphia. John Hancock was a prime mover in a lottery that was used to rebuild Faneuil Hall. A handful of churches were built by subscription, which frequently involved a prize as well, although the churches also provided the opposition, especially among the Societies of Friends. Buildings at some of the early colleges such as King's College (now Columbia University), Harvard, Yale, Princeton, Dartmouth, Brown, Transylvania (the first college west of the mountains in Kentucky) and William and Mary were built by subscriptions that involved prizes.[17] The University of Pennsylvania used a lottery to underwrite part of its operating budget.

In 1776 the First Continental Congress tried to raise $1 million by means of a lottery to finance the Army. It was unsuccessful. After independence, the Congress attempted to use a lottery to help finance the new capitol. George Washington bought the first ticket, but this lottery was also only marginally successful. In 1792 Connecticut sought to raise funds for its statehouse with a lottery. Only $1,450 resulted.[18] With only occasional exceptions most lotteries were small and private, frequently unsuccessful and occasionally crooked. One Plymouth, Massachusetts, lottery netted only $9,876 for the city while promoters and winners received $886,439.[19]

During the nineteenth century, with the growth of cities, lotteries proliferated. Cities sought to expand their trade regions by sponsoring lotteries to build roads and canals. This was an age that resisted taxation, and the lotteries were supposed to avoid taxes. From 1790 to 1860, twenty-four of the thirty-three states sponsored lotteries.[20] Worthy causes rapidly disappeared and profit became the main motive. By 1825 the lottery enterprises took in several times the entire federal budget.[21] In the 1820s and 1830s there were dozens of lotteries in each major city—Boston, New York and Philadelphia—the latter having over 200 lottery offices by the year 1833 (up from three in 1809). New York City had 168 brokers selling tickets.[22] In 1832 at least 420 lotteries were drawn in eight states, taking in over $66 million.[23]

These lotteries were not only numerous, they were dishonest. The treasurer of Rhode Island reported in 1830 that the state had received only $43,000 in taxes from $4 million in authorized lotteries, or about 1%. Prizes were not paid, or they were paid to relatives of the promoters. There were so many other forms of deceit and corruption that lotteries soon fell into disrepute. In 1833 Massachusetts and New York and in 1834 Pennsylvania abolished lotteries. By 1840 nine more states banned them, and by 1862 only Kentucky and Missouri still had operating lotteries, even though Missouri had banned lotteries by statute in 1842.[24] The trend of legal restrictions culminated in federal legislation in 1872 that authorized the Postmaster General, upon collection of sufficient evidence, to deny delivery of mail and money orders to "fraudulent" lotteries.[25]

The next development in America's lottery history came on August 11, 1868, with the acquisition (by means of over $200,000 in bribes, according to a Louisiana Supreme Court Case, C. C. Antoine *v.* D. D. Smith, *et al.*) of an exclusive license to conduct a lottery in Louisiana for 25 years beginning January 1, 1869.[26] The lottery was exempt from taxes. Promoters were soon selling tickets nationwide. With the demise of the Kentucky Lottery in 1878 and a short-lived Georgia Lottery shortly after, the Louisiana Lottery had the field to itself. Eventually as much as $28 million per year flowed to Louisiana for the monthly lottery, with up to $22 million more spent locally on the daily lottery, with only $40,000 per year going to charity.[27] The promoters kept nearly half the money and made $5 million to $6 million a year after expenses and bribes.[28] The promoters used their profits to buy sugar refineries, banks, cotton presses, newspapers and land, further extending their control over the state. This placed hundreds of jobs at their disposal, which they made available to those recommended by favorable legislators.[29]

Bribes were openly exchanged, and the lottery became more powerful than the legislative and judicial branches of the government. There were literally hundreds of vendors in New Orleans, with most taking their pay in tickets which were worthless. Destitution was rampant, with the result that citizens finally mounted a campaign to rid their state of the lottery. In 1885 the directors tripped over their own arrogance and sued a Philadelphia publisher for libel when he visited the New Orleans exposition. The directors assumed a quick conviction in their bribed courts, but local lawyers volunteered their services, and national outrage was stirred.[30] The publisher was acquitted. The fight to rid the nation of lotteries took several years, but on September 18, 1890, the federal legislation of 1872 was extended to all lotteries, not just fraudulent ones, and to all mail carrying information, tickets or prizes, including newspapers that carried lottery advertisements.[31]

Realizing that pressure was mounting against the lottery, the owners applied for a new charter in 1890, three years early. While nearly two-thirds of the legislature initially opposed the measure, by the time the vote was taken two-thirds in both houses of the legislature voted for the measure. The governor vetoed the bill, but it was passed by the lower house, failed by one vote in the upper house but was approved by the Supreme Court after the records had been adjusted by the senate leaders after adjournment. The lottery promised first $500,000 annually to the state, then $1 million and finally $1.25 million to accomplish passage.[32] The blatant purchase of the charter led to a voter rebellion. In 1892, the citizens of Louisiana—through a newly elected legislature—closed down the lottery.

After the turn of the century the outlawed lotteries were replaced by numbers games, which began in Harlem around 1900.[33] These could be as simple as a board with the numbers from one to a hundred, or a sheet with numbers from 000 to 999. The proprietor picked the winning number, supposedly randomly, and winning numbers were supposed to be chosen before the purchases. In reality, however, numbers were often selected after the fact so that the number requiring the smallest pay-off could be chosen. The potential for corruption was great, but the possibility of winning on the basis of a small bet attracted an increasing number of bettors. Later the pay-off number was tied to stock market sales numbers, Cincinnati Bank Clearing House numbers or pari-mutuel betting totals. While these methods reduced cheating somewhat, the main winners remained the operators, who pocketed between 40% and 60% of the gross.[34]

With the 1920s came an explosion in crime. While the FBI made its splash by chasing bank robbers and kidnappers, the real growth in the crime rate came from bootlegging, and then gambling. As soon as one branch of crime was organized, it was natural to move on to others: prostitution, drugs and gambling. One example was "Dutch Schultz" who after organizing bootlegging in New York moved into the numbers racket in 1930. Thirty murders were committed in the numbers organizational process.[35] With the repeal of prohibition in 1933, the mobs had an extra incentive to develop their organization of other forms of crime. In 1933 alone, the Post

Office Department stopped mail on 1,500 different illegal lottery operations.[36] During the Depression gambling was used by state and city governments (pari-mutuel betting), churches (bingo) and the mobs (numbers) to raise money. The numbers racket, nicknamed in the cities "the black man's stock market," "policy," "clearing house" and "the bug," and in the country "butter and eggs," increased many times over. Law enforcement was half-hearted at best, and small bribes were usually sufficient to keep the law off small-time gamblers. Many policemen considered gambling harmless compared to other types of crime. However, the sheer volume of money flowing into the wrong hands meant gambling was far from harmless. One estimate reported the gross income from all gambling as being from $4 to $6 billion per year.[37] By 1937, an estimated $300 million ($1 million a day) was being taken by the numbers racket alone.[38] Much of the money for the tracks that supported legalized pari-mutuel gambling came from former bootleggers and racketeers who "reformed" and "went legitimate." The rise of pari-mutuel betting in turn created a larger market for the illegal action with bookies.[39] During the ensuing decades, gambling revenues have been the most stable and least risky source of income for organized crime.

Various branches of government sought to use lotteries during the Depression to raise money. In 1934 the governor of Puerto Rico initiated a lottery to pay health costs.[40] Many efforts were made to circumvent the laws. Among the most interesting was a proposal in New York City put forth by James J. Lyons, borough president of the Bronx. He suggested the formation of a Municipal Supplemental Relief Association. Anyone could join for $2.50. Officers of the association were to be selected by "jury wheel" (a revolving circular box from which names can be drawn by chance, used for selecting jurors) with a $25,000 president, 25 vice presidents and 77 lesser officers at proportional salaries. The proposal was supposed to bring $12 million into the city's relief effort.[41] The plan was not approved.

In addition to the numbers racket, a variety of exotic ethnic lotteries existed among the Cubans, Puerto Ricans and Chinese. Before the legalization of lotteries in 1964, however, the biggest illegal lottery was the Irish Sweepstakes. The sweeps were popular because they had the only six figure pay-out at the time, giving away as many as fifteen $150,000 prizes per year.[42] The sweeps were fascinating because only a small percentage went to the Irish hospitals (the ostensible beneficiary received 25% in 1957, and less in later years) and a relatively small percentage went into prizes, 55% or less. Twenty percent or more of the money went to the promoters.[43] The U. S. was always the biggest market, with over four times as many tickets sold in New York City as in Dublin. By 1934 that had grown to over $16 million from New York City alone per year.[44] A huge smuggling operation was organized by the mob, and in their usual fashion over half the tickets sold in the U. S. were fraudulent. In an incredible denial of the truth, American teenagers reading *Senior Scholastic* were soberly informed that "the famous Irish Sweepstakes has been run for many years without corruption."[45] In 1973 an investigation exposed the massive wealth acquired by the promoters while less than 10% of the gross reached the hospitals.[46]

At the same time, racetrack betting rapidly increased. Bookie betting became many times larger than the numbers racket. Numerous races were rigged to aid the bookies in the payoff, although with the advent of modern communications, the mob prefers an honest race with nationwide balancing of bets. The fix is now primarily a local phenomenon. In 1954 Paul A. Fino, U. S. Representative from New York and long-time advocate of a national lottery, claimed that $30 billion a year was spent on gambling and that 57% of Americans gambled, most illegally.[47] A 1957 report of the Massachusetts Special Crime Commission found that $2 billion was being spent in that state alone on legal and illegal gambling. Gambling was by far the most widespread form of organized crime, frequently bankrolling other forms such as prostitution, narcotics and fencing of stolen property. By 1962, just before the legalization of lotteries, thirteen million customers were betting a billion dollars at New York racetracks alone. A very conservative estimate, first circulated in 1963 but still being cited in 1973, was $50 billion spent on gambling, with somewhere between $29 billion and $39 billion of that illegal.[48] This was more than the amount spent on national defense, or on groceries, was twice medical costs and more than charity and education combined.[49] Judge George Edwards of the U. S. Court of Appeals stated that ". . . the dominant force in organized crime and organized gambling in America is the Mafia." The mob was thought to have a profit nearly equal to that of the 100 largest corporations in America combined.[50]

Lotteries Fan the Fire

Overwhelming as the gambling problem might have seemed in 1963, worse was to come. At this time few had any concept of the social consequences of such massive spending on gambling.

The drain on the national economy was not clear, and no association was made between the increase in gambling and the recession of 1957 or the economic malaise of the 1960s. The latter was uniformly laid at the feet of the Viet Nam War by the war's opponents, without regard to other factors.

Gambling took a new direction in 1963 when New Hampshire authorized the first lottery since 1892. Only a portion of the clergy fought the lottery vigorously. Its proponents promoted the lottery by suggesting the profits be directed to education in New Hampshire—the first of many attempts to justify gambling in the name of "a good cause." The lottery was touted as harmless entertainment that only the prudish opposed. Only nine towns voted against the lottery, while 300 supported it.[51] There was much emphasis on a clean, honest lottery, demonstrated by the state's hiring an ex-FBI agent to run it, although the governor suggested at the public signing of the bill that residents of other states could circumvent the laws of their states to buy tickets.[52]

The New Hampshire lottery was complicated. Ticket purchasers drew numbers of horses entered in the Rockingham Park spring and fall meets. The payoff came only twice a year. If a horse scratched, all those holding that number were automatic losers. Holding the number of a winning horse was not enough to win a prize. Winning numbers were merely entered into a drawing for the prizes. With all these complications, and the six-month delay in gratification, only $5.7 million worth of tickets sold the first year, and less in the years that followed.

The lottery became more controversial after its passage than before. The original legislation did not specify whether the state's lottery receipts were to add to or to replace existing funds, releasing money for the legislature to spend elsewhere. The legislators wished to avoid passing sales or income taxes, so they interpreted the legislation to create replacement money, not additional money, for education. This maintained the New Hampshire tradition of taxing "sin," i.e., beer, cigarettes, state-owned liquor stores and tracks, but not income or sales. Property taxes continued to rise as the lottery failed to solve the recurring shortfall in revenues for the schools. While many New Hampshire residents felt betrayed, they were unable to organize sufficiently to remove the offending legislators or pressure hard enough for repeal of the lottery. The repeal movement fell apart when the leader's wife turned up holding a ticket. One unexpected result was the creation of new customers for the bookies as the new lottery gamblers began to desire quicker results.

By today's standards, when a million dollar winner gets $33,000 or so per year for twenty years (after taxes), the New Hampshire prize seems small, just $100,000 and $50,000 in later years. It was also hard to buy a ticket. They were sold at only three tracks and 49 liquor stores. They could only be purchased on site (no mailing), so you had to know someone you could trust in New Hampshire to purchase tickets for you. You had to collect prizes in person as well, for they could not be mailed. Not even an acknowledgment that you had won could be mailed. Again, the state circumvented this law by publishing the winners in the *Congressional Record,* which the Post Office Department could not suppress.[53] Nevertheless, buyers from 35 other states accounted for 85% of the sales. The only justice for out-of-state buyers was that 17 of 18 first-year winners lived out of state.[54] New Hampshire had found a way to fleece the residents of other states to avoid taxing its own citizens, a situation that did not go unnoticed by the politicians.

After watching money flow over the border to support New Hampshire, New York opened the second legal lottery in 1967, the first in that state since 1833. New York learned from its neighbor's experience, kept things simple, doubled the prize to $100,000 and ran a straight numbers game with monthly payoffs. Shortly, the state was grossing $2.5 million a month, over $30 million a year. This was still 79% short of the projections, however, causing many to label the lottery a failure. Aqueduct Track handled more gambling money in one day—$5.3 million on Labor Day—than the lottery did the entire month of July ($4.5 million).[55]

To appease the voters, state receipts from the lottery were earmarked for education, but for the first time it became clear to economic analysts that the poor were disproportionately playing the lottery and were thus inefficiently financing their own education. Even though they appeared to benefit from the lottery, the referendum approving the lottery was opposed by the two associations of school principals, the School Boards Association, the Public Education Association of New York City, the state Teachers Association and the Parent-Teachers Congress. These organizations believed that the lottery would be ". . . susceptible to fraud, breed crime, generate other forms of gambling, exploit the poor, hurt legitimate business, raise the cost of government, create social friction and in general contribute an undesirable way to finance education."[56]

The third state to follow suit and approve a lottery was New Jersey in 1971. By now the mob clearly understood the results of the lottery, even though the public didn't. The mob-run numbers racket and gambling through bookies continued to outpace the legal lottery. There were many reasons for this, including the offering of credit, better odds, and undeclared income for winners. Although the mob wanted the new gamblers created by the lottery, they protected themselves by refusing to allow vendors in the neighborhoods where the bookies operated.[57] To get the lottery passed, a million-dollar war chest was raised by proponents. Many donors with clean records put in surprisingly large amounts. There was much vagueness about their interest and the sources of the money. The campaign financed by this million-plus overwhelmed the underfinanced religious opposition.

The managers of the New Jersey lottery learned what appealed to gamblers from the mistakes of the first two state lotteries: immediate gratification. They went to a 50 cent weekly game with a $50,000 payoff from the start. Within months the lottery was grossing $3.5 million a month, much of it from across the river in New York City. At the end of eight months the lottery had grossed $100 million, five times the projections.[58] That the gambling mania was capturing large new audiences was demonstrated by a little story in *Business Week*. Gambling had long been a back room, male-dominated activity. Now women were heavily involved in gambling as well. "The wind, snow and sleet that bathed New Jersey last week might have turned a St. Bernard to his keg, but it hardly fazed 400 housewives who mushed to a northern Jersey shopping mall for the weekly payoff in the latest and so far most successful of the nation's state sponsored lotteries." The intent of the mob and the state to create habitual gamblers was reflected in an observation by the master of ceremonies of the public drawings, Jack Taylor: "The lottery crowd is already religiously devoted."[59]

After New Jersey, lotteries began to sprout across the country. Connecticut, Pennsylvania, Massachusetts and Michigan instituted lotteries in 1972, Maryland in 1973, Illinois, Maine, Ohio, and Rhode Island in 1974. By the end of 1974, thirteen states had a lottery, but these thirteen states contained 40% of the U. S. population.[60] All legal gambling that year (1974) at casinos, dog and horse tracks, off-track betting in Connecticut and New York, jai alai in Florida and the lotteries amounted to $17 billion.[61] Less than $2 billion was going to the states as revenue, far below the projections. Delaware opened a lottery in 1975 (which the state shut down later in 1975 and began again in 1977), Vermont in 1978, Arizona in 1981, Washington state and Washington, D.C., in 1982, Colorado in 1983, California, Iowa, Oregon, Missouri and West Virginia in 1985. Vermont, which was surrounded by lotteries, instituted one in self-defense, since so much money was going over the borders to other states. In the early 1980s the question was raised for the first time whether the state paid more in increased social services than it reaped in lottery revenue.

The mid-1970s burst in lottery approvals triggered an explosion of gambling across the nation. In faraway Nevada, having had legalized gambling for fifty years, the amount of revenues the state derived from casino gambling topped 50% of the state budget. With the explosion of gambling one glaring failure became clear. One of the most basic of arguments used by early proponents of the lottery was that illegal gambling would fade away if legalized gambling were approved. By 1972 a New Jersey commission discovered that it still had captured only 15% of the numbers action away from the mob.[62] However, it was clear throughout the 1960s and 1970s that illegal gambling was growing as rapidly or more so than legal gambling. By 1977, when less than $20 billion was being spent legally on all forms of gambling, estimates ranged from $75 billion to $100 billion spent illegally. The latter figure was much more difficult to determine, of course, since the mob did not file reports with the IRS.

Another major factor promoting illegal gambling was legal gambling's erosion of the federal laws on the interstate transportation of gambling material. Following the changes in federal law allowing advertising of lotteries in 1975, both legal and illegal gambling materials and legal advertising were flowing freely. An advertising explosion, which was targeted toward the poor and black, followed. Only a few objected. One was Ross Wilhelm, professor of business economics at the University of Michigan, who said, "The viciousness of the state-run games is compounded beyond belief by the fact that state governments actively advertise and promote the games and the winners."[63] Eventually the terrible social consequences of advertising caused the Wisconsin legislature to prohibit all advertising by the state lottery. Local vendors who advertised were required to clearly indicate the odds for winning prizes with that ticket. This is the strictest law to date.[64]

In 1977 another major innovation spurred the feverish pouring of money into lotteries. Four states began "instant win" games, which provided the ultimate in bettor gratification, if not in large prizes. These games were obviously directly competing with the daily numbers games. The mob advantage of same-day payoffs, no taxes and credit continued to promote the growth of illegal gambling. State lottery wins were taxed—for big winners, before the bettor received the money.

States began their lotteries with the intention of addressing the always "urgent" need to raise revenues without raising taxes. The lottery, however, is an incredibly inefficient way to raise money: 63% of each dollar is "wasted" in collection, whereas assessors and sheriffs cost about 4%. Despite this inefficiency, bettors continued to pour their money into lotteries. Pennsylvania jumped from $1.7 million per week to $2.7 million. Michigan doubled its 1976 gross to $2.2 billion in 1977. Maryland grossed $3.5 million per week, nearly three times the estimates, one of the few times that the gross has exceeded proponents' perennially optimistic guesses. The TV shows that announced winning numbers became the most popular programs in their time slots.

As the instant games proliferated, some of the earlier and smaller state lotteries suffered losses in sales, which triggered an increase in advertising. Delaware dropped 20% in gross receipts from 1976 to 1977. New Hampshire's gross take dropped 50% after a record year in 1976. Delaware officials fingered everyone but the real culprit— instant games in surrounding states. They most frequently blamed the National Football League for depressed sales because the NFL filed suit to prevent use of football games in the lottery. Delaware won the court battle to continue the games.[65]

The explosion of gambling on lotteries in the mid-1970s spurred a similar growth in all other forms of gambling. Lottery sales increased 24% in 1977 nationwide. Off-track betting in New York and Connecticut increased 26%. Dog track grosses increased 12%. Jai alai, which had expanded from Florida to Connecticut, Rhode Island and Nevada, experienced a 22% increase. The Connecticut objective of $30 million for the seven-month racing season was reached in just three months.[66]

Even horse racing gained a point or two, although its central place in nationwide gambling began a long decline which continues to the present. In 1974 horse racing accounted for 25% of all legal gambling and lotteries only 7%. By 1984, racing was down to 12.5% and lotteries up to 22%.[67] Horse racing was most seriously hurt by the advent of off-track betting in New York City. While the city gained $17.5 million in revenues, the State lost $13.5 million and the horse industry over $8.1 million.[68] In Florida the situation was even worse. A study demonstrated that 85% of the off-track bets would have been placed at the track if off-track betting did not exist.[69]

All this action precipitated such a run on gambling stocks that the New York Stock Exchange and the American Stock Exchange boosted the margin from the standard 50% to 75% on some fifteen stocks, including Bally, Metro-Goldwyn-Mayer, Harrah's and others.[70] This only slowed sales slightly.

The casinos also gained some 20% in gross receipts in 1977. However, by the early 1980s the new gamblers created by the lotteries were a different breed. Instead of the high rollers who could be expected to lose thousands, and thus were granted free rooms and shows, the new breed budgeted less than $150 per visit (although they usually spent more!) to gamble, with an emphasis upon vacationing. The shows increased in significance. Only 53% of tourists claimed that gambling was the main reason that they visited Vegas, but it is hard to believe that a hot desert town would attract the other 47% on shows alone. By 1983 Las Vegas had 50 casinos, but six were in trouble. There had been little growth in the 1980s following boom times in the 1970s. The effects of Atlantic City were being felt, and East Coast high rollers were not going West as often. Atlantic City's eleven casinos (although one shortly failed) equalled all of Vegas' casinos in their 1983 gross receipts.

As a consequence of the leveling of gambling in Vegas, the hotels had to expect each phase of the operation to turn a profit: the hotel, the restaurants, the shows. From 1977 to the mid-1980s, the casinos continued to expand their cultivation of the middle class to replace the decline of high rollers. They moved from headline entertainers who drew up to $300,000, occasionally even $400,000 a week, to production shows with lesser stars and lots of dancing girls. These cost a more modest $30,000 a week to stage. The recession of 1980 through 1982 caused the first real decline in Vegas since gambling was legalized in 1931. This led to several mergers in 1985 with a slight reduction in competition. The video slots and card games arrived in the early 1980s and helped revive the flagging trade. The video slots, which appealed to the younger generation, eventually amounted to 67% of the take for some casinos.[71]

The hotels also increased profits in other ways. They increased the number of dollar slots from 10% to 50%. The supposed incentive to the gambler was that the house only retained 3% of the dollar, 15% of the quarter slots and 25% of the nickel slots. Even though the house kept a smaller percentage the gambler fed dollars at about the same rate as nickels. Caesar's Palace indicated that their income increased 70% over an eighteen-month period as a result of these changes.

Not only did traditional forms of gambling enjoy the 1970s' gambling binge, but whole new forms of gambling emerged. In the 1950s through 1970s retailers of every type moved into what were essentially merchandise lotteries. Purchase of commodities entered you into competition for whatever prize was being given away: tetherball kits, jukeboxes, records, oranges, swimming pools and vacation trips. Newspapers printed "Lucky Buck" numbers, the serial numbers off dollar bills which, if matched, paid $25 to $3,000. Men's clothiers used "suit clubs" where customers paid a dollar a week toward a suit but got it free if their number was drawn. Elaborate treasure hunts and many other games were saved from being illegal lotteries by not requiring the payment of money to win.[72]

As usual, all the customers paid for the few winners. The results were sometimes ludicrous, as when Mrs. A. W. Conner of Tampa, Florida, won a nationwide contest for a Hollywood screen test in June of 1966. She was 79. Probably most widely remembered are the earlier oil company contests promoted most strongly by Gulf (now BP), Humble, Citgo, Mobil, Sunoco and Atlantic Richfield (ARCO). Abuses caused five states to outlaw giveaway games by 1967.[73] A congressional subcommittee, chaired by John D. Dingell of Michigan, investigated mail-order sweepstakes, and found that they were not awarding prizes if the initial winner did not respond. Only about 10% of the prizes were actually being awarded. Legislation followed that required the awarding of all the prizes.[74] Nevertheless, such marketing techniques grew from a $95 million to a $182 million business from 1977 to 1983.[75] The churches weren't left out; in 1976, the state of New York approved "Las Vegas" nights for churches and fraternal organizations. Some commentators suggested that the gambling binge was a response to inflation. It made as much sense to spend the money on gambling as it did to watch it shrink in banks that were paying interest rates lower than the rate of inflation. Such is the nonsense of those who rationalize gambling by suggesting that nothing is better than something.

Lottery proponents found a whole new set of lobbying partners with state governments from the corporations that produced the games and equipment. Several were propelled into *Fortune's* "Second 500." The biggest beneficiaries of the lottery boom were Control Data, IBM, Datatrol, Mathematica, American Totalisator (maker of pari-mutuel equipment) and Bally, long known for its near monopoly (80%) of production of pin ball and slot machines. Lesser-known big winners were Scientific Games and Dittler Brothers of Atlanta. The two firms, both producing games for business, joined forces to produce instant games for the states in 1974, with Scientific Games handling the design and marketing and Dittler Brothers doing the printing. They produced 1.5 billion tickets in 1984 and several times that now. Revenues were over $30 million in 1983. Dittler is a wholly-owned subsidiary of Southam, a Canadian newspaper chain.[76] Scientific Games was later acquired by Bally. The impact of this new giant force behind lottery development was revealed when the news came out that $2.1 million of the $2.5 million spent to pass the lottery bill in California was supplied by Scientific Games.[77] They also poured money into Arizona and Oregon. Bally and Scientific Games have been linked to organized crime in a report by the New Hampshire Attorney General.[78]

Advertising—Creating a "Need"

Lottery proponents have long said that they were merely responding to a felt "need" among the populace to gamble. They claimed simply to be servicing a demand. It is interesting, however, that in every state, once the newness of the lottery wears off and the newspapers stop devoting much attention to winners—unless it is a really big multimillion dollar prize—revenues begin to drop. Heavy advertising and new games are necessary to maintain this alleged "natural urge" to gamble. The supposedly spontaneous mid-1970s surge in gambling was fueled by advertising. The states had spent a total of $200 million per year to create gamblers in the late 1960s and early 1970s. From 1975 to 1977 the Television Bureau of Advertising noted a 140% increase in lottery ads. During this same period expenditures for those ads grew from $2.9 million to $6.9 million. By 1984, a total of $23.3 million was spent on TV ads, up 35% from the previous year.[79] By 1990, lotteries were spending $156 million per year on advertising, a much higher percentage of gross income than was the case for the average corporation. California alone spent $35 million and New York $15.7 million.[80] So much for gambling's being a natural demand.

The ads created the stream of new gamblers that the state and the mob needed to replace disillusioned and broke bettors. As columnist George Will noted, "In this age of lotteries, manufacturing mobs is a government goal and mass hysteria is an important ingredient of public finance."[81] Check your own state advertising and see how many times the words "hurry," "hysteria" and "panic" are used. These words are especially used in radio advertising where an image must be created by words alone. States lotteries are willing to use any dubious technique to attract customers. Massachusetts used a phony ESP test, encouraging readers to pick a number between one and five. While you would expect 20% to pick the answer "3" that was on the next page, actually nearly half the people will choose near the middle. So the lottery was trying to convince the public that if they picked the correct answer they had some special power to beat the odds.[82] The use of "psychometric market segmentation" techniques allowed the targeting of specific classes of people, with the poor as the most common target. The most common "value" is greed, motivated by the desire for a life without work. Although a *Glamour* poll revealed that 79% of the population believes that the low odds of winning ought to be stated, the states have been quite effective in hiding the odds, printing them in type visible only to the better class of eagles. Despite the clear evidence, only 39% of Americans realize that lotteries lead people into other forms of gambling.[83]

Growth in the 1980s was even greater than during the mid-1970s. Just before the decade began, in 1979, the fourteen state lotteries generated $2.1 billion in sales. By June of 1983, with seventeen lotteries, the gross had jumped to $4 billion, but it was still a tiny fraction of the estimated $177 billion spent on all legal and illegal gambling. Illegal gambling has always exceeded legal gambling, although with increased legalization, the ratio of illegal to legal has been reduced. In the 1950s, estimates were that illegal gambling garnered ten times the amount spent on legal gambling. By the 1980s, one estimate suggested that this ratio had been reduced to seven to one.[84] Current estimates suggest that the take for illegal gambling may be as low as half that of legal gambling, but others suggest that it is still twice the legal amount. While the percentage of gambling that is illegal has declined, the absolute amount of illegal gambling is still growing. States have steadily added lotteries, with Texas and Georgia becoming the 36th and 37th in 1992. The same arguments are still being used to promote lotteries, although they have long since been shown false. Probably the most powerful lure of the 1980s was the tremendous growth in the size of the prizes. Multimillion dollar prizes became common, especially after several states combined to form Lotto America, now called Powerball.

When in January 1984, Ontario's 6/49 Lotto prize reached $13 million, over eleven million Canadians and Americans spent $67.5 million trying to win it. People borrowed money to put on the lottery, and complaints arose of government-induced hysteria and the promotion of fantasies. The odds against any single entrant winning climbed to an incredible 135 million to one. There was a single winner. Interviewees consistently expressed the hope of escaping poverty, not by working, but by winning the lottery. The situation became so bad the minister of recreation in Ontario, responsible for running the lottery, recommended a $5 million cap be put on prizes.

Also in 1984, a single prize reached $117 million in the Spanish Lottery, one of the largest prizes anywhere in the world to date. The mere size of the prizes kept the lotteries constantly in the news. The big prize mania caused a new round of studies of the impact of the lottery upon the nation. Since it was one of the larger lotteries, Pennsylvania received attention. By 1984 the state was receiving a half billion in income per year from its lottery, on sales of $1.25 billion. To that point the largest pot had been $18.1 million. That same year (1984) the Illinois jackpot hit $40 million, and in August of 1985 the New York jackpot hit $41 million. People bought tickets at the rate of 22,000 per minute.[85] In December of 1988 the New York jackpot hit $45 million. Tickets sold at a rate of 28,000 per minute, with $37.4 million worth sold in three days. When this happened the state did not need to advertise; they simply indicated to the media, which treated it as news, the growth of the prize each day as tickets were purchased. Also in 1988 the Florida jackpot rose to $55 million, and on that same incredible day, New York awarded $23 million and Illinois $21 million, creating the second $100 million day in history.[86] In the last hours before the drawing, sales reached 51,000 tickets per minute. Florida's lottery, with a large affluent retired population, surpassed California's first day, and grossed $1 billion in just its first eight months.[87] By 1986, however, California's lottery had become the largest in the world.[88]

Even more incomprehensible was Pennsylvania's 1989 prize of $115 million. Just before the drawing, the state sold eleven million tickets in one morning.[89] Airlines, buses and roads into the state were jammed with people coming to buy tickets.

By 1984, 68 percent of the population lived in states with lotteries, implying that those without them were the smaller states, except for Texas. Forty-six states allowed some form of gambling, thirteen of them allowing only bingo by charitable or religious organizations.[90] In 1978 estimates were that about 60% of the population gambled. By the mid-1980s, estimates were that 80% gambled.[91] Present estimates range from 84% to 91%, with most studies indicating that about nine out of ten Americans gamble at least occasionally. At least 44% gamble on charities. Approximately 41% gamble at least once a year at casinos. Another 41% gamble on sports, either privately or in significant amounts through bookies. Something over 33% gamble on horse racing either on or off-track, with an unknown percentage using a bookie.[92] The size of these figures indicates that at least a third of the population is engaging in several different types of gambling at the same time. These gamblers are spending $7 billion on lotteries alone with over $2.8 billion going to the states as revenue.[93] By 1984 Americans spent an estimated $177 billion on gambling, fifteen times what was donated to churches and half what was spent on food.[94]

A Gambling Society

By 1986, twenty-two states and the District of Columbia had lotteries. These states contained 60% of the population.[95] By 1987 the states were grossing $15.6 billion, but this was less than 8% of the total $200 billion put at risk on gambling that year. By 1989 Americans lost an average of $90 for every man, woman and child per year on lotteries alone. While this seems modest, one must consider the percentage that can't and won't gamble. By then 87% of the population had been convinced to approve of lotteries, mostly with no idea of their real consequences. The situation was worse in the Northeast, where in 1988 the Massachusetts average loss was $235 per person, Connecticut residents averaged $162 per person, New Jersey $155 and Pennsylvania $121 per person.[96] By comparison, the Japanese average $230, British $200 and Canadians $60 per person. Remember, these figures are for legal lotteries alone. Total gambling is estimated at five to ten times that amount.

In fiscal 1990 gross lottery sales reached the $20 billion mark, with $7.7 billion going to the states (37.5%). The leading amounts governments received to "replace taxes" were: New York, $958 million; Florida, $849 million; California, $771 million; Ohio, $604 million; Illinois, $588 million; Michigan, $437 million; and New Jersey, $249 million. The other 26 states accounted for the remaining $3,345 million in receipts. Nine states recorded declining sales with California's 14% leading the way. During the 1980s, the annual gross from lottery sales had increased at a rate of 26% per annum. In 1991 that growth was only 3%. The lottery boom seemed to be nearing an end, since there were few states that had not opened lotteries.[97] Total gambling in 1990 amounted to $286 billion, or 5% of our gross national product. This was more than the $213 billion spent on elementary and secondary education, and more than four times as much as was given to all the churches in America.[98]

One recent development is the video lottery or card game. Introduced by Bally in Illinois in 1984, it usually simulates five card draw poker and is placed in a bar or other retail location.[99] The maximum bet is $2, but up to 13 games a minute can be played, which allows the loss of up to $26 a minute. Since so many teenagers and young adults are already addicted to video games, this is being called the crack cocaine of gambling. One bar owner went $200,000 in debt in a matter of weeks in South Dakota, which is one of six states with the machines. These are viewed by state officials as a means of reviving the faltering lotteries, no matter what the consequences. South Dakota, however, considered discontinuing the games. Nebraska has placed a ban on the machines.

Video lottery terminals are simply an intermediate step to casino gambling. A later chapter will explore the growth of casinos, but we have already mentioned their 1977 move into New Jersey. In addition, twenty-three states now have Native American casinos, largely as a result of a 1989 law that sought to simplify management of Native American gambling. The law was seriously flawed and led to rapid expansion, especially in the mid-western states.

Finally, in May 1995, the first off-shore video casino opened on the Internet. The gambler places a deposit, at first limited to $500, in a foreign bank and then can play with a secret PIN number at the casino located on St. Martins. While wagering by phone is illegal under Title 18, Section 1084 of the U. S. Code, enforcement is lax. The casino also allows you to play for free, although you can't win anything, of course. Not knowing who is playing for real and who is playing for fun makes this form of gambling a legal nightmare. This may become the most addictive form of gambling of all, since a person can play completely from the privacy of his or her home. The potential damage to the U. S. balance of payments may also become significant.

Today we have arrived at the point where over 200 million Americans gamble over $500 billion per year legally and $300 billion to $700 billion more illegally. Only two states, Hawaii and Utah, still have no legal gambling, and the pressure is great upon Hawaii. The amount put at risk in all gambling venues is approximately $4,000 per year for every man, woman and child. Not all of this $4,000 is lost. Estimates of losses to those running the games range from $50 billion to $100 billion. This still is $400 or more for all types of gambling for every person in the country. Most Americans have accepted the myth that gambling is harmless recreation. They give little thought for its economic, social, political or moral implications, even though gambling is a dominant force in all these areas. For three decades we have thoughtlessly accepted the illogical proposition that the way to decrease gambling is to legalize it.

As predicted by farseeing Massachusetts judge Elijah Adlow in 1960, each increase in gambling has increased the mania for gambling, both in numbers of people and the amount spent. Abatement in the gambling fever will only come with the restriction of its availability. Illegal gambling was once confined to cities, but from there it has become a major non-producing "industry." Gambling establishments are monuments to the frailty of human will. They are on every corner.

Review Questions

1. What are the social and moral reasons for rejecting the idea that the pervasiveness of gambling makes it legitimate?
2. Why is gambling not a natural instinct?
3. What similarities and differences do you see in the use of gambling for revenue in the 1600s and 1700s and the present?
4. What events led to the banning of lotteries in the 1830s?
5. What historical facts refute the casino owners' contention that people have always gambled and, therefore, it is an acceptable activity?
6. How was the rise in gambling related to the rise in crime in the 1930s?
7. How great was the growth of mob-run illegal betting prior to the coming of lotteries in 1963?
8. How effective was legalizing lotteries in ending illegal numbers games?
9. Why do illegal numbers games flourish alongside the lottery?
10. What are the techniques used to fuel the "natural" urge to gamble?

Endnotes

[1] _____, "The Search for Santa Claus," *The Nation*, 203:436, October 31, 1966.

2 _____, "Pro and Con: Should We Have State-Run Lotteries?" *Reader's Digest*, 83:103, August, 1963.

3 Campbell, Felicia, "The Virtues of Gambling," *Business and Society Review*, 17:63-4, Spring, 1976.

4 Cited in Starkey, Lycurgus M. Jr., "Christians and the Gambling Mania," *Christian Century*, 80:268, February 27, 1963.

5 *Reader's Digest, op. cit.*, p. 105.

6 _____, "Gambling: Odds On, Odds Against," *The Economist*, 268:35, July 22, 1978.

7 Willimon, William H., "Lottery Losers," *The Christian Century*, 107:48, January 17, 1990.

8 _____, "Gambling: Spain May Follow Puritan France," *The Economist*, 287:67, May 21, 1983.

9 _____, "Spain: Quite a Gamble," *The Economist*, 304:49, August 29, 1987.

10 Roberts, John, "Letter from Tokyo," *The Far East Economic Review*, 95:58, January 29, 1977.

11 _____, "Everybody Wants a Piece of the Action," *Newsweek*, 80:46, April 10, 1972.

12 Blanche, Ernest E., "Lotteries Yesterday, Today and Tomorrow," *The Annals of the American Academy of Political and Social Sciences*, 269:71, May, 1950.

13 Haynes, Alan, "The First English National Lottery," *History Today*, 29:613, September, 1979.

14 _____, "Alaska: The Ice Lottery," *Time*, 73:24. May 18, 1959.

15 Blanche, *Loc. cit.*

16 Blanche, *ibid.*

17 _____, "Why Not Raise Revenue from Lotteries?" *The Christian Century*, 50:926, July 19, 1933.

18 _____, "Early Connecticut Lottery," *Hobbies*, 67:50, December, 1962.

19 _____, "New Hampshire: Off to the Races," *Newsweek*, 61:40, May, 13, 1963.

20 Phillips, Layn, "The Premium Savings Bonds: Respectable Revenue Through Legalized Gambling," *Tulsa Law Journal*, 11:244, Number 2, 1975.

21 Tigner, Hugh Stevenson and W. M. Euler, "Ban Lotteries and Raffles," *Rotarian*, 74:14, February, 1949.

22 Sullivan, George, *By Chance a Winner: The History of Lotteries*, (New York: Dodd, Mead, 1972), 9.

23 Blanche, *op. cit.*

[24] *By Chance a Winner, op. cit.,* 51, and Kate, Barry M., "Lotteries - The Consideration Requirement," *The Missouri Law Review,* 37:144, Winter, 1972. See also, John E. Kleber, ed., *The Kentucky Encyclopedia,* "Lotteries," pp 572-3, Lexington: The University of Kentucky Press, 1992.

[25] _____, "Postal Fraud Laws," *The Outlook,* 79:111, January 14, 1905.

[26] McGloin, F., "Shall the Lottery's Charter Be Renewed?" *The Forum,* 12:555, January, 1892.

[27] Aswell, James, "The Louisiana Lottery," *Collier's,* 127:22, January 20, 1951.

[28] Robbins, Peggy, "Louisiana Lottery Was So Big it Didn't Have to Be Rigged," *The Smithsonian,* 10:113-4, January, 1980. Forty-seven percent of the $28,000,000 monthly drawings went to the promoters. Wickliffe, John C., "Shall the Lottery's Charter Be Renewed?" *The Forum,* 12:561, January, 1892.

[29] Peterson, Virgil W., "A Look at Legalized Gambling," *Christian Century,* 82:676, May 26, 1965.

[30] Peck, Harry Thurston, "History of the Louisiana Lottery," *The Bookman,* 21:299-300, May, 1905. Part of an article entitled, "Twenty Years of the Republic," 293-304.

[31] Comstock, Anthony, "Lotteries and Gambling," *The North American Review,* 154:217-24, February, 1892. See also *The Outlook, op.cit.,* p. 112.

[32] Buel, C.C., "Degradation of a State: or the Charitable Career of the Louisiana Lottery," *Century Magazine,* 43(ns21):618, February, 1892.

[33] _____, "Racket: Dewey to the Rescue of 10,000,000 Willing Suckers," *Newsweek,* 10:17, July 24, 1937.

[34] Blanche, *op. cit.,* 74.

[35] *Newsweek, loc. cit.*

[36] _____, " 'Numbers' Racket," *Popular Mechanics,* 62:202, August, 1934.

[37] *Popular Mechanics, ibid.,* p. 201.

[38] _____, "The Numbers," *Time,* 29:42, January 4, 1937.

[39] Starkey, *op.cit.,* p. 269.

[40] _____, "Puerto Rico: Governor Winship Legalizes National Lottery," *Newsweek,* 3:12-13, May 26, 1934.

[41] _____, "Lotteries: N.Y. Relief Plan Called Ill-Advised, Immoral," *Newsweek,* 4:9, September 29, 1934.

[42] Davis, Bert H., "Lotteries Challenge the Church School," *International Journal of Religious Education,* 12:17, March, 1936.

[43] _____, "How the Sweepstakes Get Away With It," *Good Housekeeping,* 145:51, September, 1957.

[44] *Popular Mechanics, op. cit.,* p. 202.

[45] _____, "State Lotteries: Useful Money Maker or Ethical 'Skid Row?'" *Senior Scholastic*, 83:25, September 13, 1963, and _____, "State Lotteries: Sure Bet or Bad Risk?" *Senior Scholastic*, 88:14, March 11, 1966.

[46] _____, "Eire: The Sweepstakes Scandal," *Newsweek*, 81:43, February 12, 1973.

[47] Fino, Paul A., "The Case for a National Lottery," *American Magazine*, 158:18, August, 1954.

[48] Phillips, *op. cit.*, p. 241.

[49] Starkey, *op. cit.*, p. 267.

[50] Parthemore, J. A., Jr., "A Look at Gambling," *Vital Christianity*, p. 3, March 14, 1965.

[51] Cantwell, Robert, "Gambling for the Yankee Dollar," *Sports Illustrated*, 20:25, March 30, 1964.

[52] _____, "Needed: Counteraction Against Lottery," *The Christian Century*, 80:668, May 22, 1963.

[53] _____, "New Hampshire: For the Record?" *Newsweek*, 63:34, May 11, 1964.

[54] _____, "How New Hampshire's Lottery Worked Out," *U.S. News and World Report*, 57:16, September 28, 1964.

[55] _____, "New York Gambles and Loses," *The Christian Century*, 84:1245, October 4, 1967.

[56] Conklin, T. L., "New York Prepares to Vote on Lottery," *The Christian Century*, 83:1157, September 21, 1966.

[57] _____, "The States: The Numbers Game," *Newsweek*, 78:18, September 13, 1971.

[58] Ross, Irwin, "Legalized Gambling: Is It a Good Bet?" *Readers Digest*, 99:96, November, 1971.

[59] _____, "New Jersey: The Lottery Fever is Highly Contagious," *Business Week*, p. 45, March 13, 1971.

[60] Brinner, Roger E. and Charles T. Clotfelter, "An Economic Appraisal of State Lotteries," *National Tax Journal*, 28:395, December, 1975.

[61] Gordon, Richard L., "Legal Gambling Racks Up Big Ad Support," *Advertising Age*, 48:3. October 3, 1977.

[62] _____, "Everybody Wants a Piece of the Action," *Newsweek*, 80:50, April 10, 1972.

[63] _____, "State Lotteries and Gambling," *USA Today*, 107:1, April, 1979.

[64] Wisconsin Legislative Council Staff, "The Wisconsin Lottery," Information Memorandum 87-7:3, December 4, 1987.

[65] _____, "Wedge for Wagering," *Time*, 108:69, September 13, 1976.

[66] _____, "Jai alai Moves North," *Time*, 108:55, August 30, 1976.

[67] Simmons, Susan A. and Robert Sharp, "State Lotteries' Effects on Horse Racing," Journal of Policy Analysis and Management, 6:446, Spring, 1987.

[68] Coate, Douglas and Gary Ross, "The Effect of Off-Track Betting in New York City on Revenues to the City and State Governments," *The National Tax Journal,* 27:63-9, March, 1974.

[69] Berg, Sanford V. and Emery Jay Yelton, "Profits, Payments, and Complementary Products: Additional Ways to Improve Pari-Mutuel Taxation," *The National Tax Journal,* 29:197, June, 1976.

[70] _____, "Rien ne va plus," *The Economist.* 268:113, September 9, 1978.

[71] _____, "Low Rollers," *The Economist,* 285:69, December 25, 1982.

[72] _____, "The Lure of the Giveaway," *Business Week,* pp. 41-43, September 26, 1951.

[73] _____, "Facts About Giveaway Games," *Good Housekeeping,* 165:202, November, 1967.

[74] _____, "Who wins the sweepstakes?" *Senior Scholastic,* 96:17, April 27, 1970.

[75] _____, "The Sweepstakes Binge," *Newsweek,* 104:46, January 23, 1984.

[76] _____, "Jackpot: Two Firms Win the Lottery Prize," *Time,* 125:69, February 11, 1985.

[77] _____, "Lotteries: California Joins the Crowd," *The Economist,* 297:32, October 12, 1985.

[78] Rohrig, Byron L., "Lottery Foes Target Public Policy," *Christian Century,* 104:397, April 29, 1987.

[79] Rohrig, *ibid.*

[80] Willimon, *op. cit.,* p. 40.

[81] Will, George F., "In the Grip of Gambling," *Newsweek,* 113:78, May 8, 1989.

[82] Frazier, Kendrick, "Selling the Lottery with ESP," *Skeptical Enquirer,* 12:25-26, Fall, 1987.

[83] _____, "This is What You Thought," *Glamour,* p. 137, December, 1989.

[84] Cizik, Richard, "Gambling: The Legal Menace," *Christian Herald,* 106:47, November, 1983.

[85] _____, "14 17 22 23 30 47," *Time,* 126:21, September 2, 1985.

[86] Shapiro, Joseph P., "The Dark Side of America's Lotto-Mania," *U.S.News and World Report,* p. 21, September 19, 1988.

[87] Sullivan, Maureen, "Florida: Sunshine Gamblers," *American Demographics,* 11:48, February, 1989.

[88] Blakey, Robert, "The Real Story Behind Lotteries," *Light,* pp. 10-11, February, 1987.

[89] Will, George F., *loc. cit.* See also, _____, "Privitise State Lotteries," *The Economist,* 312:12, July 1, 1989.

[90] Eadington, William R. and James H. Frey, "Preface," *Annals of the American Academy of Political and Social Sciences,* 474:9, July, 1984.

[91] Cizik, *op. cit.,* p. 46.

[92] *Glamour, loc. cit.*

[93] _____, "Lotteries: States Hit the Jackpot," *U.S. News and World Report,* 97:16, September 17, 1984.

[94] Colson, Charles, "The Myth of the Money Tree," *Christianity Today,* 31:64, July 10, 1987.

[95] Mikesell, John L. and C. Kurt Zorn, "State Lotteries as Fiscal Savior or Fiscal Fraud: A Look at the Evidence," *Public Administration Review,* 46:311, July/August, 1986.

[96] Willimon, *loc. cit.*

[97] Kerr, Thomas J., "Are Schools Losing at the Lottery?" *School and College,* 41:19, April 1992.

[98] Atkins, Joe, "The States' Bad Bet," *Christianity Today,* 35:20, November 25, 1991.

[99] _____, "Gambling on a Way to Trim Taxes," *Time,* 123:43, May 28, 1984.

Chapter 2

I'll Never Get Addicted!

Gamblers are a funny lot. I don't remember where I first heard this story, but it is worth the telling. Seems there was a gambler in New York state who loved to play the ponies. He would schedule his vacation to coincide with every meet at Aqueduct. He'd get up at four in the morning to walk to the station and catch the train for a three hour ride. After the races he would have dinner with his cronies and play cards until time to catch the train back. He'd drag home at eleven o'clock at night and was up at four the next morning to repeat the routine. After his vacation he'd returned to work exhausted. A fellow worker said, "Why don't you just rent a room near the track?" The gambler replied, "What, and miss vacation with the wife and kids?"

Gamblers are made, not born. Gambling is an irrational activity since nearly everyone loses, except those who run the game. Losing resources is the opposite of what people want to achieve. Therefore, gambling does not make sense, and must be taught.

Gambling is a business. Carl Cohen of the Sands Hotel said, "Gambling is a business pure and simple. We sell a chance to win money."[1] This business does not sell something that contributes to feeding, housing, clothing or transporting the person. The chance is not tangible, and for all but the tiniest fraction of customers the sale ends in disappointment. How could anyone possibly sell such a worthless product? The only way to succeed is to advertise: advertise a thrill, and call that thrill entertainment or recreation. How else could so many of us be convinced that giving our money away voluntarily and getting nothing in return is exciting? Promise something big, and celebrate only that one in eight million customers for whom that promise becomes a reality. We have accepted this silliness, with some tragic consequences. For some, foolishness turns into obsession, although only 39% of Americans know that.[2]

Who Is the Gambler?

Since nine out of ten of us gamble at least occasionally, let us examine the nature of the gambler. Some psychologists have stated that some personality types are more susceptible to becoming gamblers than others. Since such a great percentage of us are gamblers that is probably only partially true. More likely, some have personalities that put them at higher risk of becoming pathological gamblers. Many Americans think it is undemocratic to use the law to aid those who have problems with impulse control. They reason that if gamblers have a problem they will gamble anyway, and it is better for the state to garner the money than the mob.

How do we classify those who gamble? If we consider just gamblers and pathological gamblers, the first group is very large and the second group is smaller. Perhaps 85% of the population fall in the first group and 1% to 5% in the second (a 1993 Gallup poll suggested that the figure is nearer 5%[3]).

Some formal studies of gambling have sought to define gamblers as being either amateurs or professionals. Gambling has become part of the weekly, or even daily, routine of more than a third of the American population. It is the occasional activity of another half of the population. However, the frequency of gambling does not make the first group professional gamblers and the second amateurs. A more useful distinction is those who run the games and those who play. The former are the real professionals. We may also include as professional gamblers those who gamble full-time to make a living, although they are not always successful. All other gamblers are amateurs, no matter how proficient. The professional running the games makes money. The amateur players normally do not.

The amateur gambler, whether high frequency or low, is responsible for the growth in gambling described in the previous chapter. Although 37 state lotteries have outlets in every grocery and gas station, and 23 states harbor some sort of casinos, the professionals intend to make it even easier to gamble. Coming soon are street corner terminals as prolific as phone booths that will take your bet. The ultimate will be direct cash computerized transfers from your bank so you will not have to leave the comfort of your couch to lose your money. These methods are intended to attract the underage gambler since some states still have limits on how old you must be to gamble. The underage gambler exhibits less understanding of the odds and less control over the impulse to gamble than adult gamblers. The gambling interests, like any industry, want to hook the young on regular use of their "product," regardless of the consequences for the individual.

Where do high frequency gamblers originate? Some studies purport to show that the third who regularly gamble come proportionately from all classes, which may be true with regard to percentages. What this really means is that the 39,000,000 people below the poverty line gamble in large numbers. This group can least afford it. A Maryland study found that of the regular purchasers of lottery tickets, people in the bottom third economically purchased significantly more than half the tickets.[4]

The most likely players are males, Hispanics, blacks, Catholics and laborers who are young, with incomes under $10,000 (spending up to $2,000 of that on gambling) and are non-college graduates. Several of these categories point disproportionately to the poor as spending the largest percentage of their salary on the lottery.[5] A 1994 study by the University of Louisville Center for Urban and Economic Research demonstrated less dramatically that those with incomes less than $15,000 spent $480 per year on the lottery, or 3.2 percent of their income. Those with incomes over $35,000 spent $383 per year on the lottery, or 1.1 percent of their income. This study considered only lottery gambling in a state with horse racing and riverboat casinos on the Illinois and Indiana shorelines of the Ohio River, so the total amount spent on gambling is actually much higher.[6] So, while the number of gamblers from each class MAY be proportional (depending on which study you read), there are many indicators that the amount spent is not proportional to income, and falls disproportionately upon the poor, who can least afford it. One educated estimate is that the economic effect of the Connecticut and Massachusetts lotteries was equivalent to levying a sales tax of 60% on lower income groups.[7] Even unemployment does not decrease lottery playing, for only 2% fewer of the unemployed gamble.[8] That gambling does not hurt the poor is a myth. The lottery pushes people over the edge into poverty, and it keeps them there.

For a variety of reasons, the poor are susceptible to the lottery, which has a lower rate of return than other forms of gambling. The poor cannot afford a trip to the casino, although the Native Americans are helping the casino interests by bringing the casinos closer to home. Poor people cannot even afford the minimum fifty or hundred dollar bet with a 10% commission that the bookie insists upon. So, they play $1 or $2 or $10 a day on the lottery. The poor are forced to play the least efficient game where the house take is 63%, unlike other forms of gambling where it is usually less than 25%. The poor seem least aware of the risk, and understand the odds less than the better educated.

The professionals who run the game feel no sympathy for the poor. Forty years ago George I. Holmes of the California Revenues State Racing Board said of those who bet the rent money, "If they cannot afford to bet, they should not go to the tracks." Las Vegas and the state of Nevada have a long history of disinterest in the losers who cannot even afford to go home—that is, until they turn to crime to secure the means of leaving. The government officials who have approved gambling as a revenue source are no more caring now than forty years ago. The evidence comes from the continued approval of lotteries, despite the clear evidence of increased social services costs, the disproportionate spending by the poor, and the evidence from the Institute for Social Research of the University of Michigan that lotteries are three times as regressive as the next most regressive tax, the sales tax.[9] Regressive means that the tax hits the poor the hardest. Only four states had politicians who were willing to make token provisions for the pathological gamblers they were about to create. Through lottery profits, the poor are inefficiently financing their own education, health care and welfare programs. No wonder they are in such deep trouble.

Incredible though it may seem, some legislators admit they are going after the poor bettor. They indicate a saintly desire to make the pleasure of gambling accessible to the poor as well as the rich. The rich play roulette, Black Jack and other expensive games while the poor are left out. The lottery makes this joy available to all. Before you pat these policy makers on the back for championing the poor, remember that craps has been with us a long time. Furthermore, even horse racing is hardly the sport of kings, since the predominant bet is still $2, certainly the province of the poor.

Getting on the Gambling Bandwagon

In light of the evidence that gambling has become more widespread than in the past, that people are gambling more money per year, and that the poor gamble as much as 20% of their income, what accounts for our acceptance of gambling? Americans have been drawn into this activity for a number of reasons.

Resistance to lotteries has declined. Historically, ministers and churches have been the strongest opponents of gambling. For the past thirty years, however, much of the leadership of the mainline denominations has been involved in seeking social justice in the form of minority rights, freedom to choose abortion and other issues. They have also focused upon political justice and human rights. This agenda left little time for a battle against traditional social issues such as alcoholism, gambling or other individual problems. The focus of modern society upon the self-life and the freedom to choose—even if the choice damages oneself and others—has reduced gambling to a minor problem in the eyes of many. Unfortunately, it is no longer a minor problem, and the moral issue is simply not being confronted.

The churches' resolve to take a moral stand against gambling has further eroded since the 1930s by the churches' participation in gambling in the forms of bingo, raffles and casino nights. By 1963, just before lotteries began to cut their take, gambling income for churches and fraternal organizations had grown to $80 million.

Stephen Wynn, a Wharton School of Business graduate, who moved from a promising business career into investment in gambling ventures, exemplifies the common modern view. He foresaw all forms of gambling as a growth business. "In Nevada where the state gets 5.5% of the gross win, and where gambling is wide open, the state last year got $110,000,000. . . . When legislators see those kinds of figures, they're going to want to expand the opportunities for people to gamble as rapidly as they can."[10] Note that there is no mention of Nevada's problems with the mob, or the high crime rate. A few Americans seem vaguely aware that there may be some economic or social issues connected with gambling, but almost no one sees gambling as a moral issue anymore.

Not only did the churches disappear from the battle, but traditional political resistance to government participation in crime, which gambling was considered, has eroded as well: "[William Penn] founded a community in which the government would try to be a force for moral improvement. Imagine what he would think of Pennsylvania in the grip of gambling fever fomented by the state government."[11] Gone are the days when politicians sought to pass legislation in the best interest of all, even if their decisions were not popular. Now, most vote whatever their constituents want regardless of the consequences. As a result, politicians are guided by the pork barrel, lobbyists, the mob, special interest groups and political action committees. Seldom is legislation considered on its moral merit, but rather on the basis of what the majority want. Certainly, this has been the case with gambling.

Getting in on the Game

Most of us, at the age when we first were invited to gamble, had some resistance to losing whatever of value we were being asked to risk. For us to be enticed into gambling by those who run the games, this resistance must be overcome. Over the past thirty years it has become progressively easier to persuade young people to gamble.

A number of psychological studies examine the role of childhood games in initiating gambling. Most males first experience an invitation to pit skills. For the older generation it was the school yard marbles game for keeps. For the next generation it was pitching baseball cards, with the winner keeping the cards. For others it was trying to win free games on the pin ball machine, or a back alley game of craps. For the current generation, there is a high correlation between the mania for electronic competitive games and adult gambling. Since so many adults gamble, can we be sure these games cause gambling? Probably not, but they serve as a common threshold. Most addicted gamblers began between ages 10 and 14.[12] For most women the threshold came later, often in the form of playing cards for small pots. Since the rise of lotteries a much larger percentage of women now gamble, and for many the lottery was the threshold.

The psychological studies may be making things too complicated. Mario Puzo, a well-known gambler of a previous generation, says that children gamble for the same reason adults do: greed.[13] Greed is simply coveting what someone else has to the point of being willing to do anything to get it. Gambling is an attempt to satisfy greed without having to work. It represents a partial failure to grow up. As Robert Lindsay, a senior official of the United Church of Christ, once said, "Lotteries do not appeal to grown-up instincts;

they appeal to whatever is arrested in our personal development—a Walter Mitty syndrome."[14]

Once we have tried gambling, what entices us to continue? Gambling in general provides a form of excitement, a minor thrill. Most of this thrill is based upon anticipation. There is a slight rush just before the key card is turned, the roulette ball drops, the ticket is bought or the instant card is scratched. For some, gambling is a means of using this tiny thrill to fight monotony or boredom. Surely it says a lot about our society when we fight the malaise of our lives with the tiny thrill of the lottery. Crime, drug addiction, alcoholism, gambling and suicide are all escapes. So is entertainment, but the latter is acceptable morally; this is why proponents try so hard to connect gambling with entertainment. Of course, when the stakes become higher and more of our resources are on the line, the sense of anticipation is replaced by anxiety, which heightens all our senses. Some find taking the big risk to be almost intoxicating.

Some analysts have claimed that gambling is an attempt to beat the perceived determinism of life. If a person feels trapped by destiny, perhaps the acquisition of great wealth against all odds will overcome destiny. Maybe even God will smile upon me now, this person thinks. This represents magical thinking more than anything else, but for some, gambling appears to be an attempt to establish their freedom to do as they wish, freedom from control by others or a higher power.

For others, gambling is more clearly an opportunity to prove superiority or skill. There is a sense of well-being that comes from rising to the challenge, overcoming the odds or seeking the favor of someone else. Many of these attitudes are promoted by the media, which seems susceptible to a "gee whiz" attitude when it comes to gambling. Journalistic skepticism disappears in the presence of gamblers. Perhaps it stems from the long association of gambling with sports and the reluctance of journalists to damage these American celebrities. In addition, experts say there are cultural reinforcements to gambling: "Various cultural signals actually condition would-be gamblers. The media propagate by romanticizing stories about gambling and gamblers, frequently showing daring, larger-than-life heroes thriving on risk (such as the sequence of movies about James Bond), and also by giving enormous publicity to game show contestants or gamblers who win substantial prizes."[15] Whatever the case, the stories gamblers tell are left without comment as if true, even though gamblers are notorious liars. One of the most self-serving, reputation enhancing favorites is the *Sports Illustrated* story of Billy Baxter:

> Eyes glistening, Baxter mentioned that he and Tommy Fischer, another Las Vegas gambling man "and a good all-round hustler in his own right," routinely bet the prelims on a fight card at the Silver Slipper, whether they know the boxers or not. "It's a standard $300 bet, and the way it works, one of us has to make the price [set the odds] after the first round. This one night it's Tommy's turn, and in the first round of a fight that was scheduled for four rounds, one fighter gives the other a terrific beating, knocking him down twice."
>
> Between rounds, Baxter said, "I pester Tommy for the odds. Finally, he blurts out, 'Oh I dunno—200 to 1, I guess.' . . . Now Tommy starts thinking about it and scratching his head. He says, 'Gee Billy, that's $6,000.' 'Uh, no, Tommy. That's $60,000. If your guy wins, you get $300. If my guy wins, you owe me $60,000.'
>
> "Tommy is beginning to look sick. And in round 2, my fighter makes a great comeback." Baxter got up from the table, danced around, making a facsimile comeback. "At the end of the round, I still see little hope, but Fischer is paranoid. He sees the fight as even. Between rounds he runs over to his guy's corner and yells, 'I'll give you a thousand bucks if you win this fight!' I see him, so I go over to my guy and I say, 'I'll give you a thousand bucks if you win.'
>
> "So now we got two preliminary fighters who at best are in there for a couple of hundred bucks apiece, fighting for over a thousand. Round 3 is a war. His guy's still getting the best of it, but Fischer can't see that. He's really paranoid now. He's walking back and forth, holding his head." Billy walked back and forth and held his head. " 'Sixty thousand bucks, Gee-zuz!' so he tries to settle the bet. 'What'll it take?' he says. . . . 'Make it $15,000.' I say, 'It's a deal.'"
>
> Billy sat back down, pleased with his performance and smiled broadly. "And, of course, his guy wins the last round and the fight. Which means Tommy not only has to pay me $15,000, he has to pay his fighter an extra grand as well."[16]

Notice there is no verification of the story with Fischer. There is no comment about the truthfulness of Billy Baxter. It's a great story that makes gambling sound glamorous, but has little to do with reality. Where is the commentary on taking advantage of the emotions of another human being? And did you catch the fact that Billy snookered the reporter as well? If Fischer's fighter won as Billy said, then Fischer didn't pay Billy, Billy paid Fischer $300, whereas Fischer paid only the $1,000 to his fighter. Billy undoubtedly has another story to tell his pals about fooling reporters!

What we do find out about "Bluffin'" Billy Baxter is that he is a good poker player, having beaten and been beaten by some of the best: Doyle Brunson, Chip Reese, Stu Unger and Bobby Baldwin. He has won Amarillo Slim's "Superbowl of Poker" at Lake Tahoe. He has collected three championships at Binion's Horseshoe Hotel "World Series of Poker." He has hustled pool, golf and poker and moved to Vegas to spend full-time betting on football, golf, baseball and boxing. He lives next door to Robert Goulet and down the street from Wayne Newton and has done time for making book. He claims to routinely bet $400,000 a weekend in the football season, says he gambles $6 million to $7 million a year and hopes to net $300,000 to $400,000. He stays with high stakes games and will not play with the guy who cannot pay the milk bill, his most outstanding ethical position. Experts say there are less than ten Billys who clear over $100,000 a year. The average Vegas poker player makes less than $12,000 a year, not enough for housing and food.

In addition to advertising we are attracted by the supposed glamour of gambling. This is most apparent for casino gamblers. They know they lose and lose steadily, if not occasionally spectacularly. They apparently like the plush surroundings, with thick carpet, beautiful women, plenty of liquor and shows just around the corner. Even if it is temporary, it seems a world of high living and contentment, a way to escape the drudgery or banality of life, at least for a time.

Gambling seems less obviously recreational and thrilling for the off-track bettor or lottery player who often buys the ticket in common or even dirty surroundings. How much of a thrill can it be to give your money away in a dingy bar, cigar store or even the supermarket? Desperate hope for the big win seems a more likely explanation.

For some gambling is an escape. The gambling burst of the mid-1970s was in part blamed on the attempt to escape inflation, as mentioned in the last chapter. It is also escape from a boring job, a dissatisfying home life, responsibility and boring TV. Frederick Koenig, a Tulane University sociologist, has said, "A gambler forgets all about the complicated problems he lives with and can't handle for a world where there is only one problem, win or lose." "Luck" appeals to many because, Koenig continues, "We can't do anything about inflation—we don't even understand it—we can't do anything about foreign affairs, or crime in the streets, or our own children. So we see where we stand with fate."[17] We exchange this sense of powerlessness for a momentary situation in which we at least partially control our activity and environment.

The Pathological Gambler

From the third of Americans who gamble regularly, somewhere between 3% and 5% become pathological gamblers. This translates into 8 million to 12 million souls at the present time, up from the 1 million to 4 million estimated in 1976.[18] This implies a growth rate of approximately 400,000 addicted gamblers per year. Three-fourths of them are men. The percentage of women is increasing as they join the ranks of the steady gamblers. In 1983, just over half of the women in the United States gambled. Now the percentage is over 80%. One writer suggested as early as 1983 that there are more pathological gamblers than alcoholics.[19]

Pathological gambling and depression are closely related. Some analysts appear to believe that pathological gamblers are depressives for whom gambling is a tonic. Others assume that the gambler became depressed and sometimes manic as a result of the development of the gambling habit. Still others believe that gamblers are inveterate liars who use the depression as an excuse for the gambling. Gamblers fit all three categories.

How does one become a pathological gambler? Commitment to gambling frequently follows a big win, provided the amount was a significant portion of the annual salary. The "chase" begins to repeat that big win without having to work at a routine job. Sometimes gamblers chase the big win the rest of their lives without ever repeating their victory.[20] There is no single pattern, for gambling may become pathological anywhere from one to twenty years after the gambling is begun. Gambling can be a very real addiction like any other, with the craving exceeding the need for food, sex or any other basic need. The hold of gambling is incredible. One recovering gambler said, "You're looking at a guy who used to buy transistor radios from kids on the train so I could hear the score."[21] Americans are not totally unaware of this potential, for a *Glamour* magazine poll revealed that 39% of the respondents believed that lotteries promote other kinds of gambling and can lead to "compulsive" gambling. Still we try it.

Tragically, there is very little help available. The largest available resource is Gamblers Anonymous, patterned after Alcoholics Anonymous, a twelve point self-help group support program. Only four states have gambling treatment centers: Maryland, Connecticut, New Jersey and New York. New Jersey allocates $275,000 to its center out of its 1 billion a year gross. Minnesota allocates $300,000 for treatment, although it did not have a center at the time this was written. Iowa places a half percent of its lottery gross in a fund for aiding addicted gamblers.[22] There are only a few additional private treatment centers nationwide, such as the Johns Hopkins Compulsive Gambling Counseling Center. Most of these programs demand total abstinence and total restitution of all money borrowed or stolen to support the gambling habit. This, according to the leaders, is the only way to restore self-esteem and lift the depression that is the usual reason gamblers seek help. Only a tiny percentage of pathological gamblers seek help, and estimates suggest that only one in twenty-five of those needing help find it. Gambling is frequently allied with alcoholism and promiscuity.

We have hinted so far at the tendency of lotteries to serve as a threshold or gateway that leads to other forms of gambling. This does not invariably happen, and no such implication is intended. In fact, the opposite can happen as well. Some studies have indicated that horse players were more likely than the population at large to add the lottery to their gambling routine because it was accessible. Similarly, those who played an out-of-state lottery were several times more likely to play a new in-state lottery than the population at large.

The gambler does not stay with the lottery alone as the pathology develops. Gamblers tend to try various forms of gambling until they find one at which they feel they have some skill. Most cards games require some skill to be competitive. A big win at some point leads the gambler to think he has a special talent for that game. This has been the traditional means of leading suckers into higher stakes poker games where they will be fleeced. The big win, especially if it seems to last for weeks or months, solidifies the sense that the person can make a living doing what is pressure-filled, but more fun than working.

The pathological gambler may be either amateur or professional, but most become as full time as their stake will allow. Most professional gamblers who run the casinos are not pathological. They are "bankers" who operate on fixed percentages without much risk. Where illegal gambling operations are operated, the professionals are simply racketeers, who may have to buy protection to run their illegal game, but in this age of indifference, less of that is necessary than a couple of decades ago. Rather than being pathological gamblers, these are again simply unscrupulous businessmen. The full-time amateur is the largest group of pathological gamblers. Most of these have an outside source to keep them going: a working co-dependent or inherited money.

The most famous example of one who gambled away the family fortune was Nicholas Andrea Dandolos, commonly known as Nick the Greek. Nick is a legend, meaning that many of the stories about him are of dubious worth; most were self-told and unverified. Nick claimed to have won and lost over $500 million dollars during his 73 years. He claimed to have won a half million in one poker game and then staked it all on the turn of a card. The latter is probably apocryphal, since if he had won he would have stated that he won even more. If he had lost it would have been less of a story. He more surely lost $605,000 to Arnold Rothstein in the biggest known poker pot in history. He once supposedly lost $280,000 on a single roll of the dice. These are hardly the marks of a hero and rational man.

Nick supposedly dressed well, spoke five languages and gambled away his rug merchant father's money. He goes down in history for such famous sayings as, "Women are the keel and adornment of the race; they should not be warred upon or engaged in serious conversation." He once dined with the Duke of Windsor, and also with Dutch Schultz, the crook. He was never arrested for breaking the law, but he never claimed not to have done so. He was said to have paid the hospital bills for over 600 people, sent 28 young people through college (why they bothered with this is a mystery, if gambling is the way to go), staked over 300 in business, given half a million to charity (less than one poker game), and given out over 2 million in loans. He claimed that the next best thing to playing and winning was playing and losing. The main thing is to play.[23]

As mentioned, full-time gamblers specialize. As a consequence, their social status varies, from the bridge player who may have high social standing, to the crap shooter who has no standing. They attempt to minimize risk in the game of choice. They learn the psychology of opponents and bet only when they have an edge. They know the probabilities and the applications to playing situations, but their understanding is often intuitive and not formally learned. Full-time gamblers take risks only outside their preferred game and do this primarily for the thrill or for a quick fix to their stake. The latter frequently fails. Most full-time gamblers live in urban areas with card rooms, casinos, off-track betting and accessible bookies. The full-time gambler builds up a network of associates to whom money is loaned in flush times, and from whom money is borrowed in lean times. This network provides the emotional support that formerly came from family and friends. Frequent association and knowledge of each other's styles and specialty often leads to teaming up in games. They are always careful to play the best odds. If they are playing the house, they concede the percentage (vigorish) and play to win early and cash out.

The house percentage varies from one type of gambling to another. Las Vegas and Atlantic City keep about 5% on the roulette wheel, 12% on craps, 5% to 25% on the slots, 13% to 15% on Jai Alai, 18% at the tracks, and the bookie keeps 10% on the $50 bet. Full-time gamblers seldom play the lottery where the house take averages 63%. Full-time gamblers do not declare income tax on illegal winnings. The house percentage prevents long-term success for the full-time gambler. The only chance is to become expert at private games with no house percentage.

Many gambling proponents are reluctant to admit that legal gambling has created a vast new group of pathological and full-time gamblers. They do, however, admit the growth of these groups. Even this has been a reluctant admission, for in the 1950s and 1960s gambling supporters agreed with U. S. Representative Paul A. Fino who thought a legal national lottery would help control people's gambling instincts.[24] The most gentle way of putting it was, "Among them [gamblers] some stop short of ruin, but not short of intermittently losing the money that buys amenities and sometimes necessities for their families."[25] This opinion ignores the fact that many abandon their families altogether.

How can we identify the pathological gambler? On the Edwards Personal Preference test, the pathological gambler has a higher than normal score for achievement, exhibition, dominance, heterosexuality, deference and endurance. On the Minnesota Multiphasic Personality Inventory, gamblers demonstrate elevated psychopathic deviation, and depression. Almost half show a sociopathic personality disturbance pattern—unable to profit from experience. They lack personal and group loyalties, are defective in judgment and sense of responsibility, and have an overdeveloped ability to rationalize behaviors. They tend to exhibit high energy, hyperactivity, high tolerance for stress and higher intelligence.

Health care professionals are concerned about the problem. Valerie Lorenz, the executive director of the Center for Pathological Gambling, says gambling is the mental health problem of the 1990s, and will probably replace alcoholism as the worst social problem for Americans. Sirgay Sanger, director of the National Council on Compulsive Gambling, calls it the addiction of choice in the 1990s.[26] Mental care workers are also concerned because approximately 20% of those who enroll in treatment programs have attempted suicide at least once. Since men are more frequently successful at suicide, gambling is a life-threatening habit.

Gamblers are predatory. Greed makes them ruthless and unconcerned about their victims' suffering. Money from gambling substitutes for a lack of security, power or love. The mock struggle of the game is more manageable and substitutes for real life. Since gambling as a profession is not yet totally respectable, gamblers gravitate to the edge of the underworld. They have frequent contact with illegal bookies and game operators organized by the mob. They have no moral reason to avoid cheating, although most do not cheat others in their support network. The most common forms of cheating are marked and manipulated cards, and loaded dice. The underworld regards cheats as worse than the seducer of a friend's wife or a coward and treats them roughly.

As the pathology develops, the gambler detaches from his past. He is often the victim of insomnia, impotence, heart attacks and marital problems. Gamblers lie. They frequently go through a common cycle: the big win, losing and desperation. The winning phase is the fun part. The big win is immediately assumed to be the result of skill or a system. When the losing begins it is assumed to be due to external circumstances or bad luck, not to the skill level or the flawed system.

The losing phase is worrisome. Short term borrowing begins. The gambler tends to splurge when he does win. "Chasing" becomes the smart strategy, that is, gambling to secure another big win, which often never comes. Hidden borrowing begins: borrowing from sources other loaners don't know. Marital problems escalate over the money spent and borrowed. Work is an interference with gambling. The gambler at this stage frequently moves into illegal activities: bookmaking, borrowing based on lies, civil fraud, the forgery of a spouse's or relative's signature to secure a loan. The gambler will plead for a bailout with promises to quit but then use the bailout as a new stake for another round of gambling. Job loss due to absenteeism is normal. In the desperation phase the gambler is obsessed with getting even. He attempts to gamble full time, works only occasionally to get a new stake and stays away from friends and family to whom he owes money. The gambler frequently embezzles. In New Jersey a teller embezzled $38,000 from the bank to buy lottery tickets. In Kentucky a convenience store clerk scratched over $150,000 worth of tickets, expecting to pay the money back from his winnings. Panic sets in, which frequently increases risk-taking with even worse odds and results. Optimism about winning begins to wane, the gambler becomes irritable, restless, hypersensitive, insomniac, irregular in eating. Life is no longer pleasant and the person is physically and emotionally exhausted, hopeless, helpless, alienated, divorced, arrested and subject to suicidal thoughts. The end result of pathological gambling is loss of control and interference with all parts of normal functioning.[27]

In 1974 the National Policy Toward Gambling Commission of the federal government estimated that there were 1.1 million pathological gamblers at that time. By 1976 the federal government had responded to this crisis by allotting $330,000 to the Veterans Administration for the care of addicted veterans.[28] They expected the number of veterans needing this help to top 3.8 million by 1990. By 1990, the number of addicted gamblers was between 6 million and 10 million. Psychological experts, but not sociological experts, consistently agree that increases in general gambling lead directly to increases in pathological gambling.

Felicia Campbell's gambling-supported minority opinion is different. She says that gambling is stimulating. It appeals especially to the elderly, who wish to make decisions after life has restricted the ones they can make. She claims that gambling gives the "peak experience" of life.[29] This is hard to believe when so many millions have found their peak experience in producing something or in doing something good for others. She further claims that gambling produces a godlike feeling, that all the physical and emotional systems are alive.[30] (Note that this godlikeness is defined in terms of greed, not giving.) She further suggests, against all the findings of clinicians, that gambling benefits depressives, the grief stricken, and that it keeps one alert instead of dull or tranquilized. She says that absorption in the contest is positive, not pathological. She advocates gambling as a harmless escape which allows the poor to surmount impotence. Her goal is ". . . a society in which we may glory in our humanity rather than suffering guilt over our normal impulses."[31] Perhaps Ms. Campbell should have taken her research to the back side of Vegas on a dark night to see the magnificent results of gambling addiction which she and other state officials deny. Orville Wahrenbrock, chief assistant of the Division of Human Resources, said, "I'm not aware that a problem called compulsive gambling exists in Nevada."[32] He also must have been unaware of the crime statistics for Nevada.

Summary

Of all gamblers, lottery players are the least sophisticated. In early economic studies of lotteries, efforts were made to adjust the "expected value" (the percentage of ticket sales that goes to prizes), the probability of winning a prize and the "inequality" of the prize structure (one big prize with many small ones, or several large prizes with no small ones). By 1976 it was known that these variations had little effect. The key issues were the price of the ticket, the frequency of drawings and the convenience of purchase.[33]

We have observed the progression of gambling both in terms of amount and scale. We have also looked at the individual development of gambling from childhood games through occasional gambling to heavy gambling. We have noted that a small percentage become full-time gamblers and pathological gamblers. Nine out of ten of us are gamblers. We need to stop and live a little. As Maurice Maeterlink once said gambling is ". . . the stay-at-home squalid, imaginary, mechanical, anemic, and unlovely adventure of those who have never been able to encounter or create the real, necessary and salutary adventure of life."[34]

Review Questions

1. What are some of the ways that experts classify gamblers?
2. What dangers exist for the occasional or recreational gambler?
3. Does the occasional gambler have any responsibility to the pathological or potentially pathological gambler?
4. Why do lotteries target the poor?
5. Why are the poor attracted to the games with the least chance of winning?
6. How are childhood games related to adult gambling?
7. Why do the media emphasize the winners, and not the other side of gambling?

8. Why does the church no longer actively resist gambling?
9. Are professional or amateur gamblers more likely to become addicted?
10. In what ways can pathological gambling become life threatening?

Endnotes

1 _____, "The Bet, Gentlemen, is Billions," *Newsweek*, 46:64, July 11, 1955.

2 _____, "This is What You Thought," *Glamour*, p. 137, December, 1989.

3 Popkin, James, "America's Gambling Craze," 116:46, March 14, 1994.

4 Colson, Charles, "The Myth of the Money Tree," *Christianity Today*, 31:64, July 10, 1987.

5 _____, "Bettor Half," *The Wall Street Journal*, p. 1, July 27, 1989.

6 _____, "Poor Spend More on Lottery, Study Says," *Lexington Herald-Leader*, p. B-3, June 29, 1994.

7 Colson, *loc. cit.*

8 _____, "Gambling Goes Legit," *Time*, 108:56, December 6, 1976.

9 Zauner, Phyllis, "Lotteries Painless Taxation?" *American Legion Magazine*, p. 22, June, 1966.

10 _____, "Gambling: The Newest Growth Industry," *Business Week*, p. 113, June 26, 1978.

11 Will, George F., "In the Grip of Gambling," *Newsweek*, 113:78, May 8, 1989.

12 Dunne, Joseph, "Portrait of the Gambling Addict," *Light*, p. 12, February, 1987.

13 Smith, James F. and Vicki Abt, "Gambling as Play," *Annals of the American Academy of Political and Social Sciences*, 284:131, July 1984.

14 Miller, Robert, "Those Crazy Lotteries," *Maclean's*, 97:14, January 23, 1984.

15 Smith and Abt, *op. cit.*, p. 124.

16 Underwood, John, "Look Up and He's Got Your Money," *Sports Illustrated*, 60:86, May 28, 1984.

17 _____, "Why Legalization is Spreading So Fast," *Business Week*, p. 129, June 26, 1978.

18 _____, "Kicking the Habit," *Time*, 108:61, December 6, 1976.

19 Kantzer, Kenneth S., "Gambling: Everyone's a Loser," *Christianity Today*, 27:12, November 25, 1983.

20 Hammer, Signe, "Gambling Better than Sex," *Science Digest*, 92:24, June, 1984.

[21] *Time,* "Kicking the Habit," *op. cit.,* p. 61.

[22] Zauner, Phyllis, "Lotteries: Painless Taxation?" *American Legion Magazine,* p. 23, June, 1986.

[23] Safakis, Carl, *The Encyclopedia of Gambling,* New York: Facts on File, 1990, pp. 207-208.

[24] Fino, Paul A., "The Case for a National Lottery," *The American Magazine,* 158:105, August, 1954.

[25] *Business Week, loc. cit.*

[26] Brushaber, George K., "The Lottery Plague," *Christianity Today,* 33:15, September 8, 1989.

[27] This progression is based upon Henry R. LeSieur and Robert L. Custer, "Pathological Gambling: Roots, Phases and Treatments," *Annals of the American Academy of Political and Social Sciences,* 474: 151-153, July, 1984.

[28] _____, "Gambling Goes Legit," *Time,* 108:56, December 6, 1976.

[29] Campbell, Felicia, "The Virtues of Gambling," *Business and Society Review,* 17:63-4, Spring, 1976.

[30] Campbell, *loc. cit.*

[31] Campbell, *op. cit.,* 73.

[32] Robin, William J., "Compulsive Gamblers: Reno's Lost Souls," *The Christian Century,* 91:1012, October 30, 1974.

[33] Vrooman, David H., "An Economic Analysis of the New York State Lottery," *National Tax Journal,* 29:488, December, 1976.

[34] Douglas, J.D., "Spreading a Table for Fortune," *Christianity Today,* 23:50, July 20, 1979.

Chapter 3

Of Course
I Want to Win
a Million!

B uddy Post was a big winner—his take was $16.2 million in the Pennsylvania Lottery in 1988. He has had little of the money to spend. In 1992, his former landlady received one third of his annual payments after claiming that she shared the ticket with him. For the time the case was in court he received no payments and fell behind on payments for legal fees, the bar and used car lot he bought. In 1991 he received a sentence of six months to two years on an assault charge after he fired a shot into the ceiling of his garage to scare off his stepdaughter's boyfriend, who was claiming the pickup truck Post had been driving. In 1993 his brother was convicted of trying to kill Post and his wife Constance in order to gain access to the money. In 1994 Constance separated from Post and now receives $40,000 per year, while Post himself receives $24,000 per year after filing for protection from his creditors. He attempted to sell the remaining $5 million in payments for $2.1 million but was prevented. His unmaintained mansion is half-filled with legal papers.[1]

Even the winners are losers. The New York Lottery used to advertise "Hit it once and your troubles are over!"[2] Nearly all of us believe that money will solve our problems. We think that somehow our personality will change and we won't have to take the old person with us into our new found wealth. Such is not the case. If we were negative before winning, we will be negative after. If we were generous before, we will be generous after. If we were happy before, we will be happy after. But, if we were unhappy before, we will still be unhappy after winning. The experience of lottery winners proves this.

We know that over 200 million Americans are gambling and losing. How many are winning? During the first two decades of state lotteries—from 1964 to 1984—the lotteries created 1,444 so-called millionaires.[3] By 1983, in New York alone $2.7 billion had been spent by the bettors to create 122 people who thought they were millionaires.[4] By 1991 that number had grown to over 3,000 and presently is approaching 4,000. Think of it! What a tiny number compared to the hundreds of millions of losers. Most of these people didn't become what we usually think of as millionaires, that is, someone with a million dollars to spend any way they please. A million dollar prize is paid out at the rate of $50,000 per year for twenty years. In the early years some only cleared $25,000 per year after state and federal taxes. As the years have passed most lottery winnings have become exempt from state taxes but not from federal or social security taxes. A million dollar winner now receives around $33,000 per year after taxes. If the winner had no other source of income, that would put them barely above the average income in the U. S., hardly what we think of as a millionaire.

Of course, if the winners kept their jobs and lived at essentially the same level, the extra $33,000 per year could buy a lot of amenities. Nevertheless, the lottery system rips off even the winners. How? If the winners received the whole million, they could reap profits by investing the unspent balance. As it is, the state receives the profit from investment. Most states buy an annuity with a face value of the million to be paid out over twenty years for much less than a million dollars. This keeps the amount they pay in prizes low. Secondly, since the pay-out comes over a twenty-year period, the winner is paid in progressively inflated dollars, with the government again reaping the benefit. Finally, the slow pay-out prevents the winner from purchasing big ticket items like houses or cars with cash. They must pay the finance costs, which on a $100,000 house can amount to as much as $150,000 additional dollars over a twenty-year period.

The state continues to look for other ways to deceive the lottery's customers. In 1990 Kentucky decided to pay those who won less than one million dollars in an unusual way. Three winners were to share a $2 million jackpot. That meant each would get $666,666, right? That is what they thought, but the state lottery acted differently. They paid each approximately $344,000, which they indicated was the "present value" of the prize. In order to get the full amount they would have to invest their winnings for twenty years. In 1993 two of the winners sued the state lottery for the full amount on the basis that it was advertised as a full prize.[5] The lottery winners won.

In this high stakes game of holding as much money as you can and cheating the other person out of as much as possible, sometimes the state or federal government can get burned. In the 1960s in New York, a $132,000 racetrack payoff was not collected for two days. When it was finally claimed, seven men showed up claiming they had equal shares in the ticket. This reduced the tax bite from $67,000 to $23,000. The state was suspicious.[6]

It is true that a handful of genuine millionaires have been created. The largest prize through 1984 was a $40 million pay-off in Illinois. That amounted to $2 million per year for twenty years, of which the winner received over $1 million a year. The pace of millionaire creation has picked up since 1984. However, we must ask ourselves whether the handful of true millionaires and the 4,000 "lucky" pseudo-millionaires are worth the losses of the 200 million people who gamble and win nothing.

Getting Ready to Win

Since nearly all of us dream of winning our million, what do we anticipate doing with it? The most frequently mentioned plan is to get a new car or van. Americans have had a love affair with the automobile since Henry Ford made it possible for most people to purchase one. However, most of us drive something older, less attractive, less expensive or unique than we want. We are tired of repair problems and bills. So, the first thing we plan to do with our winnings is get a new car.

The second most frequently mentioned big ticket item is a new house. Renters look forward to owning their own home. Owners look toward owning a better or bigger house in a better neighborhood. For those who already have the home of their dreams, the plan is a second beach, lakeside or mountain retreat. Interestingly, most intended home purchases are not as extravagant as we might expect, but they are usually in the $100,000 to $300,000 range.

The third goal is a boat or a vacation. The boats generally range from fishing to speed to house boats, depending upon taste. Few plan to deep sea sail or motor, and few plan to buy a yacht. Of course, more modest boats are necessary in light of the lotteries' protracted pay-out methods. The vacation most frequently coveted is a trip to Europe. The desire is for it to last a month. A few mention an around the world tour, but for most Europe is enough. Cruises in the Caribbean are also intensely popular, especially with singles.

The fourth most frequently mentioned plan is a good college education for the children. Parents want their children to have a better life than they have had, and believe college helps provide that. This is true if the children are motivated to enter the professions. However, as many underemployed college graduates know, a college education is not a sure ticket to the comfortable life. Most of the children of lottery winners don't want it. They do not wish to work after the lottery win. They want to play, enjoy the money and win the lottery themselves when they grow up. In the 1930s Simon Kess won the Irish Sweepstakes at 19 years of age. He observed, "I don't need an education with $150,000."[7] One of the most common statements I hear from public school children who do poorly in school is, "Why should I work hard in school? I'm going to win the lottery when I grow up." In a survey I conducted over a four-year period, out of 300 children, 230 expected to win the lottery. Even when confronted by the handful of million dollar winners in Kentucky, they were unshaken in their belief. Their attitude is, "Someone else will lose, and I will win."

Thus, while higher education is the parents' plan, it is not the children's. One wise winner, Ollie Carter, in Rockford, Illinois, realized this and set up a trust for her children and grandchildren. She won $11.4 million—$563,000 a year for 20 years. She and her husband retired, but she told her six children and his seven not to quit their jobs because she was not going to support them. They bought cars for each of her children and major gifts for his, bought a new $200,000 house, two new cars for themselves and took a trip to Paris to shop. Money for tuition, fees, books and room and board for the children and grandchildren was set up. A small allowance for spending money was included. After it was established, Ollie Carter said, ". . . they only get the money if they go to college. If they don't do well in school, they don't get the money."[8] This is the only plan that could work.

Usually one of the last things mentioned is gifts for others, the church or charities. The amazing thing about the intended gifts is their smallness. While there are exceptions, most gifts are in terms of games, bikes and videos for the kids, and a few thousand or hundred for charities out of the million. Sharon Barnes won $16 million in Ohio, gave $15,000 for endowing black student scholarships at Ohio State University and $5,000 for an inner-city health conference. These were definitely worthy gifts, but they amounted to one part in 40 of her annual income.[9] Lottery players who want to get rich don't plan to give much away.

Those who gamble have a plethora of individual goals: money for hobbies, a home for parents, opening a business and any number of other things. Mario Montuoro, who a few years ago accused Raymond Donovan, then secretary of labor, of being present during the bribing of a union leader, was $25,000 in debt, convicted of narcotics and firearms charges, supposedly had a contract out on him by the mob and then won $2.5 million in the New York Lottery. He magnanimously indicated he would establish a fund to fight union corruption, repay loans from friends and buy a bicycle and a bed for his stepchildren. The press did not follow up to see if he made good on any of his promises.[10] One of the winners in New Hampshire's first lottery in 1963 won $100,000 and figured he was "even" for life on the horses.[11]

Magic and Misunderstanding

How do people win? Is there some method to increase your chances of winning? That is a burning question for most people. Numerous magazines and books purport to reveal the secrets of winning in sweepstakes, contests, bingo and lotteries. Almost all the methods touted require you to spend even more money than previously in your effort to win.

The most common method is having a scheme to pick the numbers for lottery games. Many use number books that supposedly have analyzed combinations that are more likely to occur. However, if this works, why don't we read more stories about winners who used this method? Then there are the dream books that explain ways to convert your dreams into numbers to play on the lottery. Many people play combinations of birth dates, the street number of their house, telephone number, social security number, death dates of parents and other numbers associated with themselves. The problem with many of these approaches is that they have a limited range and exclude some percentage of the possible numbers that may be picked by the lottery. This greatly increases the odds against winning. More winners have let the lottery randomly select their number.

Players exhibit a great deal of magical belief and misunderstanding of the odds. Some players believe that their chances of winning increase the more weeks they play. It is true they can't win if they don't play, but the odds each week are essentially the same. Each week is a stand-alone event, and the odds against winning a pick six of 42 numbers is over five million to one. The odds of picking six of 54 in the Lotto America are almost 26 million to one. Some play the same numbers every week for fear that if they stop playing them, those numbers will win eventually. The only way these people can play new numbers is to increase the amount they spend on the lottery.

Contrary to a common belief, the odds of picking the right number are not changed by how many people play the game. What may change is the odds of winning the prize by yourself.

Some things are more unlikely than winning the lottery: being killed in an airline crash, picking the exact blade of grass a golf ball will land upon or being dealt thirteen cards of the same suit in a bridge hand. However, some very improbable things are a lot more likely to happen to you than winning the lottery: being struck by lightning (1 in 2 million) or being dealt a royal flush in a five card draw poker game (1 in 649,700).

Magical thinking has no foundation in reason or religion. One does not find promises in the Scriptures of great wealth without work or receiving something for nothing. The books of Proverbs and Ecclesiastes give the lie to such religious thinking patterns. Nevertheless, many expect God to help them win the lottery. Occasionally when they do, they attribute it to God. Jesse Burrell's handicapped mother told him, "The Lord is going to bless you real good." After winning $4.4 million in the New Jersey Lottery, he said he believed her statement was why he won, but that he had been expecting health, not wealth.[12] Even the editors of the magazine *Jet*, which appeals primarily to a black audience, are attracted by the idea of magic. After a survey they commented that while they could not see any pattern in the way winners selected the numbers, there had to be some method to their madness.[13]

Many believe they will win again even though the odds of such a happening are as astronomical as the first time. The only major multiple winners noted by the press in recent years were Robert and Mary Froner of Brooklyn, New York, who won a major prize (over $25,000) in the New Hampshire Lottery just two days after winning $172,726 on a bet at New York's Roosevelt Raceway, the biggest payoff at that time on a $2 bet anywhere in the U. S.[14] One syndicate of players won twice in England—in 1952 and again in 1955—taking $40,000 to $50,000 for each player each time.[15]

Very little research has been done on either winners or losers in the lottery. Most of what follows in this chapter is based on media stories about winners and the few formal surveys and academic studies of what happens to them. One reason, of course, is that many of the winners will not participate in formal studies for reasons that will become obvious.

Surprises for Winners

Contrary to their expectations, winners do not enter a happy land of pleasant dreams. They enter a real world of human greed and all the pain that can flow from it. Winning has an immense number of negative effects that no one wants to think about.

The first shock is the instant pressure that follows winning. In Canada, where the law requires public release of names, the pressure is intense. Lottery officials encourage winners to write their name and address indelibly on the back of the ticket and to refuse all offers to buy it. (Offers to buy at reduced amounts would supposedly give them tax free dollars.) Winners are urged not to discuss the win with anyone and not to make statements that could later be used in courts as promises to pay. They are urged to immediately call lottery officials to arrange protection for their families and for further advice on how to handle the avalanche of calls and visitors. They are urged to immediately disconnect their phone and get an unlisted number as quickly as possible. They are cautioned to stay at a hidden location for several days and to arrange for private or police protection of their property. Sounds like fun.

Winners can expect to be besieged by relatives who want "loans" or gifts, or simply to share in the wealth. They experience a steady stream of friends, family and con-artists with "business" opportunities in which to invest (most of which lead to losses) as well as beggars and requests for donations. All in all, unless they get that unlisted number quickly or leave the phone off the hook, winners can expect 100 to 300 calls, and as many as 100 visitors at the door in the first few days. States advise winners to be skeptical and not feel guilt when saying no to pleas for help. They advise funneling all charity donations through well-known, reputable agencies.

Few families have completely harmonious relationships. Most will have differences of opinion concerning how the money ought to be handled. Whatever weaknesses were in the family before the win will tend to be aggravated after the win. Divorce and lawsuits are two of the most common results of lottery wins. With money, many married winners decide to seek more glamorous partners. Fragile marriages tend to shatter under the impact of the sudden wealth. Parties already in their second or third marriage are frequently sued by previous spouses for everything from a piece of the action to back child support or alimony. One of the most interesting cases was Curtis Sharp who won $5 million in the New York Lottery in 1982. He made international headlines when he showed up to receive the prize with his estranged wife on one arm and his "fiancee" on the other. He shared the prize with both, and shortly after receiving the first installment, he divorced and remarried. Mike Woodford of Ohio won $15 million but was in the middle of divorce proceedings. The estranged wife got half. Gerald Roberts won $1 million in Canada in 1978. He decided against investing the money, and by the following February had spent half of it on a yacht, a divorce, construction equipment and shares in his favorite hotel and bar. Within a year of winning he died of cirrhosis of the liver at the age of 32. He was both a winner and a victim.[16]

Family friction with all members tends to increase. Resentment from less well-to-do relatives festers. Many relatives are estranged. Conflict with children increases, usually over the performance of chores around the house or achievement in school. Often there is a feeling of not wanting to work among the children of winners. Many families are beset with fears that their children will be kidnapped (although there is no record of this ever having happened), and so they withdraw from family and friends and become isolated.

Spending and debt are frequent problems. Most winners do not understand how little they will get up front and commit to extensive purchases before they find out. The initial spending spree frequently leaves many with debt they cannot manage for several years. A few have had to file for bankruptcy. Ken Proxmire won $1 million in Michigan in 1977. He moved to California, bought three sporting goods stores and went broke in 1980 with $100,000 in debts. His wife left him but later returned. Of his $50,000 yearly payments, $20,500 went to bankruptcy settlements, $10,500 to taxes, leaving him with $19,000 on which to live.[17]

Nearly all winners dramatically increase their consumption. One out of every five splurges on a major vacation trip, the dream of a lifetime. Many simply live in fear that someone is going to con them out of their money. They tend to become more mistrustful of others. Most relationships for these winners deteriorate. Many of the worst cases occurred in the early years of big prizes. Today, the management of lottery systems have brochures and booklets telling winners how to avoid the major pitfalls that have beset winners in the past, but disaster still happens occasionally.

Legal Fees and Great Expectations

What people actually do with their money does not always match what they intended to do. Most handle the money fairly well, although as many as 40 percent of the winners have serious problems.

One of the few early studies was conducted by Mark Abrahamson in 1980. This study was limited and probably sought to test theses that the winning amounts were too small to affect. He studied winners of from $500 to $100,000 to evaluate the effect of sudden wealth (which brings his lower limit into question) upon winners. He was seeking to determine whether winners severed their ties to others. He also expected the effects of sudden wealth to be greater upon the poor than upon the middle class. What he actually found is probably more interesting than what he sought to find.

Abrahamson's study showed that it took up to a year for the full impact of winning to be realized. Most winners spent more money trying to achieve gratification of several sorts and to offset the effects of boredom. Many felt that if they were bored they could go out and buy something and feel better. Many also expressed that large winnings seemed to suppress their efforts to achieve in the future, including the effort to maintain friendships.

While the smaller amounts had little effect, winners of large amounts did show some effects of winning. Many big winners were deluded into thinking there were no limits. They tended to become rebellious, comparatively immoral relative to their previous lifestyles, and eventually despondent. Some had difficulty establishing and maintaining a coherent life plan after a big win.[18]

Another early study of 120 New York winners of $10,000 or more found that 47 put the money into investments, 17 spent it on travel, 10 bought cars, 8 paid up their mortgages, 5 bought new homes, 5 gave to charity, and 2 bought boats and ran for office. This varies greatly from the expected new car and house at the top of the anticipation lists.

Another major expectation was that winners could quit their jobs. That did not happen nearly as frequently as winners expected it to. One recent and comprehensive survey found that 23% quit their jobs, many of these near retirement age.[19] Most of those who do so move to another place, and are reemployed within two years or so. The others who quit were usually older workers near retirement, and the sudden infusion of wealth allowed them to retire early.

More closely in line with expectations of winners was the taking of a vacation. Surveys commonly indicate that 20% or more splurge on a major vacation trip, usually to a remote place (Hawaii is a favorite) that was their lifelong dream. Many of these trips did not fulfill expectations, and there was a certain amount of disappointment that the glamour of real life did not match that of the movies.

Many winners have felt an over stimulation of desires for material things and romance, as well as an increased sense of power. This fits, of course, with the old adage that money is power. One Irish Sweepstakes winner quit his job, moved to Miami and in two months wined, dined and gambled away his entire winnings.[20] The results of this increased sense of power are not always totally bad. Louis Eisenberg, who won $5 million was ". . . so self-conscious that halfway through his career as a maintenance man he turned down a promotion to the post of elevator starter because it meant too much public contact . . ." As a result of winning he became confident enough that taxi drivers no longer refused to take him to Brooklyn. He was also able to meet his longtime favorite singer Lainie Kazan without embarrassment.[21]

Some winners adjust well. The New York study demonstrated that many had a greater sense of security. Rebecca Hood, winner of $1 million in a *Time* magazine sweepstakes in 1985, said she had been playing the sweeps for 16 years and had previously won a watch and some baseball pencils. With the first $40,000 check she tithed $8,000 to the Mormon Church, paid off her debts, continued on her job and visited her brother across the country in Washington State. The happiest recipients of large prizes paid off the mortgage and banked the rest. The winnings provided a nest egg or security blanket that had not been there before, and the winners were content with that. Occasionally there is a happy result to a big win. When Betty and Arthur Gloss won $6 million in 1984, the publicity led to a reunion with his three sons by a previous marriage whom he had not seen since 1949.[22]

While most winners continue their jobs, many of them meet resentment from fellow workers who feel they are taking the job from someone else who needs it more. An example was Joseph Hearl, who won $140,000 in the Irish Sweepstakes, a large amount in 1953. He paid off his mortgage, bought some appliances and a new car, and paid $85,000 in taxes. Thinking they had plenty of money (before the tax bite), the Hearls quit their jobs under pressure from fellow workers. When he got down to $30,000, which was producing less than $200 a month in income, he went back to work. During the time they were not working they were very lonely, feeling they had exchanged friends for isolation.[23] Another example was Mike Wittkowski, who won $42 million. He was hassled so badly by fellow workers for keeping his job that he finally had to quit. He bought a liquor store and become self-employed.[24]

Some winners are only mildly affected. Edward and Kathy Henry won $1 million in the New Jersey lottery in 1971. They indicated that they did "pretty much what we wanted" before their win, so it affected them little. They upscaled, moving from a $37,000 house to a nine room $69,000 house. They bought a car for themselves and helped their parents buy a home in Florida. They began taking an annual Florida vacation and made two four-day trips a year to Las Vegas to gamble. They joined a $1,000 a year country club and spent more on groceries. Edward kept his job, and they invested the balance, expecting to send their kids to any college they wanted.

Patsy and Dick Tilton won a million in the New Jersey Lottery in 1972. Dick kept his $18,000 a year job as an electronics technician at a military installation. They received $32,800 after taxes each year. They did endure ribbing at work, excessive mail, continuous solicitations, had to get an unlisted number, and the kids expected to get everything they wanted. They kept essentially their same standard of living. They stayed in the same house, which they had recarpeted. They bought two new cars and more expensive gifts than in the past. They increased their charitable contributions, took nicer vacations and bought more new clothes. They expressed general satisfaction with the result of the way they handled winning.

Other winners find the winnings disrupt their lives. Nearly all winners dream of quitting their jobs until they realize that there will be no retirement funds after the 20-year pay-out is over unless they continue a plan on their own. Those who do quit are uniformly disappointed with the result, except those near retirement. A New York couple won $200,000, quit their jobs, squandered the money in California in just a few weeks, and returned home jobless and broke. A New Jersey tailor won $1 million, quit his job and was hopelessly in debt in just two years. A Long Island, New York, couple could not handle the pressure. His new sense of power led to arrogance, she developed an ulcer, and they gladly ended their relationship in divorce. One $100,000 winner said he was not happy he won. He still had the same hang-ups as before. Danny Hogan bought a ticket for Margie Moore. The resulting lawsuit over how much each got ended a longtime friendship.[25]

The unexpected pressure gets to nearly all the winners. The incessant phone calls drive them to distraction, although they frequently handle the calls with more grace than others in the same city with the same name who did not win. The concept of the good old American gold-digger is not dead. Kermit Rorkmill, after winning $100,000, received fifteen calls from girls asking for dates, including some who had previously turned him down and two who had refused his proposal. "I didn't know girls were like that," he commented. Erika Earnhart won $1 million in 1976, $50,000 per year tax free. She went through two divorces, major child custody battles, paid huge lawyers fees and wound up paying alimony to one ex-spouse. She chronically borrows to get to the next check and says had she known the result "I'd have torn up that ticket or put it in someone else's name." She still plays the lottery in hopes of winning again and catching up.[26] Corinne Chaney lost $400,000 of her million on a used car lot her friends advised her to buy. She says, "I do not trust people anymore—that's what the lottery did for me."[27]

Probably the ultimate case of disruption was William Curry, a 1990 winner of $3.6 million in Massachusetts. He died of a heart attack three weeks after winning. In another complicated case, Richard Van DeBoe gave his winning $13.6 million ticket to his girlfriend, Kelly Elsinger. His estranged second wife Kandy sued him for half since they were still married. His first wife Helga sued for $21,450 in back child support and an increase in her $75 per week stipend. The IRS said Kelly owed $6.9 million in gift taxes. The final outcome was that Van DeBoe and Elsinger were awarded half after $100,000 was set aside for child support. The lawyers made a killing.[28]

What can we conclude? The minimum a big winner can expect is a disrupted life, with threatened relationships with family and friends. Weathering a win requires maturity, stability and minimizing the impact of the money upon lifestyle. The happiest winners pay off the mortgage on the house, fix it up, buy a new car and take a trip. They spend very little of the rest. The happiest ones keep their jobs. The worst case scenario involves broken marriages, estranged children, angry families, lawsuits, debt and depression. Nearly all wind up with more stress in their lives than before the big win.

Winning big is not the heaven that we anticipate. Is it enough of a heaven to justify all the losers who share in creating it?

Review Questions

1. How would you spend a million dollars?
2. How does your plan differ from what most people think they want for their million?
3. How does your plan differ from how people actually spend their million?
4. Who would be most likely to sue you if you won a million dollars?
5. What is the first protective step that winners must take?
6. Does sudden wealth bring happiness?
7. How do the happiest winners manage their money?
8. How does the big win affect the children of that family?
9. How would you compare the agony that losers suffer with creating what the winners receive?
10. Why are there so few big winners?

Endnotes

[1] Kapsambelis, Niki, "This Man Counts Woes in Large Denominations," *New Jersey Star-Ledger,* Thursday, August 29, 1996.

[2] Chinn, Harvey N., "Lotteries," *United Evangelical Action,* 33:12, Winter, 1974.

[3] _____, "Lotteries: States Hit the Jackpot," *U.S. News and World Report,* 97:16, September 17, 1984.

[4] _____, *New York's Lottery Report, 1976-1983,* p. 7. This is a publication of the New York Lottery.

[5] _____, "Lottery Winners Say They Want Full Value," *Lexington Herald-Leader,* C2, June 28, 1993.

6 _____, "Recreation," *Time*, 83:43, May 8, 1964.

7 _____, "Sweepstakes: Irish Turf Yields 'Gifts From Heaven,'" *Newsweek*, 4:19, November 10, 1934.

8 _____, "$11.4 Million Lottery Winner Has Big Plans For Fortune," *Jet*, 74:25, August 1, 1988.

9 Angelo, Bonnie, "Life at the End of the Rainbow," *Time*, 136:81, November 4, 1991.

10 _____, "The Better Payoff," *Time*, 119:13, May 10, 1982.

11 _____, "Customs: The Bonanza Machine," *Time*, 84:59, September 18, 1964.

12 _____, "Winning Secrets of Black Lottery Winners," *Jet*, 12:31, April 25, 1988.

13 *Ibid.*

14 *Time, loc. cit.*

15 _____, "Habits Abroad: The Big Gamble," *Newsweek*, 45:42, April 25, 1955.

16 Miller, Robert, "Those Crazy Lotteries," *Maclean's*, 97:16, January 23, 1984.

17 _____, "When Lightning Strikes," *Time*, 123:43, May 28, 1984.

18 Abrahamson, Mark, "Sudden Wealth, Gratification and Attainment: Durkheim's Anomie of Affluence Reconsidered," *American Sociological Review*, 45:49-57, February, 1980.

19 _____, Angelo, *Time, loc. cit.*

20 Stewart-Gordon, James, "The Odds: 450,000 to One," *The Reader's Digest*, 74:93, April, 1959.

21 _____, "The Brave New World of a Lottery Winner," *Newsweek*, 103:10, May 21, 1984.

22 _____, "When Lightning Strikes," *Time*, 123:43, May 28, 1984.

23 Merson, B., "So He Won $140,000," *Collier's*, 133:30-34, June 11, 1954.

24 Angelo, *Time, loc. cit.*

25 *Ibid.*

26 Pulliam, Russ, "Unlucky Lotto," *Christianity Today*, 29:17, October 18, 1985.

27 Hluchy, Patricia, "The Gains and Losses of the Newly Rich," *Maclean's*, 97:17, January 23, 1984.

28 _____, "Closing in on the Winner's Circle," *Newsweek*, 112:31, December 26, 1988.

Chapter 4

How to Lose When Someone Else Gambles

I listened on the phone intently as the choked voice on the other end poured out his story through tears. As a young couple living in the Midwest, he and his wife made an occasional vacation trip to Las Vegas to gamble. One year after a big win they decided to move to Las Vegas so they could gamble more frequently, since they seemed to be lucky. They could only get low-paying jobs, but since they both knew black jack well they soon became dealers. Then began a cycle of more and more gambling. They would work their shifts and often gamble another six to eight hours a day. They got deeper and deeper in debt and more and more depressed. They moved to progressively poorer places, pawned everything of value and were reduced at one point to living in their car. His wife committed suicide. He considered it himself.

He finally fled back to the Midwest but could not find work. When he called me he was dealing black jack again on a river boat in Illinois. He pleaded with me to tell people to stay away from Las Vegas, which he called the killer of dreams and families.

Gambling is a losing proposition. Everyone loses nearly all the time. Except for the professionals who run the games, gambling is for suckers. Losing at gambling increases the pressure and the guilt in the life of every person who participates. Gambling affects an average of twelve other persons whose lives touch the gambler and reduces the residual money the gambler has left for the needs and wants of himself and others. Economic studies have obtained reliable results by assuming that the sum wagered by a player closely approximates his losses because of rebetting the winnings.[1] As one gambler said, "The aim of the game is still to bleed you as quickly as they can without actually spilling it on the floor."[2]

The comedian and gambler Joe E. Lewis once said, "I hope I break even today. I need the money."[3] Gamblers great and small are always trying to get even. This, of course, means they are always in the hole, they have always lost money. Gamblers like to say that "quitters never win!" "Stayers" never win either. Even the temporary wins of "stayers" turn into losses. The gambler Mario Puzo supposedly once said jokingly, "All parents should teach their children card games, mainly because they are great preparation for the disappointments of life."[4] Unfortunately, gambling itself is one of those great disappointments. Gamblers mostly lose but remain in the chase in the forlorn hope of catching up.

In the previous chapter we saw that even winners have problems, and big winners sometimes have big problems. We can easily accept that losers have problems as well, and big losers have even bigger problems. In Chapter 2 we looked at the four general kinds of gamblers—the professionals who run the games, professionals who attempt to make a living gambling, amateurs who play often, and occasional amateurs.

The operators have low risk, are essentially guaranteed a profit, operate behind the scenes and frequently have connections with the mob, even though they may be essentially businessmen in states where gambling is legal.

The second group, those who attempt to make a living through gambling, is relatively small, fairly rapidly growing and contains many pathological gamblers.

The third group of high frequency amateurs contains most of the pathological gamblers.

The fourth group are the part-time and occasional gamblers who make up most of the rest of the population. The losers we look at in this chapter come mostly from the high frequency amateur group.

Millions of Americans are losing hundreds of billions of dollars. For some strange reason, most think they are not going to lose and somehow they are going to overcome the odds and win. They believe this despite the overwhelming evidence that nearly everyone loses, and loses all they bet. In this chapter we look at the consequences for the losers.

Letting the Poor Pay the Bills

We look first at the poor, the biggest losers relative to their income. Even as ardent an early advocate of lotteries as A. J. Sabath said, "Unquestionably, gambling makes the poor poorer."[5] Those near and below the poverty line have the most to lose. A study conducted in the state of Maryland revealed that "people earning less than $10,000 buy more tickets than any other group."[6] Most of the poor play the lottery because the tracks, Las Vegas and Atlantic City are out of their reach. (This is rapidly changing, however, as casinos spread. The gambling interests believe they will have a casino within a three-hour drive of nearly every American by the year 2000.[7]) Most of the poor play in the hope of escaping poverty, despite the fact that it drives them farther down the economic ladder. Blacks play the lottery regularly and disproportionately. They support the lottery on a regular basis, but they believe that when prizes get big, whites move into the market and disproportionately secure the big prizes.[8]

Every state that institutes the lottery experiences growing welfare rolls. Nearly every state that institutes the lottery experiences some economic downturn. The reason is simple. The money spent on the lottery by the marginally poor family cannot be spent on necessities such as food, shelter and clothing, let alone on luxuries like automobiles. As Oregon state representative Tony Van Vliet expressed it, "I always felt that it was an insidious way to re-collect our welfare dollars."[9]

Getting the hard data on the magnitude of these problems is difficult, but some studies have been attempted.

The high frequency player normally spends $40 per week on the lottery. For the poor this can be as much or more than 20% of their income. In New Jersey, one out of three families with incomes under $10,000 spend 20% or more on lotteries.[10] For the upper middle class it is less than what is spent on recreation. Of course, one must keep in mind that the wealthier player who plays the lottery soon tires and moves on to other forms of gambling that have a greater chance of return.

Some writers have sought to establish that the middle class is the main support of lotteries, but the data are skewed. An Arizona study found the average player was a 36-year-old white male with an income of $20,000.[11] What this means is that more whites play than blacks. True. However, this does not mean they play proportionally to their numbers in the general population. The $20,000 was a mean salary which can be skewed by a few high salaries. A more meaningful measure in this case would have been the median (middle) salary, which would have been lower. Further, Arizona, which is home to relatively few blacks, is not representative of the nation as a whole. With techniques such as these, the facts can be misrepresented to show that white middle-class people are the mainstay of the lottery. It just is not so. A New York study demonstrated that 36% of the problem gamblers were women, 32% were minority (compared to the 11–15% minority population participating in the survey), and one in three was under thirty.[12]

Gambling losses are felt more quickly by the poor gambler's family. No food. No new shoes when needed. No hope. A Mexican social worker once said that, ". . . the Lottery is the only ray of hope that the poor people have, and hope is as necessary to the well-being of an individual as bread."[13] Tragically, the lottery was then and is now a false hope.

The poor are more vulnerable to the sales pitch of the state lottery. They are less able to understand the odds. A Harvard study showed that blue collar workers with a high school education were less able to estimate odds in all gambling situations than were college trained students.[14] The lottery is, therefore, a callous tax by the wealthy upon the poor. While it is a "voluntary" tax, the poor are least able to understand the decision they make to play the lottery and can least afford this regressive tax.

The poor also lose emotionally. The increased pressure of gambling losses is the undoing of many families. When two family units are created from one, as in the case of divorce or separation, both households frequently fall below the poverty line if they did not before. We can make light of the pressure, but that ignores the real situation of the mother who puts the milk back on the shelf to buy the lottery ticket.

The children of the poor lose. Anyone who is dependent upon a gambler loses, but the children are the most vulnerable because they have the fewest alternatives. They frequently lack adequate food and clothing because of the habits of adults. A Kentucky study revealed that 17% of the teenagers in that state are underfed, and some fraction of that is due to gambling. This is perhaps the most reprehensible and inexcusable consequence of gambling. Pathological gambling is also linked to increased child abuse. It is a cycle that threatens to repeat itself: a California study pointed out that teenage gambling increased 40% after the lottery began in 1985.[15]

Transferring the Tax Load

Not only do the poor lose—taxpayers lose, too. Every state picks up the tab for regulation and enforcement. The gambling commissioners who run the lotteries pay their officers and supervising boards, if such exist, out of the proceeds of the lottery. The cost of enforcement when problems develop and the necessary watchdogging that must be done to keep commissions honest is directly taken from taxpayers.

Since illegal gambling increases in every state that institutes the lottery, the cost of enforcement of gambling laws rises at both the local and state level. If enforcement is ignored corruption follows. In any location where the proceeds from illegal gambling become significant, the mob is sure to follow to organize the gambling. The mob is no longer the phenomenon of the big cities— New York, Philadelphia, Chicago and Detroit—but has spread to 23 major centers, from which it reaches to every city of over 50,000 people that has significant gambling, drugs and prostitution.[16] You just don't read about it. The lottery is just the beginning of gambling expansion, for there will be ongoing pressure to introduce casino gambling, legalized slots, riverboat gambling, dog tracks, horse tracks, jai alai, video terminals, Internet gambling or any other form that can turn a buck for the operators.

The taxpayers lose because the economic base shrinks, reducing tax revenues from other sources. Taking several hundred million or a few billion out of the economy has pitched many a state from boom times into malaise. The lottery does not produce anything. There is no commodity involved. There is nothing to consume. The money is taken from the many, 40% or more is redistributed to a few, 20% is distributed to advertisers (a service, not a commodity) and the managers of the lottery and the other 40% goes to the state, which provides services and does not produce many durable goods. (The 20% for administrative costs is a conservative figure. A survey of 61 national lotteries worldwide found that "administrative costs" exceeded 20% in every case.) The only production involved is the equipment and the printing of cards, which may account for two to five percent of the gross, depending upon the size of the state. If the amount of money spent on lotteries were spent on durable goods and consumables, it would give every state a major economic boost.

Taxpayers lose along with businessmen when sales decline and delinquent accounts grow, which is the common pattern after lotteries are instituted. Grocery businesses seem to feel the crunch first, especially when the lottery is new. In the late 1960s the lottery workers in Puerto Rico went on strike for ten days. During that period of time food sales jumped 30%. The poor are the most likely to fail to feed themselves when gambling.[17] Declines in poor neighborhoods of two to four percent have been reported. The percentage the store gets for selling the lottery tickets sometimes does not make up for the losses in sales on groceries. In poorer neighborhoods the rise in delinquent accounts has been sufficient to close some stores altogether, based on anecdotal evidence, although statistics on this are not available.

Finally, taxpayers lose when welfare costs rise, as they always do following the arrival of the lottery. At the same time that the gross product of a state declines from the loss of hundreds of millions from the economy, the number of unemployed and welfare applications invariably rise, increasing the state's welfare costs. In Kentucky, during the first four years of the lottery, the number of people living in poverty rose from 578,000 to 763,000—and this during an economic recovery with declining unemployment. The state's welfare costs rose by 40%.[18] While this effect has been repeated in other states, it is especially striking in poor states like Kentucky and Mississippi because so many live near the poverty line. However, the impact upon wealthier states is not negligible. Dr. Valerie Lorenz of the National Center for Pathological Gambling says that Maryland's 1990 cost in lost productivity, theft, embezzlement, tax fraud, lost revenues and welfare costs was $1.5 billion. The gross of the lottery was $335 million, from which the state received less than 30%.[19]

Although several states designate their lottery receipts for education, numerous studies of the net effect of lottery income upon education have discovered that the lottery is a net loss for education. As soon as lottery receipts are earmarked for the state's schools, legislators withdraw other appropriations from education. This is not something that happens occasionally—it is standard procedure, as we shall see in the next chapter.

Losing and Addiction

Those who become pathological gamblers are losers also. Gambling addiction has increased in every state where a lottery has begun. Psychiatrists, psychologists and Gamblers Anonymous all report an increased need for their services when a state begins a lottery. "Gambling of any kind encourages more gambling. Far from feeling the sting of competition, illegal operations find more clients."[20] Some of these who increase their gambling become pathological. One gambler described stealing from his kids' piggy banks and selling pints of blood to get a "roll" for playing dice. Another tells of stealing the money saved for his father's funeral to play the horses.

Professional gamblers seek to avoid such compulsions. They say, "Never bet more than you might spend on some other form of recreation. 'A gambler must never think about how much he'd like to win. . . . He's got to keep in mind instead what he can afford to lose.'"[21] Do most gamblers follow such a rule? Probably not.

A standard Gamblers Anonymous joke goes, "How can you tell when a compulsive gambler is lying? When his lips move." The same can almost be said of some of the proponents of lotteries in their efforts to avoid the implications of lotteries. GA leaders emphasize that lotteries make their work much harder. In a state with a lottery it is much more difficult for a pathological gambler to adhere to total abstinence. It is much easier to stay away from the track or the casino, or even the off-track betting parlor, than it is to stay away from the grocery or the gas station. Several studies show that accessibility determines the rate at which people become pathologically addicted.[22] GA has also found since its beginning in 1957 that it is much more difficult to establish in the mind of the gambler the immorality of gambling when the state endorses it. Outsiders say their rate of success in helping addicts is only one in thirty.

Two broad schools of thought have arisen concerning pathological gambling. The sociological group views gambling in light of its social context, with increases in the frequency of gambling causing social problems but not necessarily psychological ones. Mark G. Dickerson argued for this position in *Compulsive Gamblers* (1984). On the other hand the psychiatric view is that excessive gambling is aberrant behavior and the result of illness. In 1980 the American Psychiatric Association's *Diagnostic and Statistical Manual of Mental Disorders* [called DSM III] listed "Pathological Gambling" under "Disorders of Impulse Control Not Elsewhere Classified."[23] This document, essential for classifying patients for receipt of insurance payment for psychologists and psychiatrists, describes the disorder as follows:

The essential features are a chronic and progressive failure to resist impulses to gamble and gambling behavior that compromises, disrupts, or damages personal, family, or vocational pursuits. The gambling preoccupation, urge, and activity increase during periods of stress. Problems that arise as a result of the gambling lead to an intensification of the gambling behavior. Characteristic problems include loss of work due to absences in order to gamble, defaulting on debts and other financial responsibilities, disrupted family relationships, borrowing money from illegal sources, forgery, fraud, embezzlement, and income tax evasion.

Commonly these individuals have the attitude that money causes and is also the solution to all their problems. As the gambling increases, the individual is usually forced to lie in order to obtain money and to continue gambling, but hides the extent of the gambling. There is no serious attempt to budget or save money. When borrowing resources are strained, antisocial behavior in order to obtain money for more gambling is likely. Any criminal behavior—e.g., forgery, embezzlement, or fraud—is typically nonviolent. There is a conscious intent to return or repay the money.[24]

Psychiatric investigators have consistently found negative emotional states central to the pathological gamblers. The strongest of these is depression. The difficult-to-determine issue is which is the cause and which is the effect. The best current evidence is split with the majority favoring the rise of serious depression along with the rise in pathological behavior. The minority opinion is that depression preceded the descent into compulsive gambling. Associated with the depression are tension, irritability, hostility, suspiciousness and "interpersonal aberrations." Some recent research has tentatively linked pathological gambling to childhood attention deficit disorders. This research suggests that gambling is an impulse control problem similar to attention deficit disorder.[25]

When the pathological gambler does experience an occasional win, he is unable to take the money and run. The win merely provides the stake for the next round of gambling. The loans are already made. No need to pay them off, experience losses and have to go borrow again. Better to leave the loan and use the winnings to attempt to parlay this small win into a bigger one. Then the loans will be paid off. Most pathological gamblers live for the thrill of the "action." For most it appears to bring more gratification than sex or food. Anthropologist Charlotte Olmsted even claimed it was a substitute for sex.[26]

The thrill of the action leads to depression as soon as the stake is gone. Three of four pathological gamblers experience serious periods of depression. Four out of five at some time think about suicide. One in eight make a potentially lethal attempt. Nearly half experience restlessness, elevated moods and racing thoughts, as well as the depression. A third, according to some experts, are both manic and depressive. For the gambler, the depression is not temporary, but long term. For more than one in three, gambling is associated with drug or alcohol abuse as well. Other researchers argue that some of this is incorrect since gamblers are liars. They suggest that some reports of depression on the part of gamblers is lying to avoid responsibility for their actions. Probably only a psychologist can understand just how lying about depression excuses pathological gambling. When the debt becomes impossible, suicide becomes more common. In the late 1950s in Japan the suicide rate over gambling losses on bicycle races became so high that the Japanese legislators reduced the permissible number of races to reduce gambling opportunities. The suicide rate dropped.[27]

Interestingly enough, lay people and literary types recognized the passion to gamble as pathological long before the psychologists began to study it. In literature the picture of the gambler has long been associated with glamour, excitement and pleasure, but also with pain and hate—in other words, with human emotions, and distorted ones at that. Dostoevski's *The Gambler* was in part autobiographical and clearly pictures the battle against fate and perhaps even a battle seeking the correction of a firm father. George Eliot in *Middlemarch* (1871) recognized ". . . that specific disease in which the suspension of the whole nervous energy on a chance of risk becomes as necessary as the dram to the drunkard."[28] Thackeray in *The Virginians* and Stevenson in *Kidnapped* also portrayed the pathological dimension of the gambler.

Ernest Simmel in 1920 began the first formal psychological studies of gambling. In 1928 Sigmund Freud attempted to explain the drive to gamble as a substitute for masturbation. Theodor Reik, a student of Freud's, sought to explain the compulsion as a modern "oracle" through which the gambler attempts to see into the future. Rene LaFarge of France saw gambling as the erotization of fear. Ernest Jones in England saw gambling as the sublimation of oedipal aggression toward the father image in the gambler's life.

Between 1936 and 1943 Edmund Begler sought to build a comprehensive psychology and typology of gamblers. We still agree with many of the characteristics of the gambler that he found. He habitually takes chances; gambling precludes all other interests; the gambler does not learn from defeat; the gambler does not stop when he wins; he progressively risks too large a sum; and he experiences a thrill. In 1947 Ralph Greerson called the gambler an impulsive neurotic. In 1986 Leonide Goldstein found pathological gambling related to impulse control disorders such as alcoholism, with attention deficit disordered children more likely to become involved in either gambling, alcoholism or both.[29] Others see it simply as a childish desire to have without earning, the simple practice of magical thinking or playing out superstitious patterns.

It's Not My Problem

As stated earlier, gamblers can expect no help from the operators of the game. The house will not set a limit for you when you cannot set your own. As Bob Brigham, vice president of Harrah's in Las Vegas, said in 1974, "Wouldn't you get angry if a restaurant waitress told you that you were too fat to have a second piece of pie? We feel the same way about the so-called compulsive gambler. If they want to lose their money, that's their business." So there is little help and not much hope for the gambler.

An example of the willingness of the house to take all you have is the case of Sir Hugh Frazer. He lost up to $500,000 a night at roulette and eventually had to sell stock in his company to pay his debts. He eventually lost control of the clothing store empire he and his father had built.[30] Another addicted high roller was the "sultry Iranian" Kitty Milinaire, daughter-in-law of the Duchess of Belfast, who gambled away $6 million in three years.[31]

Unlike the wealthy, however, the poor man does not have the money for therapy. Suicide is the more common way out. In early 1995 the St. Louis papers were full of the story of the Illinois housewife who didn't pay the bills, went seventeen months without paying the mortgage, cleaned out the savings accounts and pawned her wedding rings. Her husband, who let her handle the finances, had no idea what was happening and was in shock when she killed herself on the morning the sheriff was coming to evict them. She was a good mother, an excellent teacher and a hooked gambler.[32] How unfortunate that only one problem gambler in 25 can find a GA group, even if they wish help.

Some justify gambling by comparing the thrill of risking one's resources on cards to the entrepreneurial capitalist who is also a major risk taker. However, the gambler does not produce anything, while the entrepreneur does. The gambler does not win, the other frequently does. Nevertheless, people continue to try to put a morally acceptable face on gambling. In a bizarre casting of gambling as a positive moral good, Albert Mammond, a former philosophy professor at Johns Hopkins University, said, "I think luck as well as freedom must be counted in the salvation of man as well as in the fall. I believe that luck should be counted in the story of Jesus. God may have known he had a good bet, but he had to wait for the finish."[33]

Males are at greater risk of becoming pathological gamblers than females. First of all, a higher percentage of men are high frequency gamblers. Secondly, males appear to be under more peer pressure than females to prove their virility through gambling. When a female enters a game, studies have shown that all the men involved become more cautious and conservative in their gambling. On the other hand, when females move into a predominately male game they tend to increase their levels of risk taking.[34]

As indicated in Chapter 2, gambling usually leads to crime, petty or otherwise. An increase in gambling through the introduction of lotteries inevitably leads to an increase in crime. Tax fraud, loan application fraud and theft (especially from family members) are the most common forms, although occasionally the crime is more serious. Most gamblers are angry but nonviolent. For that reason, embezzlement is attractive to many gamblers. Lest you think crime does not follow gambling, remember that Reno and Las Vegas had, until recently, the highest number of police per capita of any cities in the country. Las Vegas has the leading number of major crimes per capita of any city in the country. Suicide, murder, quarrels and divorce are the fruit of gambling.

These first four chapters have outlined the nature of the problem of gambling. Legal gambling increases illegal gambling. Lotteries and other forms of gambling have negative economic impacts, both in terms of productivity and in terms of increasing state welfare costs. Gambling breeds pathological gamblers, up to five percent of the population, as many as 10 to 12 million at present.

The half of us who are only occasional gamblers, or those few of us who don't gamble, excuse ourselves from responsibility by saying, "Hey, it's not my fault. I don't abuse gambling." However, we cannot afford our sideline indifference. Wasted lives and a ruined

economy are too much to lose. We must resist the gambling proponents' easy arguments that hide most of the truth. We must say
that occasional pleasure is not worth the cost to society of the presence of legal gambling. Again, is it satisfaction enough to the millions of losers to vicariously share in the "pleasure" of the winner?
The few professionals who get wealthy from gambling are leeching
the life blood from our society. It is time for a change.

Review Questions

1. Who are the only gamblers who consistently win?
2. Why do people with lower income disproportionately spend
   on the lottery?
3. What is statistically wrong with studies that identify the "typical" player?
4. What are some of the ways taxpayers lose when gambling ex-
   pands?
5. What is the connection between gambling and social welfare
   costs?
6. What are the most common companions of pathological gambling?
7. How can pathological gambling be life threatening?
8. Why is so little help available for addicted gamblers?
9. Why do gamblers usually turn to nonviolent crime?
10. What are gambling's effects on the addicted gambler's family?

Endnotes

[1] Kinsey, Robert K., "The Role of Lotteries in Public Finance," *National Tax Journal*, 16:14, March, 1963.

[2] _____, "Recreation: God Save the Ace," *Time*, 86:70, September 10, 1965.

[3] _____, "Everybody Wants a Piece of the Action," *Newsweek*, 80:46, April 10, 1972.

[4] Smith, James F. and Vicki Abt, "Gambling as Play," *Annals of the American Academy of Political and Social Sciences*, 474:132, July, 1984.

[5] Sabath, A. J., "Should We Have a National Lottery?" *American Magazine*, 134:63, November, 1942.

[6] Willimon, William, "Lottery Losers," *The Christian Century*, 107:48, January 17, 1990. See also Charles T. Clotfelter and Philip J. Cook, *Selling Hope: State Lotteries in America*, Cambridge, MA: Harvard University Press, 1989, p. 100.

[7] Popkin, James, "America's Gambling Craze," *U.S. News and World Report,* p. 41, March 14, 1994.

[8] _____, "Are State Lotteries Stacked Against Blacks?" *Ebony,* 46:126-128, June, 1991.

[9] _____, "Gambling on a Way to Trim Taxes," *Time,* 123:42, May 28, 1984.

[10] _____, "Privatise State Lotteries," *The Economist,* 312:12, July 1, 1989.

[11] *Ibid.*

[12] Neff, David, and Thomas Giles, "Feeding the Monster Called 'More,' " *Christianity Today,* 35:20, November 25, 1991.

[13] Fligelman, Belle, "Ten Cents a Chance," *Inter-American,* 2:27, November, 1943.

[14] _____, "Odds-Payers' Odd Preferences," *Psychology Today,* 12:31, May, 1979.

[15] Atkins, *op. cit.,* pp. 20-21.

[16] Powell, Stewart, Steven Emerson, and Kelly Orr, "Bustin' the Mob," *U.S. News and World Report,* February 3, 1986, p. 27.

[17] _____, "The Search for Santa Claus," *The Nation,* 203:437, October 31, 1966.

[18] Bishop, Bill, "More People Have Fallen Under Wheel of Poverty," *Lexington Herald Leader,* p. E-1, Sunday, February 26, 1995.

[19] Atkins, *op. cit.,* p. 29.

[20] Pulliam, Russ, "Unlucky Lotto," *Christianity Today,* 29:17, October 18, 1985.

[21] Edgerton, Jerry, "How Winning Football Bettors Do It," *Money,* 7:51, January, 1978.

[22] Dunne, Joseph, "Portrait of the Gambling Addict," *Light,* p. 12, February, 1987.

[23] _____, *DSM III,* Washington, D.C., American Psychiatric Association, 1980, p. 291.

[24] *Ibid.*

[25] Miller, Lawrence, "Pathological Gambling: Cerebral Roulette," *Psychology Today,* 20:9, April, 1986.

[26] _____, "Why People Gamble and Should They?" *Time,* 90:27, July 21, 1967.

[27] _____, "Bicycle Racing: Worse Than Prostitution?" *Newsweek,* 54:34, December 28, 1959.

[28] Dickerson, *op. cit.,* p. 1.

[29] *Psychology Today, ibid.*

[30] _____, "Sir Hugh's Addiction," *Time,* 108:54, December 20, 1976.

[31] _____, "Britain: In the Chips," *Time*, 112:41, July 24, 1978.

[32] Bosworth, Charles Jr., "Woman's Suicide Perplexing," *St. Louis Post-Dispatch*, Illinois Edition, pp. 1 and 12, February 4, 1995. See also February 22, 1995.

[33] _____, "Why People Gamble and Should They?" *Time*, 90:27, July 21, 1967.

[34] Bauer, Richard H. and James H. Turner, "Betting Behavior in Sexually Homogeneous and Heterogeneous Groups," *Psychological Reports*, 34:251-8, 1974.

Chapter 5

Three Percent of the State Budget! You Must Be Kidding!

The most widely held myth about gambling—even more prevalent than the myth that it is harmless recreation—is that it will produce revenue and relieve the tax burden. Two decades ago Raymond S. Blanchard revealed the gambling interests' intentions at a 1976 National Conference on Public Gaming, saying, "We've got to convince people we're not in the gambling business. We're in the public revenue business."[1] Nevertheless, despite his claim, casinos and state lotteries *are* in the gambling business.

Is Gambling a Tax Break?

As a major source of revenue, gambling is largely a failure. Lotteries and river boats were supposed to provide an easy source of revenue without increasing taxes. So far, only in Maryland (briefly at 6.9%) has lottery income exceeded 5% of a state's general revenues. By 1984 the average revenue in states with lotteries was less than 2% of state budgets.[2] (At present, the best estimates are that lottery revenues account for a little over 3% of state budgets.) In the 1970s, gambling promoters were certain that if they could have sports gambling they could produce 10% of a state's revenue needs.[3] While Metropolis, Illinois, and Tunica, Mississippi, for example, have reaped great local benefits in terms of taxes, their river boats have not produced significant tax revenues for the states where they are allowed. New Jersey actually saw a decline in the percentage of tax revenues received from gambling after the advent of the casinos. Gambling is generally an inadequate and sordid substitute for fair taxes.

But What About Nevada?

Then, there is Nevada, the dream state of many lawmakers.

Nevada is interesting. In 1978, *Business Week* quoted an investment company executive as saying, "In Nevada, gaming revenues have grown at a 14% compound rate for the past 30 years. Gambling is the closest thing to being a recession-resistant business."[4] This is high praise indeed, but examine the entire picture before you applaud. Casino gambling was legalized in 1931 and first taxed in 1945,[5] but it was not until travel restrictions were lifted in 1946 that gambling began to grow rapidly. By 1971, state revenue from gambling amounted to $41 million, which at that time was 40% of the state budget.[6] One-third of all those employed in Nevada worked in the gambling business.[7] Even in Nevada, however, all was not well. After 1980 the toll of competition from Atlantic City caused an end to growth. New innovations became necessary to promote further growth, for example, the video slot machines which appeal to the younger generation and the themed casinos of the 1990s. The state's take of revenues leveled off at just over 50%. Other state taxes are low or non-existent.

With Nevada in mind, politicians as long ago as 1963 began to look ". . . to the gambling market as the cornucopia of profits and revenue that could help solve chronic city and state fiscal crises. . . ."[8] New York City was the classic example. The city sought to use off-track betting to fund health care for the elderly, anti-narcotics efforts and mental health care. Managers expected to reap $225 million per year for the city, but much less was realized.[9] The expectation of the populace, led by the politicians, was that services could be expanded without raising taxes. This dream has often been dashed by the harsh reality that gambling has hidden costs that are not apparent before it becomes entrenched. Nevada illustrates that.

There is a darker side to Nevada that is less well advertised by those seeking to promote gambling elsewhere. Low taxes and high revenue are not the whole story. In the 1960s, Nevada's major crime rate was double, and the suicide rate triple, that of any other state.[10] Nevertheless, in 1963 *Senior Scholastic* magazine informed our nation's teenagers that Nevada had no major crime problem.[11] As a result Las Vegas needs the highest number of police per capita of any city in the country. This remained true into the 1980s, with the highest bankruptcy rate added in the late 1970s.[12] Nevada's prisons are poor, full, and, according to the prisoners, inmates are poorly fed, the buildings are vermin infested, and prison life is brutal. Gambling is freely allowed in the prisons, presumably to help keep the prisoners' minds off their other problems.[13] Apparently, some of that wonderful revenue from gambling is needed to clean up the mess that gambling makes.

Nevada's problems are not unique when gambling becomes a major revenue source. When the state of New York was considering off-track betting, the speaker of the New York State Assembly conducted a study of the effect of off-track betting in England. He found that ". . . the amount of gambling had jumped all out of proportion to the economy, the number of bad debts was rising, and low-income people were being hardest hit of all."[14] Every major academic study that has not been financed by gambling interests has repeated the pattern of this very early study. Don't expect the states to restrain the growth of gambling, however, for politicians don't bite the hands that feed them, and many lawmakers have been well cared for by gambling money, including Bob Dole's half million dollar fund raiser in Las Vegas in July of 1995. Bad debts, poverty, crime and suicide are too often forgotten in the excitement when a new form of gambling enters a state.

Will Gambling Bring Boom Times?

A second problem Nevada faces is that industry is reluctant to locate there. Part of that attitude is due to the state's short supply of water, but another factor is that industrial analysts have found that where gambling is strong, workers are less dependable. Because they miss work more frequently, the company experiences losses in productivity. This was noted beginning in World War II when many industries discovered that with surplus money and so little to buy, gambling was a factory problem. In the boom times of the 1950s, many major American industries banned craps and refused access to the plant floor for bookies.[15] The various industrial unions recognized the problem as well and refused to defend employees who were fired for gambling.[16] Some of the unions worried about infiltration by crooks and gamblers, with the Maritime Union even dropping some members who were implicated in arranging gambling on cruise ships.[17] Gambling reduces the will to work, for all are tempted by the dream of great wealth without having to work. This is true, despite Nevada sociologist Felicia Campbell's claim that employees performing monotonous tasks would benefit from gambling breaks to keep them alert. Industry has found for decades that incentives are more effective.

A third feature of gambling in Nevada is the influence of the mob. As is commonly known, Benjamin "Bugsy" Seigel, a subordinate of Meyer Lansky, the "Chairman of the Board" for the New York La Cosa Nostra, first recognized the opportunity for a desert gambling oasis. He opened the first casino, secured an agreement to run Las Vegas as an "open" city for any mobster (in order to minimize gang wars for control) and influenced the state legislature. The influence of the mob has continued, with a steady skimming of profits from various casinos, into the early 1990s. Since the 1970s, the mob has cleaned up its act to some extent by operating through legitimate businesses and honest front men, but legal gambling "poses little threat to illicit gambling."[18] Known criminals have ties to casinos in Las Vegas and other Nevada towns. Many maintain homes or hotel suites there. For the record, here are some of the known connections.

- ❏ The New York mob owned or maintained interest in The Flamingo from the time it was opened in 1946 to 1971, when it was sold to the Hilton chain.

- ❏ William E. Roemer, Jr., a former FBI investigator of the Chicago mob, calls the Stardust the flagship casino of the Chicago mob, which they later shared with the Cleveland mob when Moe Dalitz moved in to run the action for that group.

- ❏ At the Tropicana, Lou Lederer was the front man for Frank Costello of the Chicago mob.

- ❏ The Aladdin was skimmed by the Detroit and St. Louis families.

- ❏ The Dunes was owned by Major Riddle, who was closely associated with the Chicago mob and by Morris Shencker, who fronted for the mob in Kansas City and St. Louis.

❑ The Sands was owned by New York mobster Doc Stacher until it was purchased by Howard Hughes in 1967 and went straight.

❑ The Desert Inn was opened in 1950 with Moe Dalitz and other members of the Cleveland mob as owners.[19]

In the 1970s mob ownership became hidden, and organized crime's take from casino profits was reduced to skimming, which at times may have reached 10% of the gross. By the early 1990s, the Nevada State Gaming Control Board believed they had reduced the skim to less than 2%, and that the casinos were honestly run. Some authorities consider mob rule benevolent, but how can a homicide rate near that of Detroit and occasional assaults upon reporters be deemed "benevolent"? The rest of the crime is committed by the customers of the mob. Several years ago Fred J. Cook, a prize-winning reporter, said, "The sinister truth is that Nevada's legalization of gambling was one of the greatest boons ever bestowed on the American underworld by a grateful government. . . . The net result has been to make 'fun-loving' Las Vegas virtually the capital of American crime."[20] This statement would be just as true today if we substituted "gambling and political influence" for "crime."

The easy revenues from gambling, thus, bring crime and influence peddling that is not confined to Nevada. Organized crime permeates our society and delivers drugs, prostitution and gambling. As gambling grows legally, three decades of evidence point to a corresponding growth of illegal gambling. What is unfathomable is how both the public and the politicians can ignore gambling's social cost. The loss of industry to areas with less expensive work forces, the weakening of the will to work and the policing of crime are all very expensive. This says nothing of the welfare costs for those pushed into poverty by gambling and for middle class families that are split into two poor families by gambling-related pressures. Somehow we don't believe these are real people who suffer, although nearly everyone of us knows an addicted gambler.

Doesn't It All Go to a Good Cause?

How have voters in 38 states been persuaded to accept lotteries and people in 23 states convinced to allow casinos of one sort or another? In state after state the argument has been used that the lottery will provide "new" income to solve chronic problems that voters have not wanted to solve by taxing themselves. The favorite "beneficiary" of this new tax money among the promoters of gambling has been education. In 1991, 58% of state lottery receipts was designated for education. In other states, where education has not been the main problem addressed, funds have been directed to the general fund (21%), to senior citizens (8%), the cities (6.7%) and the rest to miscellaneous other funds. Now that we have thirty year's worth of evidence to work with, we should pay close attention to whether the lottery is an effective way to help fund these important priorities.

In at least 13 of the 38 states with lotteries, revenues have been specifically earmarked for education. Many players believe that even though they lose, their money is "going for a good cause." Many believe that education in these states is getting extra money because of the lottery. That belief, however, bears investigation.

In New Hampshire, where the lottery started in 1963, from 1964 to 1970 both receipts and money paid out declined each year. The receipts fell from $5,730,000 to $2,004,000 while the amount going to education fell from $2,768,000 to $837,000 in 1970.[21] When the second year's receipts declined sharply from the first, the lottery promoters put one over on the press by supplying a two-year summary, which was compared to the last year before the lottery, showing what appeared to be a big increase.[22] In reality, the amount contributed to educating children in New Hampshire increased from only 4% to 6% after the advent of the lottery—that is, from $55 million to $57 million. This is a little over a 3% increase in education funds due to the lottery, and even this amount promptly declined in the following years. The chief political architect of the lottery, Lawrence M. Pickett, had predicted that the lottery would mean $4 million per year for the schools. In the euphoria of the day when the bill passed he predicted that the yearly total might reach $11 million per year.[23] In just 7 years it reached $837,000. Most of this decline resulted from the start of lotteries in New York and New Jersey, which drew the action away from New Hampshire. The lottery was not the needed boost to education that voters intended by enacting the lottery. While complete records are not available, it is likely, based on the experience of other states, that increased social services costs due to lottery-induced poverty exceeded the gain in education.

New York had a similarly disappointing experience with its lottery. In 1967 the percentage of lottery receipts given to education was 55% of the gross, but in 1970 that was reduced to 45% in order to increase the amount going to prize winners to 35%. This change was deemed necessary because the gross receipts had fallen from $54 million in 1967–1968 to just $47 million in 1969–1970. Pre-lottery projections had called for over $300 million.[24] By 1976, lottery income had declined to $45 million, an amount that could have been produced by a 0.1% increase in the sales tax, which, while regressively inequitable, would have negatively impacted the poor much less.[25] The availability of bookies and numbers games with better pay-offs clearly suppressed sales. The state was unable to compete with illegal gambling.

New Jersey is one of the early success stories for the lottery. Revenues ran nearly 100% over projections for the first two years. New York promptly modified its weekly games to daily ones to mimic New Jersey's, which caused New Jersey's income to level off after 1972.

The end result of manipulating the public into accepting gambling was a dribble of money for education, not the torrent of funds that had been expected.

Some states used lottery money to benefit education even more indirectly, all the while claiming to promote education. Kentucky is an example of a state that puts lottery money into the general fund. Since over 50% of the general fund goes to education at all levels, education should benefit from the additional state revenues from the lottery. This dollar amount was so small, however, that just a year after the institution of the lottery, a federal judge ruled Kentucky's educational system unconstitutional. This led to the Kentucky Education Reform Act of 1990 and the largest tax increase in the history of the state. So Kentuckians got both the economic drag of the lottery and a massive tax increase, which sent the state into an economic decline that wasn't reversed until 1996.

The lottery's impact upon education in Illinois is also very clear. Until 1985 lottery revenues went into the general fund. In 1985 the legislature decided that lottery proceeds should go for kindergarten through twelfth grade education. By 1988 the lottery was providing $500 million of the $2,800 million education budget. During the three years since 1985, however, the legislature had progressively reduced the amount it appropriated from other revenues by the same amount. There was no net increase for education due to the lottery. At this point it made no difference whether the money from the lottery went directly to education or into the general fund, but the legislators looked better and could justify the lottery more easily when they could point to how much they loved the little children.[26]

California is another interesting example. The state of California operates the largest lottery in the world. California enjoyed the usual 1980's growth trend in revenues from the lottery. In 1990, however, California experienced a 14% drop in lottery sales. In alarm, the state dipped into school funds to provide a larger percentage of money for prizes in an attempt to boost sales. This illustrates what many states have experienced. Lottery income is unstable compared to other general revenue sources. Continued reliance upon lotteries for education funds will lead to unpredictable levels of funding for the schools. The $7 million dollars diverted in California represented $1 out of every $88 spent on pupils that year. Ed Foglia, former Education Association president, said he had learned a hard lesson. Education funding could not be tied to gambling receipts without causing serious damage to education.[27]

Florida also merits attention. Thirty-eight percent of the gross lottery revenue in Florida is supposed to go into what is called the Education Enhancement Trust Fund. The public was told that the money would be for improvements. This implied that it would be above the routine maintenance of the school-funding system. One of the "enhancements" was a new pre-kindergarten program. After a very brief time the program had to be funded from other accounts if it was to continue, and the program was discontinued in most places. Why did this happen? Once the enhancement money started to flow, the legislature cut appropriations for education from other sources. Brevard County was forced to use over $13 million in lottery money to cover teacher salaries due to the cuts. This was hardly an enhancement! Orange County reported having to resort to the same redirection of enhancement money. In addition to teachers' salaries, other necessities that were no longer adequately funded included buses, library books, salaries for teachers' aides and counselors.[28] The enhancement worked for a while and then began to erode, just as it had in Kentucky. At present, three of every four states where education was supposed to benefit from lottery revenues spend a smaller percentage of state income on education now than before the advent of the lottery.

Another major study extends this dismal picture further. In 1990, Mary O. Borg and Paul M. Mason published an extensive and complicated study of five states that earmarked money for education: New York, New Jersey, Michigan, New Hampshire and Illinois.[29] The study followed up suggestions made in a book by David Weinstein and Lillian Deitch[30] that concluded that substitution of funds rather than supplementation of funds had taken place in these states from 1968–1973. Borg and Mason had already confirmed that happening in Illinois in a 1985 study.

They carefully matched state lottery revenues against trends in total revenues for the states, seeking to determine whether the lottery was causing a change in trends or was ". . . just coincident with other mitigating factors."[31] As a control they evaluated seven nonlottery states as well. Their general conclusions were that following the beginning of distribution of lottery funds to education, two states (New Hampshire and New Jersey) increased expenditures on education in total terms. For two other states the rate of increases in education declined. Michigan turned from a healthy rate of increase in education expenditures to a rapid decline in expenditures on education.

Of even more importance is that only three states showed any increase in per pupil expenditures, while Michigan and Illinois showed declines. Clearly, the lottery cannot protect education from declining revenues if total state revenues decline. Of these five states, only New Hampshire showed an increase in both lottery and nonlottery expenditures during the 1980s. Even this is discouraging since New Hampshire experienced growing school enrollment, and thus only minimal improvement in per pupil expenditures. A matter for further concern was that most of the gains were in the first half of the decade. After 1985, they concluded that education suffered in real terms in all the states. Why? The most significant finding of all was that in every lottery state, once the lottery was firmly established and began to increase its revenues, total state revenues began to decline or flattened out. This decline drives funding for education more than the lottery does, since the lottery income is such a small part of state revenues. More worrisome is the suggestion that the money drained from the state economy by the lottery in particular and gambling in general throws the state into an economic decline.

This discovery has immense economic implications for all of society, not just those involved in education. Can it be just a coincidence that within a few years after a state begins a lottery, it goes into economic decline? Is it just a coincidence that when over 30 states began lotteries, the entire nation went into a decline that lasted through the first half of the 1990s?

The Lottery's Role in Hard Times

Certainly, lotteries are not the only cause of economic decline. Purchasing more than we sell outside the country is a major factor.

High wages relative to other countries is a factor. The loss of production jobs contributes to economic decline. There are many others, but gambling is certainly one of the factors. As we noted, during the 1950s factories went to great effort to remove bookies and numbers games from the work place because they distracted workers. We may not wish to admit it, but human nature is the same today as then. Why work when you can win the lottery?

Any suppression of the will to work depresses our ability to compete with the Japanese, Taiwanese, Koreans, or the European Economic Community. Loss of jobs and factories and declining productivity affects state revenues. Borg and Mason's control group pointed to the reality of economic decline. Education fared better in all states without lotteries if lottery income was excluded and in most states even if the lottery income was included. Borg and Mason conclude that lotteries ". . . have led to opportunities for state legislators to project the image that they are increasing overall allocations to the designated recipients without really doing so."[32] The bottom line is that programs that receive lottery money are vulnerable.

Other reasons for economic decline may be as important as the gambling industry, but few have as direct and immediate an effect. For over two decades, the gambling industry has grown at a pace much faster than the general economy. The dollars poured into gambling come from somewhere. Since gambling has a disproportionate impact upon the poor, who have little discretionary money, it is clear that gambling money comes directly from money spent on food, housing, clothing and transportation. This has been known since the beginning of the modern gambling boom, for in 1963 Dr. Mabel Walker, director of the Tax Institute of America, observed that ". . . lotteries do not generate money but simply remove it from the income stream."[33] More recently, the Reverend Cleveland Sparrow, pastor of an African-American congregation in Washington, D.C., said the lottery is ". . . a form of black slavery." He based this on the argument that more outlets were located in poor black neighborhoods, and they were more heavily promoted. The promotion was the point at which exploitation of the black population was established.[34] The Holiday Quality Foods grocery chain in California recognized the connection between gambling and suppression of the economy. They stopped selling lottery tickets in 1984 when they found that the decline in their gross income equalled their lottery sales, and this actually suppressed their profits.[35] The money lost through gambling directly and immediately depresses the consuming economy in terms of hundreds of millions in every state that has a lottery or casinos. These dollars are frequently the difference between boom times and decline. Our national experience over the past two decades demonstrates that no program that receives lottery proceeds will enjoy increased benefits. Lottery income simply replaces other more stable sources of income. As Borg and Mason concluded, the states should ". . . reconsider their decision to impose a lottery at all."[36] There are additional reasons to consider removal of the gambling parasites. Lotteries themselves decline and become less efficient with age. The strongest factor affecting decline is the introduction of a lottery in a neighboring state. With 38 states, including all the large ones, having lotteries, this is nearly at an end. The second factor is age. Lotteries are boring. They tend to peak at ten years and decline, regardless of whether better odds are offered, or bigger prizes, more instant games, multiple state lotteries or constantly changing games.[37] There are only a finite number of ways to vary the games, and eventually interest declines.

Gambling and Voluntary Taxes

So far we have noted that Nevada, which derives significant revenue from gambling, also has a less well-known crime problem. Then we discovered that the lottery inhibits prosperity and does not benefit the supposed recipients of the revenues. The next step is to explore the role of lotteries as revenue gatherers for the state.

States accumulate revenue from many sources. Many states have a graduated income tax, which means that a greater percentage of the income is taken from those who make more money. Most states have an upper limit of from 6% to 10%. This is considered by most tax experts to be relatively fair because it imposes the most tax on the largest incomes if the loopholes for the wealthy are not excessive. A second major tax is upon corporate incomes. These may be either flat or graduated taxes. Flat taxes hurt small industry because they must perform the same record keeping and know as much about the law as the larger corporations, even though they have more limited resources with which to do so. The unfairness of this tax has increased in recent years as states bid against each other with offers of tax concessions to entice large companies to move to a state. While revenues are depressed by these tax breaks, the hope is that increased spending on salaries will in the long run benefit the state. (Most analysts believe, however, that low wages carry more weight in such corporation decisions than tax incentives.)

In addition, states have numerous other sources of income: highway tolls, license and registration fees of various sorts, recreational and park income. States also impose commodity taxes, and the well-known sin taxes on cigarettes, alcohol, restaurants, hotels, race tracks and any number of other enterprises. Finally, we have the lotteries. As noted earlier in this chapter, in no state today does lottery income exceeded 4% of total state revenues. In only a few states does total gambling revenue exceed 4 percent: notably Nevada, New Jersey, and, for a time in the 1970s, New Hampshire. These statistics reveal why lotteries have failed to be the hoped-for economic panacea for state problems. The lotteries simply don't provide enough money.

Not surprisingly, the smallest states (with regard to population) suffer the most ill effects from gambling enterprises. The high fixed costs of running lotteries dictate that in small states the amount of gross lottery receipts going to the state can be small. A 1988 report showed that Vermont and Colorado received only 27% of the gross receipts as tax income. This was down from 35% in 1983. Maine received only 30%, New Hampshire and Arizona 31%. The larger state lotteries like New York, Connecticut and Maryland were able to do better and returned 44% to 46% to state coffers.[38] Another disadvantage of the small states has been established by studies that compare administrative costs to net lottery revenue. The small states consistently exhibit a higher administrative cost ratio. Even though the smallest states may receive the smallest returns, they may still suffer the same percentage of negative effects as the large state with regard to removal of money from the productive economy. They suffer economically while getting even less relief than the big states.

As noted, graduated income taxes are regarded as the most fair form of taxation. Some of the license fees are regarded similarly as fair taxes because they are "user" taxes. The one receiving the benefit pays the tax. Taxes that are considered unfair are called regressive, for they disproportionately affect the retained income of the poor. Analysts regard the lottery as the most regressive tax that has been invented to date. Economists have even argued against taxes on gambling, because the gambling itself is so regressive already. Sales taxes are more regressive than income taxes, because the poorest segment spends a larger percentage of its income on necessities that have the sales tax. One older study estimated that the lottery is equivalent in its regressivity to a sales tax of 60% to 90%.[39] Later studies lowered the amount of regressivity to two or three times the sales tax.[40] For research purposes, one Pennsylvania study viewed the state's lottery income as an excise tax on the ticket itself. The study found that except for incomes below $4,000 per year the effect was regressive. Those in the $10,000 to $15,000 range were hit the hardest.[41] Other studies in Massachusetts, New York and New Hampshire confirm that the poor spend a much higher proportion of their income on lotteries. The regressive nature of lotteries has been noted in studies "frequently and decisively."[42] The lottery hits the playing poor incredibly hard.

Other analysts and many legislators claim that the lottery is not a tax at all. Lotteries are supposed to be a unique form of revenue similar to license fees for fishing or hunting. Not many lottery purchasers think they bought a license. A license fee implies that recreation will follow the purchase of the license. Any recreational value (excitement) that the lottery ticket brings is usually before the purchase in the form of anticipation. For all but the tiniest fraction (one in 8.5 million) the after-purchase effect is disappointment, not recreation. Lotteries represent the absolute minimum in recreation.

Still others claim that lotteries are a "voluntary" tax. As Harvey N. Chinn has been writing for two decades, it is a voluntary tax on poor judgment.[43] No person is required to pay, unlike license fees for users or sales or income taxes for nearly all. There is a slight truth to this position, although it is minimal since nine out of ten people play. It is not totally voluntary for some small percentage who become pathological and are not able to resist the temptation. When further pressures such as peer pressure, the hope of great wealth and alluring advertising are considered, the voluntary nature of lotteries is further reduced.

Even the portion that is paid out to winners is regressive. Since the large prizes given to the few come from the purchases of all buyers, this is strongly regressive, even if the winner is poor. Any redistribution, whether by business, sports or the medical community to the few is regressive, and since so much of the lottery income comes from the poor it is even more strongly regressive than other factors in the economy. The only possible conclusion is that the lottery is economically regressive whether we choose to call it a tax or not.

How is it possible for government officials to ignore the regressive effects of lotteries, and their inefficiency as a revenue source? Most track bets are $2. Most off-track legal bets are $2. Most lottery tickets are under $2, except for some of the new experiments with high-priced tickets that are supposed to appeal to the middle-class player. Lottery proponents can claim no moral high ground of making a pleasure accessible to the poor. The poor had access to gambling anywhere there was a track an off-track betting parlor, or a local card or craps game.

The legislators have not established a "right" to gamble, but they have made gambling more accessible by increasing the number of its locations. Accessibility with the sanction of government has lured millions into what would be considered theft were it not for the element of consent involved in purchasing the ticket. As William McKenna, a Temple University professor, once said, the lottery ". . . feeds off the hopes of the poor."[44] What possible moral good can be found in a game that entices poor players to squander up to 20% of their available resources on it? The policy makers are just pretending these are not real people who are suffering real pain.

Clearly, the lottery is a tax upon the poor—a regressive, devastating, depressing, immoral tax. This tax is perpetrated by middle-class and wealthy legislators elected by the votes of a largely middle-class electorate. The middle class, which shoulders the bulk of the tax load, has decided it wishes to shift the tax burden to the unsuspecting poor. Lotteries are the wealthy crassly taking advantage of the poor.

Protection from Other Lotteries

Many legislators have argued that a lottery is necessary to keep dollars in the state when surrounding states begin lotteries. Citizens were purportedly crossing state lines in great numbers to gamble millions in other states. During the late 1970s rush into lotteries, the Bristish journal *The Economist* commented, "Financial pressure, the weakening of puritan mores, demographic changes [more poor] and interstate competition have led to a rush into government sponsored gambling. . . ."[45] Estimates of the amount lost were vague but "sizable."

This argument comes from either plain ignorance or intentional disregard for the facts. Every state would be better off to ignore the small percentage of its citizens who bother to travel out of state to gamble. Governor Patrick Lucey of Wisconsin, for example, said that a lottery was inevitable since $200,000 a week ($10 million a year) was going over the border to Illinois. The thoughtless alternative is to turn a third of a state's citizens into regular gamblers, thus removing money from the consuming economy to place it in the inefficient and regressive lottery, depressing the state economy by hundreds of millions per year. Since most of the poor were not going over the border to gamble, the economic loss to a state is much worse for an in-state lottery. Since most game materials are produced in Illinois, Ohio and Georgia, states are probably exporting more money to purchase materials than they were losing to out-of-state lotteries. Serious economic damage follows in-state lotteries, not out-of-state lotteries.

Legislators are willing to ignore the facts—and even fudge them—to get a lottery. Probably the most common fudging results from the use of lobbyist-supplied projections of the amount of income a state could realize from a lottery. When the New Jersey legislature considered the lottery, proponents said it would produce $267 million per year by 1980 and as much as $360 million eventually. The actual take was less than half that. With the advent of casino gambling in New Jersey, lottery receipts never approached their estimates and amounted to only $249 million as recently as 1991. Rather than compare poor receipts with optimistic estimates, the first New Hampshire lottery director Edward J. Powers put a different spin on the statistics by saying the lottery provided $87 per pupil, ". . . just that much less the taxpayers have to come up with."[46] After estimating that income has consistently run about one-third of what promoters have indicated, *Business Week* editors stated, ". . . pre-lottery forecasts of untold millions in revenues to the state have seldom panned out."[47]

Politicians consistently plead that the only alternative to the lottery is to cut services. Not true. More efficient expenditure is an alternative. Fewer pork barrel projects is an alternative. Higher taxes are an unpopular alternative. The latter has the merit of forcing the electorate to pay for its programs. Efficiency beats taxation, for taxes depress the economy just like a lottery. The real problem for politicians is that the other alternatives to lotteries do not win elections.

Not only do lottery receipts fall short of projections, but there are other difficulties as well. The Atlantic City casinos were supposed to pay 2% to the city for the rehabilitation of the city. They refused to pay the tax. The city dallied, not wishing to anger the casino operators. Rather than suing the casinos, they negotiated. The casinos finally agreed to pay if the city spent the money only on streets near the casinos and the corridor leading to the airport, all of which directly benefited the casinos. The rest of the city continued to deteriorate. Perhaps the other taxpayers should negotiate with the city: "I'll pay my taxes only if you spend the money on my street." There is no record of that happening.

What is the big picture? By 1990, from gross receipts of $20 billion the states were receiving $7.7 billion. That is a lot of money—hard-to-replace money. That is an amount of money more than the budgets of 40 of the 50 states. For the politicians, the wonderful part is that it has been discretionary money which they have used to replace old obligations, allowing pork barrel projects or apparent largesse to the needful new projects that win reelection. The money received by the states was more than that involved in the worldwide aluminum industry, which of course actually produces something. More money going into lotteries than into soda pop cans? Hard to believe, but true. From the late 1980s into the early 1990s, the growth of lotteries equalled the fastest growing industry, computers, at about 17% per year. Despite all of that, by 1986 lotteries only accounted for 3.3% of the internally generated revenues of the lottery states.[48] While it has since leveled off, lottery growth remains greater than the growth of the economy as a whole.

The Next Disaster: Non-Revenue Producing Gambling

Gambling on Native American Lands

Nevada and New Jersey receive millions of dollars from their casino operations. The cost in social services and enforcement is also high. What about the other 23 states that have casinos, do not receive more than marginal income from them, yet have major social and enforcement costs? Riverboats produce tiny amounts of state revenue, while many cities derive large revenues compared to their budgets to cope with the additional costs. For cities like Metropolis, Illinois, the net effect is very positive because they receive the income while distributing the negative social and other costs to many surrounding counties. This is a form of economic rape of your neighbors. Many states, however, have an even worse situation because they receive no income from Native American gambling, yet must pay all the costs. How can this be?

National Coalition Against Legalized Gambling spokespersons have expressed concern over the manner in which the federal government is handling Native American gambling under the Indian Gaming Regulatory Act (IGR Act) of 1988. As the major casino operations have met defeat at the polls they have switched tactics in two ways. They are seeking local elections where they believe that money on the smaller scale can tip an election, and they are making agreements with various Native American nations to "manage" their gambling for them.

How did we get in this predicament, and just how bad is it? Native American gambling did not begin in 1989 after the passage of the IGR Act. The act was prompted by several state studies that uncovered a wide divergence of state regulations concerning gambling. These were increasingly being challenged in the courts. The national legislature sought to simplify things and reduce litigation. The result was the Indian Gaming Regulatory Act of 1988.

This act gave Native Americans the privilege of matching any existing form of gambling in their state on tribal lands. Their games could be conducted without state regulation or taxation since each tribal entity was regarded as a sovereign nation. Gambling was classified into three categories. Class I included traditional tribal games. Class II included bingo, keno and similar games. Class III includes casinos, pari-mutuel wagering, video games and lotteries. These are by far the most lucrative, so the law specified that a compact be negotiated between the state or its designated representatives, usually interpreted as the governor.

The act is most notable for what it did not provide. No reasonable benefit to the state for allowing the gambling was established. No reasonable grounds for a state to refuse to negotiate a compact were indicated. No supervisory authority was created or designated to ensure the honesty and integrity of the operations. No provision for police protection of patrons was made. The patrons and employees were clearly at the mercy of the operators. Since Native Americans have no more immunity from greed than the rest of us, the situation created by the act is ripe for abuse. The states have no jurisdiction over these sovereign nations within our borders with regard to cleanliness of food services, the OSHA standards of safety for the protection of workers, child labor laws, sexual harassment of cocktail waitresses or the proper handling of money. In light of the long history of skimming casino profits, those tribes that have invited outside management have no assurance they are getting either a fair share or the share they negotiated. As the casino interests move into combination with the Indian tribes, the potential for unsupervised profits is greatly expanded. Given the high cost of maintaining even a modicum of integrity in Nevada and New Jersey, only the most sanguine will believe in an honest deal for the tribes or the patrons under these conditions.

The results of six years of this system are well summarized in the document *Casinos in Florida: An Analysis of the Economic and*

Social Impacts, published in 1994. "Currently there are 318 federally recognized tribes within the United States. As of June 1994, 84 tribes have signed almost 100 state compacts to participate in some type of Class III gaming on tribal land. Tribal casinos are operated in Minnesota, Wisconsin, Connecticut, New York, Washington, Iowa, Louisiana, Michigan, Nebraska, North Dakota, South Dakota, and Mississippi. . . .

"In Florida, the Seminole Tribe attempted to negotiate a compact with the state for casinos in 1991, although Florida clearly demonstrates a prohibitory public policy toward all forms of casino gaming. When the state refused to enter into a compact, the Tribe sued the state. It was concluded, however, that the Eleventh Amendment to the U. S. Constitution granted the states immunity from such a suit." A lower court decided ". . . that the state did not fail to negotiate in good faith, since the compact being requested involved activities that were illegal in Florida. . . . These opinions were a victory for the state of Florida. However, as a result, the Indian Gaming Regulatory Act was amended to omit the state from negotiating . . . in certain situations. Indian tribes that fit into a small category can now go directly to the Secretary of the Interior."[49] Despite losing in the courts the tribes went ahead and installed video lottery terminals on the Hillsborough reservation. On June 20, 1994, the U.S. Supreme Court denied this operation in contravention of the law, and U. S. marshals removed the machines.

Casinos on the reservations are not the end, however, because the reservations are often remote from urban areas. In Wisconsin and other states the tribes sought to have all Indian-owned land declared tribal land. As a result of this situation the IGR Act now allows new lands to be used for Class III gambling upon application to the Department of the Interior. This essentially opens the entire country to Native American gaming.

Am I crying wolf? Consider the following facts and the sources. A. Vernon Jensen of the Wisconsin Council on Gambling Problems states that organized crime has clearly infiltrated the Native American casinos of that state. The *Milwaukee Sentinel* reported on January 11, 1992, that two Chicago mobsters and one from San Diego were indicted for attempting to take over Native American gambling to skim and launder money. In 1993 the Mashantucket Pequot tribe of Connecticut gave $100,000 to the Democratic National Committee, the party controlling the Department of the Interior with whom they were attempting to negotiate an expansion of their gambling complex. On August 23, 1993, *U. S. News and World Report* said, "From dozens of interviews with federal, state and local law-enforcement officials and from documents obtained through the Freedom of Information Act, *U.S. News* has learned of a number of cases that raise serious doubts about the integrity and inviolability of Indian casinos."[50] The article discusses several of the doubts.

This mess emphasizes the need for a National Commission to study how best to modify the IGR Act to protect citizens and the tribes. The act presently gives the Native Americans rights unavailable to other citizens of this country, motivated primarily by an attempt to rectify the sins of the past. The potential to benefit other than Native Americans, however, calls into question the current legislation. As a consequence, the NCALG supported legislation to create the National Gambling Impact and Policy Commission in the hope that it would study the problem and recommend corrective legislation to protect the rights of all. The immediate problem for the states remains that they derive no income from the sovereign nations but must pay the cost of addressing the problems that the sovereign nations create.

Virtual Casinos

An additional problem that is presently small but could grow to disastrous proportions economically is the creation of electronic casinos on the Internet and other information networks. Advertisements for *Casino Journal's* "Southern Gaming Summit" in 1995 began with huge headlines that state "Accelerate the Expansion of Gaming." That one statement says it all: their motive, their goal, their greed, their lack of concern over the consequences of gambling. As the expansion of casino gambling has been slowed politically, the gambling interests have pursued two routes of expansion. One is Native American gambling alliances which we have discussed. The other is the expansion of electronic gambling at off-track and non-casino facilities, primarily the home.

Under Title 18, Section 1084 of the U. S. Code, using a telephone line across state lines to win money or credit is illegal and punishable by a fine of up to $10,000 or up to two years in prison. This is the law that makes most book-making illegal. In the past, the phone companies have cooperated with the FBI, when asked, in shutting down illegal operations.

Ambiguity in enforcement of the law has arisen. Since bets placed outside the U.S. are technically beyond the jurisdiction of the government, the FBI is reevaluating its regulations, searching for an effective means of policing cyberspace. In effect, we are at the mercy of those who set up gambling operations via the Internet. Additional conflicts in the law have been created by the states, such as Kentucky, which allow the placing of bets by phone to agencies that can legally receive the bet, such as tracks and off-track betting parlors within the state.

The gambling interests have immediately expanded into this enforcement vacuum. One example is called the Online Offshore Casino and Sports Book, which opened in May 1995 and is run by Internet Casinos, Inc. This operation, like several others, is based on a Caribbean island using foreign banks to process the money, in this case on St. Martin's. The player sets up the account by cashier's check or wire transfer, or even by credit card, but in smaller amounts since the player can renege on charges. When cash transfers became possible on the Internet things were easier for the gambling managers. Internet Casinos is accessed through the World Wide Web, and has over 2,000 bettors signed up to foreign accounts. Internet Casinos plans to set up franchises for $250,000 and 15% of the "win." It is licensed to sell franchises in Canada, Costa Rica, Belize and several of the islands.[51] The owner of Internet Casinos, Warren Eugene, admits that the potential for abuse by the players, including children using their parents' accounts, is very high. With blackjack, poker, slots, keno, roulette, bingo, craps, baccarat, sic bo and pai gow available, the gambling addiction can be created or fed at an astonishing rate. James Hilliard, a psychiatric expert on gambling addiction calls the games with instant feedback the "crack cocaine" of gambling.[52] The largest current on-line casino is a free one run by David Herschman of Santa Monica, California, who says that if the Feds don't harrass Eugene, he will soon move to the Caribbean to join the action for real money.

The complexity of the issues raised by the new interactive electronic systems are not easily evaluated or policed. Initial efforts to curb on-line pornography, such as Senate Bill 314, the Communications Decency Act of 1995, have brought forth literal screams from first-amendment-rights defenders such as the founder of *InfoWorld* magazine, Jim Warren.[53] They seek to extend the protection of American rights to the international Internet. Many of the critics want no controls whatever on what passes or exists on the Internet. Undoubtedly, should the FBI or the Justice Department seek to stop off-shore Internet gambling, cries of censorship and violation of rights will be heard.

In addition to the Internet, gambling interests are also watching closely the interactive game shows on television. Just as church-run bingo games in the 1930s through 1950s prepared the way for the giant bingo gambling halls of the 1960s through 1990s, The Family Channel, a spin-off from Pat Robertson's Christian Broadcasting Network, may be preparing the way for TV gambling through their interactive games with prizes. The gambling interests argue that since the technology exists, there is no reason to keep the social and legal barriers to interactive gambling. The way the Family Network avoids restrictions on interstate games of chance is by claiming that their games require skill. The gambling interests will argue similarly. Iowa appears to be the first battleground in this war. Edward Stanek, Iowa Lottery Commissioner, has already said that there is no difference between interactive games of skill and games of chance. The medium, the technology and the payment are the same, therefore regulation should be the same. This will surely open yet another door into your living room for the gamblers.[54]

Gary Cooper, executive director of a California law-enforcement research center, says, "I think the problem [of computer crime] is growing a lot faster than the criminal justice system can handle it."[55] This lag in enforcement is just the window for which the gamblers are looking. One attempt to stop this disaster has come from individual states whose lotteries were threatened by the National Indian Lottery. Connecticut and Minnesota, later joined by Florida and Rhode Island, have indicated that picking numbers and paying by credit card over the phone is a clear violation of federal law, as indicated above. The states have enjoined AT&T and MCI from providing access to the 800 number from their states.

A final action has been taken by Churchill Downs, the home of the Kentucky Derby. On June 20, 1995, they announced the placement of 400 boxes in homes that access a cable channel that will carry races and scratch sheets which bettors can use with a card and pin number against predeposited money. This is being done under a Kentucky law passed in the 1980s making it legal in Kentucky to place a bet with a track over the phone. This particular effort seems directed at providing competition with the lottery, the illegal bookies, and keeping Kentuckians from traveling to nearby riverboats. This "test" was only moderately successful, so attempts to get slots at the track continue.

Gambling's greed for your money knows no boundaries. In just forty years, it has moved from the dark side to the bright side and now to the hearthside of society. The fruit of these technological innovations will be human tragedy, addiction, bankruptcy, ruptured relationships, isolation, depression and suicide. Entrepreneurship in America is not worth this social price.

Most Americans appear to be unwilling to face the economic consequences of gambling. Nevertheless, we must rehearse them one more time. The money spent on gambling is taken from the producing economy. Since the poor play a greater proportion of their income, there is a direct impact upon food, clothing, housing and transportation. The lottery money is at best moved to the service economy in state government, which is an economic drag, rather than a producer. At worst the money is redistributed regressively. In the early days promoters thought that the gambling would simply hurt other entertainment industries and would somehow create income in the overall economic picture. How that was to be done was not specified. Now that we know that gambling drains much more than the recreational dollar and produces nothing, this hopelessly optimistic view must be abandoned. As Harvey N. Chinn, director of the [California] Coalition Against Legalized Lotteries said, "It is impossible for the state to gamble itself rich. Gambling creates no new wealth, rather it rearranges present wealth on an inequitable basis. Lotteries are economically unsound, socially disintegrating and morally dangerous."[56]

We must remind ourselves one more time that there is further economic loss in reduced productivity. Jobs are lost to cheaper labor unless our productivity is so great it can offset the lower wages and transportation costs. Industrial unemployment increases, but lottery spending does not decrease as a result. The hopeless try even harder. Gambling wastes resources.

Gambling brings a loss of capitalization for the nation. As jobs flee, imports grow, deficits enlarge and our wealth is exported. Thrift and gambling do not go together.

Gambling creates increased social services costs. Unemployment benefits increase in states with lotteries. Broken homes due to pathological gambling create two poor families where there was one viable family. The number below the poverty line grows. The intractability of permanent poverty is enhanced by gambling. The neglect and abuse of children increases in the face of pathological gambling. In 1993, NBC nightly news reported that 18% of American teenagers and children were malnourished. All of that is not due to the lottery, but part of it is. One has difficulty establishing these costs, but recent estimates by Professor John Warren Kindt of the University of Illinois point to a minimum of $2 in costs for every $1 in gambling revenue. This may be conservative, and other estimates place the ratio as high as $5-to-$1.

Gambling's effects may be local. One of the most interesting incidents from the history of gambling is the Great Depression era solution to the problems of little Salem, New Hampshire. The gambling interests spent the then incredible sum of $100,000 lobbying to get approval for the Rockingham track. A study of the effects of the arrival of the track revealed that the city was the only one in New Hampshire unable to pay its state tax. The receipts from the track for the city were less than what had come from the factory it replaced. The town's welfare costs had tripled, while the rest of the nation was slowly dragging toward economic recovery.[57]

This knowledge has been around for decades but has been ignored. The basic question is how long voters will continue to support this system of organized economic disaster. How long will we give legislators 2% or 3% of the budget to play with? How long will the middle class subsidize a gambling-created impoverished class? When will we learn to expect only the services we can afford? When will we stop creating new gambling bureaucracies which become a haven for political patronage? When will we stop removing billions from the productive economy into the regressive redistribution that gambling represents? When will we decide to curtail gambling's increased government bureaucracy that produces fewer jobs than the private sector could with the same amount of money? We must stop the economic destruction.

Review Questions

1. What are some of the ways gambling increases taxes?
2. Why can't other states match Nevada's 50% tax income from gambling?
3. What is the "downside" to Nevada's gambling revenue base?
4. Why is it dangerous for gambling interests to purchase political influence?
5. Why doesn't industry oppose gambling the way it did in the 1930s and 1940s?
6. Have the lotteries benefited education?
7. How does gambling function as a tax on the poor?
8. Does in-state gambling protect a state from out-of-state gambling?
9. What forms of gambling produce no revenue, only problems?
10. What should you do about increased gambling in your state?

Endnotes

1 _____, "More Gambling, More Losing," *Christianity Today*, 21:36, December 3, 1976.

2 Mikesell, John L. and C. Kurt Zorn, "State Lotteries as Fiscal Savior or Fiscal Fraud: A Look at the Evidence," *Public Administration Review*, 46:313, July/August, 1986.

3 _____, "The Legal Numbers Racket," *Newsweek*, 86:31, November 3, 1975. This was the opinion of Raymond Grimes of Rhode Island, among others.

4 _____, "A Hot Streak in Gambling Stocks," *Business Week*, p. 127, June 26, 1978.

5 _____, "Nevada's Gambler's Luck," *Time*, 45:19-20, April 9, 1945.

6 _____, "Everybody Wants a Piece of the Action," *Newsweek*, 80:46, April 10, 1972.

7 Dickerson, Mark G., *Compulsive Gamblers*, New York: Longman, 1984, p. 16.

8 *Newsweek, loc. cit.*

9 _____, "Come Into the Parlor," *Newsweek*, 62:96 and 98, November 4, 1963.

10 Starkey, Lycurgus M. Jr., "Christians and the Gambling Mania," *Christian Century*, 80:268, February 27, 1963.

11 _____, "State Lotteries: Useful Money Maker or Ethical 'Skid Row?'" *Senior Scholastic*, 83:25, September 13, 1963.

12 _____, "Florida: Political Roulette," *The Economist*, 269:44, November 4, 1978.

13 Campbell, Felicia F., "The Virtues of Gambling," *Business and Society Review*, 17:64, Spring, 1976.

14 *Newsweek, op. cit.*, p. 98.

15 See articles in *Business Week*, on January 21, 1950, p. 109; October 8, 1950, p. 108; and June 23, 1951, p. 32.

16 _____, "Hold That Bet," *Business Week*, p. 32, June 23, 1951.

17 _____, "Maritime Unions Join to Wipe Out Big-Time Gambling by Liner Crews," *Business Week*, p. 145, February 22, 1958.

18 _____, "Gambling Goes Legit," *Time*, 108:65, December 6, 1976.

19 Roemer, William F. Jr., *The Enforcer: Spilotro: The Chicago Mob's Man Over Las Vegas*, New York: Ivy Books, 1994, pp. 79-81.

20 A statement by Fred J. Cook in Starkey, *op. cit.*, p. 170.

21 Sullivan, George, *By Chance a Winner: The History of Lotteries*, New York: Dodd, Mead, 1972, p. 103.

22 _____, "Taxes: Winning Ticket," *Time*, 87:80, April 1, 1966.

23 _____, "Why a State Adopts a Lottery," *Business Week*, p. 63, May 11, 1963.

24 Sullivan, *op.cit.*, p. 115.

25 _____, "Gambling Goes Legit," *Time*, 108:55, December 6, 1976.

26 Kerr, Thomas J., "Are Schools Losing at the Lottery?" *School and College*, 41:17, April, 1992.

27 Atkins, Joe, "The States' Bad Bet," *Christianity Today*, 35:18, November 25, 1991.

28 Kerr, *op. cit.*, p. 19.

29 Borg, Mary O. and Paul M. Mason, "Earmarked Lottery Revenues: Positive Windfall or Concealed Redistribution Mechanisms?" *Journal of Education Finance*, 15:289-301, Winter, 1990.

30 Weinstein, David and Lillian Deitch, *The Impact of Legalized Gambling*, New York: Praeger Publishers, 1974.

31 Borg and Mason, *op. cit.*, p. 290.

32 Borg and Mason, *op. cit.*, p. 300.

33 _____, "Real Estate Taxes, Sales Taxes and Lotteries," *The American City*, 78:7, July, 1963.

34 Cizik, Richard, "The Legalized Menace," *The Christian Herald*, 106:47, November, 1983.

35 Clayton, Lynn P., "An Incredibly Strong Argument Against a State Lottery," *The Baptist Message*, p. 4, April 10, 1986.

36 Borg and Mason. *op. cit.*, p. 301.

37 Mikesell, John L. "The Effect of Maturity and Competition on State Lottery Markets," *Journal of Policy Analysis and Management*, 6:252, Winter, 1987.

38 North Dakota Legislative Council, "State Lotteries," A report for the Budget Committee on Government Finance, Schedules, pp. 1-2, June, 1988. See also Dentzer, Susan, Diane Weathers, Marilyn Achiron and Patricia King, "No Gamble for the States," *Newsweek*, 101:68, June 13, 1983.

39 Brinner, Roger E. and Charles T. Clotfelter, "An Economic Appraisal of State Lotteries," *National Tax Journal*, 28:402, December, 1975.

40 Suits, Daniel B., Gambling Taxes: Regressivity and Revenue Potential," *National Tax Journal*, 30:34, March 1977, and _____, "Betting's Economic Payout," *Business Week*, p. 120, June 26, 1978.

41 Spiro, Michael H., "On the Tax Incidence of the Pennsylvania Lottery," *National Tax Journal*, 27:61, March, 1974.

42 Mikesell, *loc cit.*

43 Chinn, Harvey N., "Lotteries," *United Evangelical Action*, 33:12, Winter, 1974.

[44] _____, "New Jersey: The Lottery Fever is Highly Contagious," *Business Week*, p. 45, March 13, 1971.

[45] _____, "Gambling: New York's Throw," *The Economist*, 270:32, March 31, 1979.

[46] *Business Week, loc. cit.*, p. 49.

[47] _____, "The Newest Growth Industry," *Business Week*, p. 114, June 26, 1978.

[48] Willimon, William H., "Lottery Losers," *The Christian Century*, 107:49, January 17, 1990.

[49] Office of Planning and Budget, *Casinos in Florida: An Analysis of the Economic and Social Impacts*, Tallahassee: The Executive Office of the Governor, 1994, pp. 10-11.

[50] Popkin, James, "Gambling with the Mob?" *U.S. News and World Report*, 115:30, August 23, 1993. For more information consult *Indian Gaming in Florida and Other States*, an October, 1992 report to the Committee on Regulated Industries, Florida House of Representatives, and a Minnesota House brief entitled "Questions and Answers on Indian Gambling," by John Williams.

[51] _____, *National Gaming Summary*, p. 3, May 15, 1995.

[52] _____, *The Sacramento Bee*, p. G2, Wednesday, April 19, 1995.

[53] Warren, Jim, "An Indecent Proposal," *Government Technology*, p. 20, April, 1995.

[54] Boshart, Rod, "Is TV the Next Frontier for Gambling?" *The Cedar Rapids (Iowa) Gazette*, pp. 1A and 9A, Sunday, August 28, 1994.

[55] Cooper, Gary, *Government Technology*, p. 30, March, 1995.

[56] McNamara, Joseph and the Rev. Harvey N. Chinn, "Should States Run Lotteries?" *U. S. News and World Report*, 97:63, October 29, 1984.

[57] _____, "Revolt Mounting Against Gambling," *The Christian Century*, 55:1170-71, September 28, 1938.

Chapter 6

My Bible Doesn't Say Anything About Gambling

ax Lucado tells the story of "Artful Eddie." As the beloved author describes him, Eddie "was the slickest of the slick lawyers. He was one of the roars of the Roaring Twenties. A crony of Al Capone, he ran the gangster's dog tracks. He mastered the simple technique of fixing the race by overfeeding seven dogs and betting on the eighth."

But Eddie quit the mob, turned himself in, offered to tell what he knew of Capone's syndicate. Why would he do that? Lucado continues:

Eddie had spent his life with the despicable. . . . For his son, he wanted more. He wanted to give his son a name. And to give his son a name he would have to clear his own. . . . Artful Eddie never saw his dream come true. After Eddie squealed, the mob remembered. Two shotgun blasts silenced him forever.

Was it worth it?

For the son it was. Artful Eddie's boy lived up to the sacrifice. . . . [Eddie] would have been proud of Butch's appointment to Annapolis. He would have been proud of the commissioning as a World War II Navy pilot. He would

have been proud as he read of his son downing five bomb-
ers in the Pacific night and saving the lives of hundreds of
crewmen on the carrier *Lexington*. The name was cleared.
The Congressional Medal of Honor which Butch received
was proof.

When people say the name in Chicago, they don't think
gangsters—they think aviation heroism. . . . Think about it
the next time you fly into the airport named after the son
of a gangster gone good.

The son of Eddie O'Hare.[1]

The heart of morality in a secular age is selfishness versus unselfishness. Nearly everyone agrees that the extreme of either of
these attitudes has terrible consequences. If we were all totally selfish, society would quickly degenerate into an anarchy where each
person does what he or she thinks is best. Eventually, the strongest
or best armed would obtain the goods in a primitive "jungle." On
the other hand, if everyone were totally unselfish, we would all be
totally co-dependent; no one could accept anything since that would
be selfish, even though everyone was trying to give. The end result
would be isolated individualism, like the other extreme except not
so violent. Fortunately, nearly all our personalities fall somewhere
between the extremes, some closer to one end of the spectrum,
some to the other.

All the world religions spend significant space in their sacred
writings attempting to define how to live on the edge between
selfishness and unselfishness. All of them are not, however, equally
relevant to where the majority of U. S. citizens are on moral issues. The primary concern here will be the Judeo-Christian heri-
tage that informs so much of American life and relates to the
beliefs of the 53 million Catholics, the 10 or more million Jews
and the 60 or so million Protestants. Specific religious arguments
are saved for Chapter 9, and here we will consider more general-
ized moral issues.

Historical Perspectives

The definition and cataloging of what is vicious, called a vice,
changes over time. The flogging of seamen as a means of discipline was routine in the 1600s and 1700s. Today litigation would
surely follow any captain who attempted it, even on the high seas
out of the jurisdiction of any particular country's laws. Flogging

was not a vice in 1650; today it is. Similarly, it was thought vicious for a woman to smoke a cigarette in 1890. By 1960 most Americans had a difficult time seeing that as a vice. At worst it was a bad habit. Strangely enough, with increased evidence of the clear cause and effect of smoking and cancer, the habit which harms self and others is once again becoming a vice. Our definitions and acceptance of specific acts as vices are flexible and changing. A vice is a personal, harmful, destructive habit, whereas crime is a social issue. Yesterday's vice is frequently today's interesting experience.

We are ambivalent toward gambling as a vice. Attitudes have changed over time. Archaeologists have found many pairs of dice in the ruins of Pompeii and various other Roman cities.[2] Their presence in large numbers implies that playing with them was common. Some of them are loaded, which indicates that something of value hinged upon the outcome of the roll of the dice (otherwise, there would have been little motive to load them). The mere presence of dice may not reveal attitudes toward them, but the evidence of cheating places them among the less admirable features of the society.

We also know that in ancient Greek writings some of the philosophers thought that gambling was detrimental to the state.[3] The ancient Egyptians thought that gambling made men effeminate. Even in the ancient world—before the influence of the Judeo-Christian ethic—there was uneasiness about gambling.

The early-church theologian Tertullian disapproved of gambling.[4] Presumably, others did as well, although no modern scholar seems to have made such a survey. Negative attitudes toward gambling in the medieval period were very mild, and both the rich and the poor gambled, but at different games. The Catholic Church was generally silent upon the issue, although the Fourth Lateran Council of 1215 A.D. forbade the clergy to gamble.[5] With the beginning of the Renaissance, gambling began to appear in the popular culture. Italian philosopher Jerome Cardano (1501–1576) was known as the gambling scholar.[6] He seems to have initiated some elementary understanding of the probabilities in games of chance. While dice and cards became prominent for gaming during the Renaissance, lotteries also arose just slightly later during the 1600s. Lotteries were conducted both privately and under governmental auspices. With the era's poor communications they were difficult to advertise broadly, so they tended to be local. They were subject to a great deal of manipulation and fraud.[7]

Gambling in Early America

The frequency of fraud drew the attention of Protestant clergy-men, and various of them spoke out against the lotteries. The ambivalent attitudes of the accepting Catholics and the critical Protestants were imported to the colonies on this continent when the great migration to the New World began. As the influence of lotteries grew, some clerics like Cotton Mather spoke against them. Gambling's power over the people became so great that more was spent on lotteries than was spent by the colonial or early federal governments. With only a tiny percent of the population sitting under the teaching of the few well-trained clergy, the influence of Mather and others was limited. His basic argument was that the casting of lots was judged by the Bible to be ". . . used only in weighty cases and as an acknowledgment of God sitting in judgement," and not as ". . . the tools of our common sports."[8] Despite the solemn warning, the lotteries grew until by 1832 the eight eastern states were spending $55.4 million on lotteries, more than four times the national budget.

Lotteries came under increasing attack during the 1830s and 1840s as a moral blight upon society. In 1827 Governor Dewitt Clinton of New York stated that they were of dubious morality and "pernicious" in their effect upon the people.[9] By 1833 New York outlawed lotteries. Many other states followed suit. During the Civil War lotteries staged a small comeback. They were perceived as useful sources of revenue. Following the war, however, they were rejected again except for the Louisiana Lottery in a predominantly Catholic state. The Louisiana Lottery was hardly a paragon of virtue, for, as we have noted, the charter was obtained and kept by massive bribery and the corruption of the legislature and judicial system of the state.[10] The lottery further bribed newspapers to carry the lottery ads by paying up to four times the going rates for advertisements.

The campaign against the lottery was one of the early victories for the reformers who became known as Progressives in the twentieth century. Religiously, the Methodists and Baptists were most prominent in this particular crusade, with the opening round of this battle being a sermon delivered by Beverly Carradine, a Methodist minister.[11]

This historical background is necessary to refute the lottery proponents' common claim that everybody gambles and always has. Such assertions are based upon a misunderstanding, or deliberate ignoring, of the differences between risk taking and gambling. Truly, everyone takes risks because they are inherent in the choices of life. Most daily risk taking is not at the expense of someone else. Gambling, on the other hand, is the creation of an *artificial* risk where the winner does so at the direct expense of the losers. As one University of Alabama economist so aptly explained several years ago, "It would seem that those who create and take artificial risks which produce nothing of value are simply withdrawing from that reality of life where the truly challenging and productive risks abound."[12] The fact is that most Protestants in the past simply did not gamble. In the last half of the last century, only a tiny fraction of the population, perhaps as low as ten percent, gambled at all, whether religious or not. Gambling was regarded as unrespectable and was conducted by people living on the fringe of society.

Gambling Becomes More Acceptable

After the turn of the century, however, change came rapidly. In the cities, the numbers game replaced the lottery, usually run on the sly at cigar and news stands. Some small merchants also participated to enhance their income, for the numbers games frequently paid out only on the number the fewest picked. There was a similar rise in illegal poker games, which created the image of the well-heeled, polished professional gambler. The reality was often sleazy, for the venue was the riverboat or the back-street hotel, although poker was also played in private clubs for higher stakes. The game's alliance with alcohol, and frequently with prostitution, was formed.

The more well-to-do gambled at the few tracks that were scattered around the country, most prominently in Kentucky and New York. Only a fragment of the population gambled on the horses until communications were organized by the mob in the 1930s to provide more reliable information to the bookies and by the tracks using the pari-mutuel systems, which were meant to reduce the fixing of races.

In the first half of this century many people played a wide variety of games, and more often than not, gambling was NOT part of the fun. For the first two-thirds of this century gambling was widely disapproved as an immoral activity that caused one to associate with bad characters, frequently from the underworld. Gambling was assumed to have the potential to lead to dissolute character.

During this time the primary argument of the Protestant leaders was that gambling was an attempt to take the goods that belonged to someone else without working for them or giving something in return. It was viewed as a form of theft, only slightly less repulsive because the element of consent was present. Ministers also pointed to the element of greed present in gambling, a vice clearly condemned in a variety of Old and New Testament passages. The operators of gambling games received disapproval for preying upon the innocent. None of these arguments is currently invalid, but the attitude toward their validity has changed.

During World War II a major attitudinal change toward gambling took place. With so many men in uniform with so much time on their hands, gambling became a common form of recreation. One estimate was that $300 million per month changed hands, with the Army having to advise soldiers on how to keep the games honest.[13] There were sharps who abused and accumulated other's money, but mostly the bets were small and the time passed more agreeably. This large portion of the population, numbering many millions, developed an ambivalent attitude toward gambling. The nature of gambling as an escape was especially appealing during the stress of war when any moment could be your last. Stress could be controlled in the artificial world of cards and dice. Even more important for the development of the gambling habit and the production of pathological gamblers, was that in the service you did not go unfed, or unclothed, or unsheltered or untransported, even if you lost all your money. Insulated from the consequences of gambling, military personnel were able to enjoy gambling's recreational aspects without recognizing the dangers it would produce in a less controlled environment. Also, in the military, while some former mobsters were present, gambling's immoral associations were reduced. As a consequence, many adult males learned the thrill or excitement of having an experience heightened by having money riding on it.

Removing the Stigma

After the war, with a vast new audience, illegal gambling boomed. In addition, a much larger part of the population was pushing for the legalization of some form of gambling or the expansion of what was already available. Spearheading the move to legitimize and legalize gambling were entrepreneurs, gamblers and opinion shapers such as the author Jimmy Breslin, who argued that the basic right to gamble was being restricted by outmoded laws designed by little old ladies and other "blue-nose thinkers."[14] As the social attitude toward gambling changed, the willingness of churches to oppose gambling declined.

A few writers, however, attempted to deal with the more substantive reasons for gambling's immorality. The first of these is that gambling corrupts. The association with the underworld and crime was a genuine strike against gambling. If gambling could be detached from the mob, severed from its evil influences, perhaps it could be sanitized into an appropriate form of recreation. This approach still failed to deal with the two commandments against theft and covetousness, but it was a start.

Of course, there was pulling in both directions. In Minnesota, the clean-up eliminated all the slot machines, of which there were over 8,000 around the state, under the leadership of reform governor Luther W. Youngdahl.[15] In most states, however, there were efforts to legalize various forms of gambling in an effort to take it away from the mob. In New York, Governor Thomas E. Dewey, the 1948 Republican nominee for president, fought with New York City's Mayor O'Dwyer over the latter's proposal to legalize sports betting. Dewey argued that ". . . it is fundamentally immoral to encourage the belief by the people as a whole in gambling as a source of family income."[16] The FBI and Estes Kefauver, the senator from Tennessee with presidential ambitions, waged war on the mob in the early 1950s, trying to detach their interests in Las Vegas. Following Kefauver's hearings regarding organized crime there followed a flurry of gambling rejections. California and Arizona brought open gambling under state control. Montana rejected slot machines, and Massachusetts rejected a lottery.[17] Since World War II there have been dozens of rejections in numerous states, including Michigan's surprise rejection of charitable bingo in 1954.[18] Such victories for antigambling foes became increasingly rare after the initiation of New Hampshire's lottery in 1964, until the revival of the National Coalition Against Legalized Gambling in the mid-1990s. The elections of 1994 saw the antigambling foes win in Florida, Wyoming, Arkansas, New Mexico and Delaware against casino interests that frequently outspent them 100 to one.

The gambling proponents argued that there should be no moral stigma attached to taking the money of those who are willing and are having fun in the process. This seemed plausible to many because the concept of a pathological gambler was essentially unknown. The impact upon homes was not recognized. The political gamble of expanding legal gambling seemed harmless, and it was thought it would surely cut into illegal gambling, thus reducing police corruption.

Gamblers Overwhelm Their Foes!

The drive to expand legal gambling has been mostly successful ever since, with recent exceptions. The number of tracks expanded rapidly in the 1950s. Off-track gambling became legal in a few places. Casino gambling expanded rapidly in Las Vegas after the war, and then in the 1970s in Atlantic City. Casino gambling is the hottest expansion area in the mid-1990s since a 1988 law gave the Native American nations the right to match any type of gambling allowed in a given state. Since most states had charitable gambling, some including casino nights, the loophole was available for continuous gambling. Now, 23 states have casinos. In the 1970s and 1980s, the lotteries proliferated to 38. Riverboat gambling has been revived, with more boats afloat than was ever the case in the nineteenth century. The legalization of gambling encouraged millions to gamble who never would have done so when it was illegal, including approximately four out of five church members.[19] The campaign to make gambling seem like good, clean fun has succeeded, and women have been enticed into the action in nearly the same proportion as men, although their preference is for different kinds of gambling.

The church was co-opted into the campaign to make gambling legal and recreational. Statements by some clergymen that they could see no problem with an occasional bet on a nag or a friendly low-stakes poker game made the popular news magazines. A Cincinnati Catholic bishop received wide publicity in the national press for defending gambling as ". . . a legitimate amusement or recreation because it is intended as a necessary relaxation of the mind."[20] Clergy statements of opposition, if printed by the secular press, were deeply buried or confined to the letters to the editor, where they frequently seemed like spoilsports. Extended discussions of the moral issues were confined to religious journals, most of which had very limited circulation.

Few clergy leaders were willing to take so strong a stand as James M. Wall, who said, "When gambling is not only condoned, but officially supported by city and state governments through lotteries and licensed parlors, then government has become a pimp for sin."[21] Mr. Wall's strength of feeling had not waned from his statement two decades earlier that "The adoption of a laissez-faire moral position by Protestant leaders leaves us with a situation where states are engaged in the business of exploiting human weakness . . . as a means of raising state revenue."[22]

Other Justifications for Gambling

The gambling-as-recreation movement was not the only effort to remove the moral stigma from gaming. Other gambling proponents sought to compare gambling to various business activities that contained elements of chance or speculation. They attempted to make gambling moral by comparing it to something that was not deemed immoral. The most common comparison was to investment in the stock market. This rather misses the point that most investors make money in the stock market, while only a minute fraction win at gambling. For some, the stock market is gambling, which, of course, doesn't make it moral, either. Stock speculation has had disastrous results for some, just as gambling has. The comparison ignores the fact that whatever similarity might exist simply points to greed being the common denominator of both activities.

Yet another justification was that gambling was no different from sweepstakes, which most Americans found harmless since they did not have to invest anything other than a stamp. The gamblers reasoned, however, that playing for a prize put up by the participants in gambling was no different from playing for a prize put up by the soap or magazine company in a sweepstakes. Such reasoning ignores that the soap company can afford to put up the prize from its advertising budget, whereas the gambler frequently plays his livelihood away. One might as easily argue that both are equally immoral since all customers of the soap company help pay for the sweepstakes, whether they wish to or not. Too many lost track of the fact that the gambler pays for the so-called recreation, and there are many forms of more fruitful recreation than gambling.

The relationship between speculation and gambling is more clearly seen if the various activities are arranged on a moral spectrum. An appropriate spectrum would seem to be: fair exchange, investment, speculation, gambling, theft. The biblical foundation for the Judeo-Christian moral position is that the love of money is the root of evil, that the relentless pursuit of it leads to sin. A second

part is that man is to live by the sweat of his brow, that is by working for his bread in a fair exchange. This is frequently called the
"Protestant work ethic," which has somehow become a disparag-
ing phrase. Any thinking person should realize that common sense
favors a similar statement. Gambling is rooted not only in greed
but also in indolence.

Christians have never argued that the use of money was inap-
propriate. Using money to obtain the necessities of life does not
lead necessarily to the excessive love of money that causes one to
take what belongs to someone else. Fair exchange at market value,
thus, carries no moral stigma, even though it involves money. Greed
and dishonorably taking advantage of others is what carries the
moral stigma.

Investment also carries little or no moral stigma. Thrift is a
biblical value and implies the possibility of accumulation. Accumulation is not evil, unless in the process of accumulating one
forgets to be generous and hospitable, which are considered both
Jewish and Christian virtues, especially when directed toward those
in need. Investment is putting accumulated wealth at the disposal
of someone else who intends to use it in a fair exchange to make a
profit which can be shared with the investor. Investment and production do not necessarily involve risk, although competition with
others attempting the same thing usually does. Investment frequently spreads the risk inherent in the market place and if done
ethically involves no moral stigma. The issue in investment is moderation (a virtue) versus greed (a vice). Investment in the stock
market involves risk, but the one who gains does not directly or
necessarily profit at the expense of another who loses all, as is the
case with gambling.

Speculation involves a somewhat greater moral problem. The
speculation may still involve exchange, but the question becomes
one of fairness. The intention of the speculator is short-term gain
rather than long-term gain, as well as sizable gain versus moderate gain. More prominent in speculation is unearned wealth, not
as a result of producing a better product, but in terms of manipulating the market or the capital. Money made speculating is going
to be at someone else's expense, frequently the consumer who
receives an inferior product without realizing it until after the
purchase. The morality of speculation depends upon the degree
of deception involved. Speculation does not have to be immoral,
but it is tinged with immorality more frequently than in other
forms of investment.

As expected, gambling is even further removed from morality. There is no fair exchange. In the vast majority of cases something is taken from one party and nothing is given in exchange. Gambling differs from theft because gamblers consent to give up their money. They volunteer to do this in the hope of the big win, a hope that is again based either on greed or the desire to escape poverty. Only this desperate hope could induce the unfair exchange. The promise that someone will receive the prize gives the appearance of an exchange. For most players, however, there is no exchange at all, and the winner and the managers of the game take from all the rest. It is a distribution of the wealth from the many to the few which *always* leaves many more poorer and affects the general economy negatively.

The opposite of the fair exchange is stealing or theft, which formerly was universally regarded as immoral. Now, many in our society find no reason not to take what can be acquired if they are not caught. For such as these there can obviously be nothing wrong with gambling. From this perspective, gambling is a positive good. There is no intention of exchange on the part of the thief. There is only the intention of obtaining the goods of another without earning them or being detected.

From the Judeo-Christian perspective it is hard to justify theft at all and only slightly easier to justify gambling. Only the element of consent keeps gambling from being pure theft, and even that consent is partially given out of ignorance. There can be no excuse for the manager of the game who knows he is taking without fair exchange. The lack of ethical consideration is recognized even by secular authors who note that ". . . lotteries seldom advertise critical details of their operations. Not only are the odds of winning not clearly advertised, but prizes distributed over several years are not quoted in current values. Such marketing practices by a private firm would not be permitted."[23] Since gambling falls toward the low end of the moral spectrum, we can see why the one feature that appears to represent an exchange is advertised: the prize. The lottery advertises that you can win millions—not that millions can lose millions.

Guilt is associated with gambling, in part because of its moral meanness. The strongest source of guilt is from the consequences of gambling: cheating, stealing, lying, isolation and depression. Guilt itself is not something evil. Primarily, it serves to remind us of the damaging things that our behavior does to others. However, the mere mention that gambling is a social evil often results in gambling opponents' being labeled as "guilt dumpers," as though that were the most horrible crime imaginable. Guilt is about all that is left to weigh against the "thrill" of hoping to win a million. Residual doubt about the legitimacy of gambling is almost the only remaining preventative to the complete abandonment of our country to gambling.

Moral Perspectives on Gambling

What are our basic rationalizations about gambling? Just how recreational is the lottery? The heart of recreation is beneficial change. The intent of recreation is to renew the individual, to prepare to return to the routine tasks of life, to the rigors of family life. Recreation involves rest, exercise, and frequently in our society, competition. There is simply no relationship between the rest and exercise and the lottery, as well as most other forms of gambling. Therefore, the lottery's only possible element of recreation would be competition. Recreation ideally involves friendly competition between equals. If the competition becomes too intense, it begins to lose its recreational value, failing to result in rest and restoration. The excess of competition that may lead to bitterness or anger recreates nothing. If the competition does not allow for a balance in the winning then it is not really competition, but dominance. Recreation is lost especially if self-esteem is lost.

The competition in gambling is between the gambler and the "house." In the case of the lottery, this is the state; in the case of the casino, the owners; in the case of the street corner craps game, the one holding the loaded dice. In every game of chance one must overcome the cut the house takes, which is called the "vigorish." On the dollar slot machine it can be as little as 3%. On the lottery it is 55% to 63%. The competition can never be even because of the cut. The gambler loses unless he collects the big pay-off, for which the odds are hopelessly stacked against him. Since the prizes are awarded to so few, gambling of every sort is an unfair competition that has little possibility of providing the recreational reward. Gambling is gambling, not recreation.

A second common rationalization is that it is more immoral to be inconsistent than to legalize gambling. Journalists frequently argue that moralists are immoral to allow some forms of gambling and to prohibit others. A second argument is that it is immoral to allow the state to provide gambling while prohibiting private enterprise. The reasoning is that it is immoral to be able to place a legal bet at the race track but not to be able to place it legally with a bookie when you can't make it to the track. If you have pretty green grass and a fence, it is legal. If you operate out of a hat, it is illegal. This argument seems plausible until you think that the same logic would suggest that since you can drive freely in the middle of a block, you should also be able to drive freely at the end of the block and not have to stop for the sign. If location isn't important then stop signs are immoral, too. There are many reasons why gambling is confined to certain locations, most related to underage gamblers and the collection of taxes. Actually, the consistency argument is just as valid for eliminating all gambling as it is for expanding gambling.

Consistency can have a strange face. A *New York Times* editorial once proclaimed that "Consistency would require that, from a moral and ethical point of view, either all gambling should be outlawed, or a carefully regulated extension should be allowed."[24] Why does consistency demand careful regulation? How did that get to be the other end of an either/or statement? Whose morality is this? Upon what timeless authority does this dichotomy stand?

Perhaps the most reprehensible rationalization perpetuated by the managers of gambling games is the myth that the perpetrators of gambling are not responsible for the bad consequences that result when the public gambles to excess. We have spent a generation seeking to make chemical companies responsible for the toxic waste they have dumped into the environment. We sue doctors when patients die because of their negligence. We endeavor to hold drunken drivers responsible for the deaths they cause while under the influence. As this book goes to press, the courts are poised to allow suits against the cigarette companies for the cancer deaths they cause, unless the negotiated agreement passes Congress. However, even though lotteries lead millions into gambling, and millions into pathological gambling, suddenly it is the gamblers' fault because they consented, not the managers who used every means known to advertising to lure them. When robbery, assault and embezzlement follow hard on the heels of lotteries, are those involved really innocent?

Yet another common rationalization is that we cannot "legislate morality." This ignores the fact that legislators do it all the time. When we decided that it was unhealthful and thereby immoral to package poisonous meats in 1905, we legislated the morality of forced inspections of the packers. When our nation goes to war, we frequently legislate the morality of a draft and provide penalties for those whose idea of morality differs. The best interest of the largest proportion of the populace was long held to be the foundation of sensible laws. Now this has frequently been replaced by a morality that sets the protection of every minority against the opinions of the majority as the highest good. Since we legislate against countless issues that we deem immoral, if the lottery were found to be immoral in its results there is absolutely no reason to avoid legislating against it. Legalization is simply the method chosen by those with a vested interest to move their illegal activity to more respectable ground.

Should the previous argument prove unconvincing, lottery proponents further argue that since morality is individual, it is impossible to legislate it. We simply may argue that it is questionable whether a questionable activity becomes unquestionable just because it is individual. One may wish to murder someone, but that does not mean we should not legislate against murder. Theft may be someone's desire, but that does not mean we should not legislate against it. Covetousness, in the form of gambling, may be the desire of many, but that does not mean it is immune from legislation. The inability to compel universal compliance with a law is no argument against criminalizing an immoral activity.

If gambling proponents cannot win with the preceding two arguments for legalization, they argue just the opposite. We *can* legislate morality, they assert. If lotteries become legal, they become moral. Legal equals moral. This represents the argument that morality is not anchored in religious precepts, or in human character which allows for the formation of a civil society, but that morality resides in the continuously changing framework of the law. This makes morality equal to current opinion of the legal elite. If this were really so, we would not have such a guilt-ridden society. Religious precepts do not cause guilt; it is the inherent nature of man that causes a seminal awareness of good and evil. If the concept of "good" has any validity at all, it is not clear that gambling produces any "good" for nearly all who practice it. Prosperity depends upon productivity, not luck. Productivity depends upon work and creativity, not luck. Has any bookmaker ever restored a lost fortune to a ruined patron out of brotherly love?

The Biblical Case against Gambling

Another rationalization in support of gambling is that the Bible has nothing to say about gambling. There is no eleventh commandment against it, although only those who have not read the first Ten Commandments could argue thus. Whether you believe the Bible or not, it *does* have something to say about gambling. The tenth commandment (Exodus 20:17) specifies that you are not to covet. Covetousness is the inordinate desire to have something that belongs to your neighbor. The verse specifies certain things that you are not to covet: your neighbor's house, your neighbor's wife, your neighbor's manservant, his maidservant, his ox, or donkey, or anything that belongs to him. Since this is the ancient world's listing of wealth, it means his money.

The danger that the commandment warns against is that coveting can lead to taking what belongs to another without payment, either by theft, or, of more interest to us, by gambling.

Coveting is the opposite of what is lauded many times in the Bible: being contented with what you have. Numerous passages in Proverbs warn against covetousness and the theft that flows from it, such as 13:11 which says stolen money dwindles away. Proverbs 15:27 says greed brings trouble to the family, which according to 12:29, causes one to "inherit only the wind." Gambling opposes the biblical concept of working for our own needs. Psalm 128:2 encourages us to eat the fruit of our own labor; Matthew 10:10 tells us the worker is worth his keep; Proverbs 22:16 says, "He who oppresses the poor to increase his wealth and he who gives gifts to the rich—both come to poverty"; Isaiah 55:1–3 asks why we spend our money on that which is not bread (does not meet our needs) and on that which does not satisfy; see also Acts 21:33–34, 1 Thessalonians 4:11, 2 Thessalonians 3:7–8, and 1 Timothy 6:9–10. The clearest of them all is Hebrews 13:5: "Keep your lives free from the love of money and be content with what you have, because God has said, 'Never will I leave you, never will I forsake you.' "[25]

Another commandment of the ten in Exodus tells us not to steal from one another. This is also reemphasized in Leviticus 19:13, which tells us not to defraud or rob our neighbor, and Ephesians 4:28, which says, "He who has been stealing must steal no longer, but must work, doing something useful with his own hands, so that he may have something to share with those in need." Gambling is specifically in view in Isaiah 65:11–12, where it says that those who "spread a table for fortune" are destined for the sword. The covetousness that causes us to defraud or rob is rooted in three lies: (1) Happiness can be bought; (2) The quality of life depends upon possessions; and (3) Who we are depends upon our economic status. Despite the many quips that make the rounds (such as the pathetic "He who dies with the most toys, wins"), none of these is true.

In the New Testament the word *covetousness* is replaced by the word *greed*. Luke 12:15 warns us to be on guard against all kinds of greed. Romans 1:29 labels greed an especially virulent kind of wickedness. Ephesians 5:3 and 5:5 associate greed with impurity. Colossians 3:5 labels greed an evil desire that is a form of idolatry, putting money in the place of God. If God really exists, the managers of gambling games rooted in human greed should tremble, for 2 Peter 2:14 calls "experts in greed" an "accursed brood." Proverbs 15:27 suggests that association with a greedy man brings trouble. Just like modern counselors who work with gamblers, 1 Corinthians 6:10 associates the greedy with theft and drunkenness. On a more positive note, 1 Peter 5:2 urges us to not be greedy but to be eager to serve.

Few of us want to admit to being greedy, but we are. We grasp for more, whether we need it or not. We frequently grasp at someone else's expense. Gambling is clearly greedy; there is no other motivation for it. The Bible condemns greed directly and gambling indirectly but clearly. Nevertheless, four out of five Christians gamble, with a negative effect upon the work of God's kingdom. Giving to the church by evangelicals has declined from 6.7% of income in 1968 to 4.6% in 1992.[26] Some of the blame is laid at the feet of the "Boomer" generation, the first raised on a steady diet of gambling, even for church members.

Churches and the Moral Issue

We have not exhausted the catalog of rationalizations yet. Another claims that since the churches are not in agreement about gambling, it can hardly be a moral issue. Unfortunately, just because the church cannot see clearly, lacks information or lacks courage does not make something moral. With a clear biblical rejection of the foundation of gambling in greed, the church can only be regarded as delinquent if it fails to speak out against gambling. The Christian tradition has always maintained that it is not enough just to observe the commandments, which is hard enough to do, but Micah 6:2 says we are also to do justice and love mercy! Justice implies fair treatment of the powerless. Jesus said more about the poor than any other group. Gambling preys upon this group that is supposed to be treated justly. We are hardly loving mercy when we take the money from the poor, leading to hardship, job loss, divorce and despair.

Gambling misses the point of living in civilized society and exchanges freedom for selfish individualism. Romans 12:10, Hebrews 13:1 and 2 Peter 1:7 all point to the responsibility of the Christian to be brotherly, that is, to care for one another. That is very far removed from attempting to rip off a person in a gambling game. Christians have a further obligation not just to be brotherly or kind but to love their neighbors (Leviticus 19:18) and to treat others as they would like to be treated (Matthew 7:12). The last part is commonly called the Golden Rule. Just because those elements of the Judeo-Christian tradition have become unpopular in our society does not mean that they are irrelevant to a functioning society that operates in the best interest of its citizens. Caring and loving have nothing in common with gambling. Gamblers are predators. Romans 4:21, 15:1 and 1 Corinthians 8:13 demand self-denial for the benefit of others. Probably no concept of the Christian faith is more removed from the "action" of gambling.

From a Christian perspective, nothing positive can be said about those individuals or governments that promote gambling. Gambling makes its profit at the expense of those who can be tempted to seek something for nothing. This is immoral. The government, in the past, has frequently served to limit the effects of evil upon society through law. Now the government encourages evil effects for its own revenue benefit. From 1950 to 1990, gambling moved from a position of moral condemnation to one of moral acceptance. This change is rooted in our ignorance. What is moral has not changed.

Gambling's Moral Effect on People

Gambling corrupts the individual. Gambling has no other purpose than the satisfying of human greed. Gambling is ethically demoralizing. Gambling affects the personality by bringing selfishness to the fore. Gambling cheapens the soul, demeans the person and makes materialism the highest good. The gambler frequently perceives that all his or her problems are caused by the lack of money. If money can be secured by some means, the world will right itself for that person. Gambling represents an attempt to find satisfaction for the inner person in tangible resources, rather than in right relationships with others.

The gambler tacitly assumes that he is entitled to more than he earns. Whatever can be secured by gambling does not have to be earned. An implication that follows is that only the foolish work. If a large proportion of the population abandons work to pursue gambling full time, the economy for all declines. J. W. Jepson tells a wonderful little parable to illustrate this.

> A man was handed a million dollars. Immediately, he quit his job. The next day he discovered that there was no electricity and no water. He got into his car and drove around. Everything was closed—stores, gas stations, schools, banks, post offices, police and fire stations—everything. Bewildered, he asked a passerby what was going on. The other person replied, "Haven't you heard? Everybody was given a million dollars."[27]

Gambling requires no great ingenuity, creativity or effort, leaves nothing behind to admire and contributes nothing permanent to the memory of the race.

The greed that is the foundation of gambling affects more than just the gambler. The money spent on gambling is taken from other units of the family until such time as the family disintegrates. Gambled money does not buy groceries, make car payments, buy a home, provide clothing or secure an education for the children. Money gambled is moved from benefiting to wasting. As we have already noted, the effects upon the poorest segment are the most pronounced. When Puerto Rican lottery workers went on strike several years ago food sales jumped thirty percent. Gambling undermines productivity. As Jepson observes, "We gain by producing. We prosper by serving."[28] Gamblers do not discuss losses. They brag about wins, giving young children the impression that gambling is a great way to get money. Beats working. Beats school. Why study when you can win the lottery? Children do not have the maturity to see the pitfalls or the severe consequences. As a result, gambling among children is the fastest growing portion of the gamblers' take. Unfortunately, most gamblers who become addicted began before the age of fourteen. These cases are seldom discussed though often realized.

Gambling corrupts all that it touches. Much gambling remains illegal, under the control of the mob and associated with criminals. Gambling bribes continue to corrupt politicians. In 1992 several Kentucky legislators were indicted and most convicted for paying or accepting bribes in an attempt to fix a racing track's license.

One comedian commended Kentucky for bringing government back to the people, for votes were purchased for as little as $400. Even you could own your legislator. Gambling doesn't become clean even when it is legal.

Gambling undermines sound money management. What the Christian community calls good stewardship is incomprehensible to the gambler. The Christian claims that all resources belong to God and we are merely the stewards of them. The Christian concept is that time, treasure and talent belong to God and must be used wisely. This is foreign language to a gambler.

Gambling clearly does not glorify God in the life of the gambler. Gambling does not point the individual toward intimacy with God. Gambling opposes the Christian concept that work gives harmony, strength, meaning and dignity to life. Glorification of gambling implies that the moral worth of the individual is subordinate to the money worth of the individual. Such a value system suggests that a Gandhi who freed an entire subcontinent from colonial rule is worth less than a Michael Jordan who commands $31 million a year in endorsements.

Acquisitiveness and covetousness turn a person inward. Many soothe their consciences by claiming they are helping the homeless and helpless through donating tax money by gambling. Gambling more usually turns the gambler away from others, especially if the gambling becomes pathological. Luck opposes the idea that rewards are based on merit. The search for that stroke of luck makes us suckers for the short cut, including crime. In clear opposition to this, love chooses its pleasures with thought for the well-being of others, according to Romans 15:1.

Gambling undermines all economic systems, including capitalism, which makes it a matter for concern for all of us. Economic systems are damaged by the concept that reward is capricious, rather than the result of work, loyalty and caring. Gambling creates no wealth, it merely moves the accumulated wealth of the players to the hands of the managers and the few winners. George Will has claimed that it increases the fatalism of the multitude.[29]

Gambling reduces the importance of industriousness, thrift, deferred gratification, diligence and studiousness. Gambling glamorizes effortless achievement, undeserved success, something for nothing and the quick buck. The value of work is depreciated, which affects the fulfillment of the central elements of selfhood.[30] Gambling seeks to ignore the outcome of lost money: deprivation. The use of prizes by many vendors implies that they cannot compete on the basis of quality, price or service, so they bribe the purchaser. The more inferior the goods, the greater the prize. When there is no good at all, the prize reaches millions. While some games of chance do require some skill, these are not the growth areas of gambling. Growth at present is in the games that require no skill, games for those who wish to put forward no effort.

Lotteries are a regressive tax, as has already been noted. In the context of morality it is a regressive tax without conscience. Since the poor gamble the largest percentage of their income, and this is known to the more educated, the approval of lotteries is simply willingness to take advantage of the poor. The non-gambler who votes for passage of expanded gambling is asking the poor to pay his taxes, in a grossly inefficient way. Solid evidence for this position stems from early advertising that was geared to the middle class, pointing out the benefits to education or the elderly. After the initial mindset of the public was fixed, advertising was targeted directly at the poor. Humble occupations were shown dreaming of great wealth. The tone and the words used were geared to the unthinking and are actually frequently offensive. The conscienceless targeting of the poor is reflected in the comment of a Pennsylvania lottery official who said he did not regard Atlantic City as a threat to the lottery: "We think the lottery attracts a different type of player entirely than a casino."[31] He was right. He was going after the poor. The average lottery player drops $1.60 per purchase, with multiple purchases per week. The average casino visitor drops a minimum of $50, while betting ten times that amount. States willingly increase sales at the expense of the moral fiber of society.

Is it moral to exploit the poor, to refuse to tax ourselves to pay for the services we demand, to dodge responsibility for paying for the government we want to solve all our problems? Is it moral to allow waste and corruption by public officials and then let them hide behind a lottery to raise money? In 1950, Governor Thomas E. Dewey of New York said, "The entire history of legalized gambling in this country and abroad, shows that it has brought nothing but poverty, crime and corruption, demoralization of moral and ethical standards and ultimately a lower standard of living and misery for all the people."[32] More than four decades later, these words still ring true.

The decisions of recent years that imply that gambling is moral fly in the face of the facts. Lotteries are merely a foot in the door for the gambling interests to expand into other forms. Increased gambling reflects the changing moral standards while at the same time serving to mutate those moral standards even more. Why should we allow frequently corrupt officials to make our moral decisions for us instead of listening to our church or synagogue? The law has blurred moral clarity. Lotteries promote a downward trend in moral sensibility. Lotteries pander to the craving for excitement. The result of gambling is the establishment of tendencies toward excess and lack of self-control. Gambling is not a matter of private morality, to be decided by the individual, once it is made available. As Larry Braidfoot is quoted as saying, "An industry which wrecks lives, leads to an increased crime rate, fails to deliver what it promises in financial rewards, breaks homes, leaves families in financial stress, and preys upon the poor is not an industry which is a matter of personal morality."[33] Any government that legalizes moral deterioration cannot long maintain its own moral and economic vitality.

On the other hand, one can hardly expect much moral leadership from the church community that has abandoned its trust in the providential care of God for hope in bingo. Nevertheless, a believer who expects faith to help face frustration and provide stability in life's storms, who communes with God, who believes that the Messiah is coming or has already come, could not put much confidence in the lottery. Does the church no longer believe that faith provides more joy than money? One Christian has questioned putting God's money into the lottery, when it is more likely that one will be eaten by piranhas than win.[34] Seeking gain at someone else's loss is not Christian love. Gambling is taking us down a road to moral, social and economic disaster, and there is not a signpost in sight.

Review Questions

1. What major world event caused a shift in attitude toward gambling, and why?
2. Why did the church stop fighting gambling?
3. What are some of the arguments that proponents use to justify gambling?
4. What is wrong with viewing gambling as recreation?
5. How does the Bible demonstrate the problems associated with gambling?
6. What two biblical words summarize the case against gambling?
7. What is a parent's and the church's responsibility toward children and gambling?
8. What is the most basic gambling-related issue for Christians?

9. Is it okay to gamble a little? Why or why not?
10. In what concrete ways are the poor affected by Christians who gamble?

Endnotes

[1] Lucado, Max, *And the Angels Were Silent,* Portland: Multnomah, 1992, pp. 45-6 and 51.

[2] _____, "Dice," *Encyclopedia Britannica,* 7:330, New York: Encyclopedia Britannica, 1946.

[3] Peterson, Virgil W., "Obstacles to Enforcement of Gambling Laws," *Annals of the American Association of Political and Social Sciences,* 269:14, May, 1950.

[4] *De Spectaculus* (XVI), cited in Smith, Alson J., "The Churches and Gambling," *The Christian Century,* 76:512, April 29, 1959.

[5] Smith, *Ibid.*

[6] Muir, Jane, *Of Men and Numbers,* New York: Dell Publishers, 1961, pp. 41-42. A more complete history of Cardano's gambling is contained in Ore, Oystein, *Cardano the Gambling Scholar,* New York: Dover Publications, 1953.

[7] Blanche, Ernest E., "Lotteries Yesterday, Today and Tomorrow," *Annals of the American Association of Political and Social Sciences,* 269:71, May, 1950.

[8] _____, "Why People Gamble and Should They?" *Time,* 90:26, July 21, 1967.

[9] Blanche, *op. cit.,* p. 73.

[10] McGloin, F., "Shall the Lottery's Charter Be Renewed?" *The Forum,* 12:556, January, 1892.

[11] Carradine, Beverly, *The Lottery: The Louisiana State Lottery Company Examined and Exposed,* Salem, Ohio: Schmul Publishing, 1997. Contains a Prologue and Epilogue by William Kostlevy, Asbury Theological Seminary, Wilmore, Kentucky.

[12] Barrett, Arnold E., "Gambling, Economics and Morality," *Christianity Today,* 7:38, June 21, 1963.

[13] _____, "Science: If Baby Needs New Shoes," *Newsweek,* 22:68, December 27, 1943.

[14] Breslin, Jimmy, "In Defense of Gambling," *The Saturday Evening Post,* 236:12-13.

[15] Motter, Alton M., "Crusading Governor," *The Christian Century,* 65:204, February 18, 1948.

[16] _____, "Dewey Denounces Gambling Bid," *The Christian Century,* 67:133, February 1, 1950.

17 _____, "Gambling Proposals Lose in Four States," *The Christian Century*, 67:1380-1381, November 22, 1950.

18 Lenox, G. Merrill, "Churches Win Michigan Test," *The Christian Century*, 71:1442, November 24, 1954.

19 While audiences always express shock when I mention this figure, it is probably conservative. Since several studies have placed the total number of Americans who gamble within a point or two of 90%, and since 80% of Americans hold membership in some religious organization, even if every non-gambler were religious, that would still put the figure at 80%.

20 _____, "Cincinnati Churches Differ About Ethics of Gambling," *The Christian Century*, 55:1486, December 7, 1938.

21 Wall, James M., "Water in the Basement, Judgement in the Flood," *The Christian Century*, 109:475, May 6, 1992.

22 Wall, James M., "Why Isn't the Church Fighting Lotteries?" *The Christian Century*, 91:1163, December 11, 1974.

23 Mikesell, John L. and C. Kurt Zorn, "State Lotteries as Fiscal Savior or Fiscal Fraud: A Look at the Evidence," *Public Administration Review*, 46:316, July/August, 1986.

24 Quoted in Breslin, *loc. cit.*

25 All biblical quotations are from the *New International Version (NIV)*, Grand Rapids: Zondervan, 1985.

26 Lee, Helen, "Churches Struggle with New Factors in the Giving Equation," *Christianity Today*, p.48, April 24, 1995.

27 Jepson, J. W., "A Tax on Covetousness," *Pentecostal Evangel*, p. 8, January 28, 1990.

28 *Ibid*, p. 9.

29 Will, George, "In the Grip of Gambling," *Newsweek*, 113:78, May 8, 1989.

30 Levinson, Daniel J., *The Seasons of a Man's Life*, New York: Ballantine Books, 1978, p. 9.

31 _____, "Gambling: The Newest Growth Industry," *Business Week*, p.114, June 26, 1978.

32 _____, "Dewey Denounces Gambling Bid," *The Christian Century*, 67:133, February 1, 1950.

33 Larry Braidfoot as quoted by Darrell Turner, "Churches Ready to Oppose Expansion of Legalized Gambling," *Fundamentalist Journal*, 3:62, April, 1984.

34 Watson, Tom Jr., "Playing the Lottery is Idolatry," *Christianity Today*, 33:8, November 3, 1989.

Chapter 7

Crime

In 1971 Tony Spilotro was sent to Las Vegas to be the Chicago mob's outside man. His assignment was to oversee the inside men at the casinos who were running the skimming of money for the mob. Before he was through, Spilotro would steal his best friend's wife, run a burglary operation not approved by the mob, make public waves and cause murder on the streets of Las Vegas, which was supposed to be an open mob city without gang warfare between the branches of the mob.[1]

Gambling involves crime. Big crime. Organized crime. One critic of gambling has said, "When the public chooses to gamble, it also chooses crime, corruption, and cheating."[2] The clean image of state-operated lotteries is a veneer covering gambling's crooked image. The crimes are subtle, frequently involving political influence, and sophisticated (unlike the rough image of the past), and they are seldom punished. Despite the polished image of gambling crime today, the motives for the violence that accompanies crime have been constant for a century and a half. A study of crime on the Oregon trail revealed that "The main causes for the violence are pretty timeless: love affairs, grudges, gambling and property rights."[3] In gambling of any sort, crime pays and pays big.

For over fifty years supporters of gambling have argued that legalizing gambling would take it out of the hands of organized crime. The same logic says if you retrieve a hulk from the junk yard, wash it, polish it and put an honest man behind the wheel, you have a fine automobile. Like the spruced-up junker, gambling has problems "under the hood" that cannot be solved no matter how clean we scrub its exterior. Thirty-five years of experience demonstrate that state attempts to divert illegal gambling into more socially acceptable legal gambling are futile.

Gambling and Crime: Familiar Bedfellows

Gambling and crime are inseparable. After 1893 all lotteries were illegal in the United States. Only limited forms of gambling were allowed in special locations: horse racing in a few states, bingo beginning in the 1930s and casino gambling in Nevada after 1931. Bootleggers and racketeers provided much of the money that financed the legislative push to legalize pari-mutuel betting.[4] Much gambling was done in private and was not organized in the early part of this century. The rise of organized crime as a result of efforts to circumvent prohibition changed the face of gambling as well. The numbers racket, the most common form of lottery, was organized by the mob through control of numbers cards and enforcement of the relative honesty of the games. They wanted some winners, but the tendency was to select the number that had the least action for the day or week.

In addition to the numbers racket, the mob began providing illegal slot machines. The slot machine was invented by Charles Fey in 1895 in San Francisco. By 1950 Chicago, whose mob controlled crime west of the Mississippi, had become the center of production, with ten companies involved in the traffic.[5] The small investment in a slot machine produced huge profits for the owner, who recovered the cost of the machine in days or weeks. The risk of raids, the destruction of the machine and the relatively small fines for running a slot shop were well worth it. The machines placed gambling within the reach of the masses as they spread across the country.

Even though they were illegal in most states, the slots were distributed through dealers in large cities, advertised in trade journals and sold direct from the manufacturers. By 1950 there were 175 distributors, 10,000 "operators" who owned and serviced the machines, and who split the take 50–50 with the business where the slot was located. In 1949 alone, 49,000 machines worth $11 million were shipped. During the fiscal year 1948–1949, the federally required $100 coin gaming tax was paid by 69,786 businesses, each with approximately three machines. The estimated take in the early 1950s was in excess of $1 billion.[6]

When it was gradually revealed that the mob controlled the "operators," the states began to crack down on the slots. Florida cracked down in 1937 because of racketeering. Wisconsin passed a stiff law in 1945, Minnesota in 1947 and Idaho a little later. Nevada, Washington, Montana and two counties in Maryland allowed slots. They became illegal in the rest of the country. Idaho eliminated them upon discovering that the operators were not paying the taxes and armed robbery had increased, along with welfare cases and delinquent accounts with businesses.[7]

During the 1930s and 1940s, the mob also moved into the coordination of bookies and the operation of illegal casinos. The Kefauver hearings caused tighter enforcement in Florida in the 1950s, but bookies flourished in every major city and such places as northern Kentucky, Lincoln, Nebraska, and Hot Springs, Arkansas.[8]

Law enforcement netted some big hauls but was irregular. A New England numbers racket, broken up in 1934, was netting $8 million a month for its operators.[9] In one of the biggest raids of the 1930s Federal agents broke a ring in New York and Massachusetts that produced 500,000 lottery tickets per week. Over $7 million were in stock. Sixty-nine indictments were filed, and it was discovered that the gang was intimidating winners to take $250 instead of the announced $1,000 prize. They cleared about 95% of the dollars gambled with them.[10]

From 1933, when Prohibition ended, until 1970, when drug trafficking began to dominate, gambling was the most widespread illegal activity that police had to address.[11] Since a large minority of the population did not want gambling laws enforced, "symbolic" enforcement and corruption were natural consequences. From the late 1930s to the 1960s protection payoffs to the police and judges were the largest source of official corruption. In 1932 a United States senator, James J. Davis, was indicted (along with six other persons and the Western Union Telegraph Company) for personally and illegally profiting from a lottery operated for the Fraternal Order of Moose.[12]

The richest mobsters were the ones who concentrated upon gambling. As late as 1963 it was still true that ". . . public gambling provides the treasure chest of the underworld."[13] One former FBI agent maintains that was true right up to the beginning of the 1990s.[14] As a consequence, a perfectly reasonable-sounding myth arose that if lotteries were legalized, control would be wrested from the numbers games of the mob and official corruption reduced. Honest law enforcement officials argued vehemently, but unsuccessfully, that experience demonstrated that legalized gambling simply created new gamblers, easy prey for the mob. In the effort to control gambling, law officers consistently supported legislation that restricted transportation of equipment and distribution of information through any public means such as newspapers or the mails. Federal law prohibiting transportation of slot machines or parts across state lines was obtained and sometimes enforced. Some states restricted the use of phone and telegraph lines for transmitting race results.

In 1950 the effort to broaden such legislation led to U.S. Senate hearings concerning the restraint of private access to racing wire services. The Senate called on Mafia bosses to testify, including the "prime minister" of the underworld, Frank Costello, James J. (Mr. Big) Carroll of St. Louis, and Frank Erickson. They all had bad memories about ever participating in illegal bookmaking, even taking the Fifth Amendment at times. They agreed, however, that legislation would not affect the bookies. The law might slow payoffs by a few hours and cause some inconvenience, but they indicated that a bookie could operate with nothing other than the *New York Times* and a telephone if he had to. Erickson admitted that he saw no way Congress could stop him from operating.[15] Congress had no intention of closing the newspapers to sports results. Also in 1950 the California Crime Commission estimated in one of its reports that $400 million was being spent just by slot machine owners alone to bribe public officials.[16]

In the aftermath of the Kefauver investigations, federal legislation was passed that required bookies to pay a $50 occupational tax and 10% of their gross receipts to the federal government. The bookies complained that the 10% was more than their take, but those who complied simply passed it along to the customers in the form of smaller payoffs. Since the federal records were open to city and state law enforcement officials, and the bookie was to have his federal stamp with him at all times, discovering bookies would be easy in states where they were illegal if they registered.[17] In the first few weeks, only 7,700 bookies came forward to register. Most temporarily suspended operations. Some thought that this would break up the control of the mob.[18] In May of 1952, a federal judge ruled the law unconstitutional, enforcement was suspended and a long appeal process begun. Finally, in 1968 the Supreme Court ruled that the law contributed to self-incrimination in violation of the Fifth Amendment, and the law was dead.[19] The law alone could not suppress the crime. The temptation of bribes was just too great. In Phoenix, Arizona, the sheriff, a former sheriff, a deputy and seventeen others were indicted for receiving and giving bribes in Maricopa County. In Omaha, Nebraska, a radio newsman with a secret recorder toured illegal gambling joints in 1953. He exposed the fact that Omaha police had made no effort for over a year to shut down any gambling. Outraged citizens flooded city hall with calls, but the mayor protested that "Omaha is so clean you could eat off it as you would a table cloth." The gambling went on without any shutdown.[20]

The power of the payoff worked in other cities besides Omaha. When new mayor Daniel F. McDevitt took office in Reading, Pennsylvania, he made a great show of driving out the gamblers. He gave them twenty-four hours to get rid of over 1,000 multi-coin pinball machines. After 19 days in which the police netted three distributors and two operators, the mayor gave in, saying the city could not outlaw the machines. One mob leader bragged to a reporter that it took a half-million in bribes to "restore order." The mob expanded the number of machines and figured that it got its money back in two months. Federal officers stepped in, raided the mayor's Reading House Tavern (turned over to his brother while he was in office) and found 44 machines, which they smashed. In retaliation for the press coverage, the mayor closed the press room at city hall, removed the press table from the council chambers and arrested a reporter for disorderly conduct (a $50 fine) who posed for a picture with his typewriter on the court house steps. The police tailed news photographers and issued 73 tickets to news delivery trucks in four days. The mayor eased off under a new wave of publicity. Reform does not always work when the money and the fear are big enough.[21]

The mob is seldom content to run a fair illegal game—they rig the game as well. In 1949 it was discovered that the New Jersey mob was paying a banker in Cincinnati $5 per week to rig the number used as the payoff, so that the lightest bet number always won.[22] The New York Stock Exchange and the Cincinnati Clearing House began rounding their numbers so they were less likely to be used, since the same numbers came up too often. The bookies simply moved to other numbers. Similarly, a bookie interviewed by the author indicated that he routinely did not pay off big winners who seemed near the end of their resources. If they had used credit heavily or had been slow to win, there was no payoff, and the customer was written off. The exception was a customer with mob ties who might retaliate. He said he once had a case where the customer needed the money to get hospital care for a child with leukemia. The bookie said he felt bad about not paying that one off.

In Miami a reporter went undercover for three weeks, following which the *Miami Daily News* published the addresses of 16 bookie joints, houses of prostitution and numbers games headquarters. The police had been unable to find these places. The paper also fingered 16 detectives who were on the take but did not name them. This was a fourth of the detectives on the force, including five out of six in one district. The bookie joints closed, but the police officers sued the *News* for $1 million dollars. The *News* indicated willingness to go to court and provided the names, times and amounts of the payoffs.[23]

Even a casual researcher can find literally dozens of stories about the use of gambling money to purchase police protection and political influence. One of the more notable happened in Illinois, when a *Post-Dispatch* reporter taped an interview with Earl Shelton, a gangster, concerning payoffs to state officials, including cronies of Republican Governor Dwight Green. Carl and Bernie, brothers of Earl, had been murdered, apparently because they knew too much. The tape recording led a grand jury to indict State's Attorney Roy Hull for malfeasance in office. The governor dismissed the grand jury, had another appointed which promptly indicted Earl Shelton, the *St. Louis Post Dispatch* reporter Theodore C. Link and two other witnesses on charges of kidnapping and conspiracy. The charges were dropped after the election.[24]

Newspapers have not always led the search for illegal gambling. *The Philadelphia Inquirer* owner Moses L. Annenburg owned the track wire services that provided information to bookies all over the country. He also published racing newspapers for gamblers.[25] His paper did little investigative work in the years that followed. Several years later he was indicted for income tax evasion in the largest amount up to that time.

Crooked Bingo

As bingo has continued over the past fifty years, the means of subverting these games have become very sophisticated. Nearly always charities are the ostensible benefactors of the bingo halls. The charities, however, receive very little, if anything. The managers make the money. Various card-rigging schemes exist; manipulation of the numbers and holders of the cards is common. The simplest technique of all is skimming. Money is simply removed by various means before the count for distribution or tax purposes. Another means of skimming is falsification of expenses of the operation.

Chicago is the most notorious location for crooked bingo games but it can happen anywhere. A Louisville art museum served as a front for a very large bingo operation. Following an IRS investigation the bingo hall shut down and filed for bankruptcy. During the preceding year, it had taken in nearly $9 million, but the gallery had received only $27,000. It had local art worth only $11,900 at the time of the filing. Where had all the money gone? Hard to tell, but the director had purchased a new expensive home, twenty pieces of real estate and various other financial assets.[26]

Crime and No Punishment

Law-breaking has been frequently ignored by public officials. One example was Hot Springs, Arkansas, in the 1950s and 1960s. Casino gambling flourished in several places (The Southern Club, The Belvedere Club and others) even though gambling was illegal in Arkansas. Most of the gamblers were visitors and tourists who brought money into the state. Then governor Orval Faubus, who followed the "will of the people" in denying civil rights to blacks, said with regard to casinos that he was not the keeper of the public conscience. He was the servant of the people. Servanthood was especially good when the casino take was estimated at $100 million per year. The conservative journal, *The Nation,* noted that ignoring state and national law on the basis of the will of the people bordered on anarchy.[27]

In the 1940s and 1950s, Biloxi, Mississippi, located near Kessler Air Force Base, was notorious for lax enforcement of gambling laws. Senator Lester Hunt of Wyoming conducted hearings but met a wall of resistance to shutting down the bars with slots. Hunt was incensed over two young enlistees who had committed suicide over gambling debts.[28] Similar cozy arrangements existed in various New England locations where Bradley's at Newport and Canfield's at Saratoga were seldom bothered because of the prestige of their clientele.[29] Slot machines routinely operated in defiance of state law and local ordinances, and after 1950, in defiance of national legislation making it illegal to transport slot machines and parts across state lines.

Other spots in the country that had flagrant illegal gambling were Jefferson Parish, outside New Orleans; Lake Charles, Louisiana with 35 gambling dens; and Galveston, Texas, where the gambling was associated with illegal alcohol and prostitution. The Texas Rangers, who had declared the state to be clean, had to be led by reporters to 320 active slot machines.[30]

The prevailing attitude of the 1950s was reflected in the 1960 opinion of Judge Elijah Adlow of Massachusetts: "Gambling is inextricably involved in the corruption of police and the consequent weakening of authority. . . ."[31] He predicted that the nation would suffer economic decline as the result of the gambling mania. While cause and effect remain unproven, there is a high correlation between the inception of a lottery or other gambling expansion and a subsequent decline in a state's economy. By 1959 the Massachusetts Special Crime Commission recognized illegal gambling as the most widespread form of organized crime.[32]

Not only were local police corrupted but state officials as well. In Massachusetts the supervisor of the Capitol's documents room operated a book right in the Capitol. He claimed amateur status. The legislators found him innocent since many of them patronized him, but he lost his job.[33]

Crime and *Legal* Gambling

As noted in the first chapter, proponents of lotteries argue that legalizing gambling would take away action from illegal gambling. That has not happened. Illegal gambling has simply expanded along with legal gambling, sometimes directly alongside. In Brooklyn, after New York legalized off-track betting, the bookies set up shop next door, offering a better payoff by only taking their usual percentage. By 1964 the illegal gambling bill was estimated to be at least $40 billion. Experts estimated that $2 billion was spent on corrupting officials, and $7 billion was profit to the mob.[34]

In the attempt to claim that legal betting suppresses illegal, opponents of gambling were accused of aiding and abetting organized crime by their opposition. By 1975 it was abundantly clear that this was not so. *Newsweek* noted that lotteries had failed to ". . . curb illegal and usually mob-controlled gambling."[35] A University of Michigan study demonstrated that lotteries increased illegal gambling as customers who were enticed into the lottery looked for a better way to gamble and beat the taxes. The most accessible way was to gamble with a bookie. A set of interviews conducted by the Associated Press with bookies, gamblers and police indicated that the take of illegal gambling increased dramatically.[36] As noted previously, New Jersey estimated that it took away only 15% of the illegal gambling with its lottery, with no indication of how many new gamblers it created.[37] New York City reported a sudden rise in illegal gambling when its lottery started. For some people, if it's legal, it's not fun.

The mob has much more expertise at running gambling than the state, so they reap benefits from the increase in gambling. Out-of-state gambling interests supported the lottery in Kentucky even though it was predicted to hurt the horse industry. The gamblers could not care less about the losses of the straight horse owners. This lack of concern extends, of course, to the state as well. In states with lotteries, the mob often runs parallel operations, frequently paying on the same numbers the state does. You just don't hear about those who win with the mob, and it's doubtful their patrons win as much.

Much attention has been given to the cleanness of state-run lotteries. Unfortunately, there are many ways in which state-run lotteries can manipulate money with someone getting rich who is not seen by the public. Membership on a state lottery board frequently has minimum responsibilities with lots of perks. In many states the members receive handsome honoraria, the use of an automobile, all expenses paid at the best accommodations during meetings and sometimes even lottery tickets without charge. In most states the members are appointed by the governor. What better description of political patronage could be found? Most lottery board members have no special qualifications, no expert knowledge of the problems associated with gambling and no training for finding graft or corruption connected with the lottery they supervise. Board members tend to speak with one voice if their actions are criticized. Their most significant task is the hiring of the lottery director. Like major league baseball managers, lottery directors seem to migrate from state to state regardless of whether they have done well or poorly in the previous state.

Patronage is not the only potential area for corruption. Some states do not have required bidding for contracts to produce the materials for lottery use—equipment, tickets, instant win cards. As a result, Scientific Games has cornered 70% of the instant game market, far in excess of what the government considers a monopoly. Without bidding there is plenty of room for director and board inducements such as cash, vacations and expensive meals.

While major newspapers occasionally publish negative articles about the lottery and the conduct of its managers, the lotteries have avoided any serious investigation of the extent of their corruption. A mild-mannered Kansas study revealed that "Lottery staff do not always follow adequate and consistent internal control procedures. For example, the controls over instant ticket inventories do not adequately safeguard the tickets from loss, theft, or other improprieties. For prize payments, the lottery's internal controls are not adequate to ensure that unpaid instant claims are not altered, or stolen prior to payment, and the lottery does not consistently verify that the amounts billed by the multi-state lottery organization are accurate."[38]

In July of 1993, the Kentucky state auditor released a scathing report indicating mismanagement and waste on the part of lottery officials. The lottery had so mismanaged its cash flow that it had to borrow $10 million in June of 1992. The lottery lost $300,000 when it failed to purchase 1993 annuities in a timely fashion. Dividend transfers to the state had been done in violation of the law; managers spent $31,000 on charter flights with no documentation; board meetings had no agendas and inadequate minutes; seventeen employees received a $500 a month automobile allowance with no controls; managers made 145 out-of-state purchases of gasoline without justification; $100,000 of state money was spent on donations to private fund raising campaigns, including political ones; the director made $10,000 in unsubstantiated purchases; at least $4,000 in equipment was taken home by employees; one employee received a $3,000 loan; the board vice-chair had an interest in a company with a $650,000 contract with the lottery; another board member had an interest in a company with a $10,000 contract; traveling employees consistently paid the highest air fares; and over $48 million in contracts with the ten largest vendors violated state contract law. The director, several top employees and all the board members were forced to resign after the revelations. When a few were reluctant to step down, the governor called for their resignations.[39] If other states conducted the same kind of thorough audit they might well find the same kinds of irregularities. The director had been hired from another state with the highest recommendations.

Unfortunately, most states do not investigate their lotteries except in the face of scandal. Most state agencies and newspapers simply print the comments of lottery directors and their letters to the editor without comment.

Extremely sophisticated attempts at counterfeiting lottery tickets have been developed by those who wish to cash in. Some states are more vulnerable than others, depending on how sophisticated their tracking system for the sale of each ticket. The most common ploy is to present a counterfeit when a winning ticket has not been claimed after a reasonable amount of time. Most winners have a year in which to claim the bigger prizes. The counterfeiter is claiming the prize of someone who is not paying attention or who has lost his or her winning ticket. Obviously, no one knows how often this deception has been successful. State lotteries discourage stories about counterfeiting for fear it will encourage cheating.

Even less clear is how frequently collusion has led to illicit payoffs. While most televised selections of numbers appear credible, there was the notable case in Pennsylvania where the show host and five accomplices wagered over $1.2 million on combinations of the numbers 4 and 6. They filled the other balls partially with fluid so only the fours and sixes were blown up in the air to be selected. They were caught and indicted.[40] States seldom conduct independent inspections of their machines. Suspicion of tampering lingers, for example, in a 1991 case where two members of the Massachusetts mob won over $1 million dollars within a month of each other. The newspapers and national publications did not seem to think that this was strange. No one questioned whether collusion occurred or investigated the possibility. Curious indeed!

Winners Beware

Lotteries can be very reluctant to give the money to winners. We have already discussed that lotteries do not give the money to winners all at once, depriving winners of the fruit of investment and uninflated dollars. The lottery enjoys the investment income through the purchase of an annuity at much less than the face value, usually about 55%. Reluctance to give the prize may extend to giving it at all. The California Lottery had to be sued to award $3.4 million to Doris Barnett of Los Angeles. She was a big spin contestant. The ball landed on the $3 million grand prize, but *four seconds* later it jumped to the $10,000 slot. The show host had already announced that she was a multimillion dollar winner. The state awarded the $10,000. A jury awarded the $3.4 million on the basis of the announcement and the time lapse. The state appealed.

The lawyers got wealthy. The suit went on for four years, causing the winner ange, depression and a sense of racial unfairness. A superior court judge finally rejected a retrial and the multimillion award stood.[41] During the court cases the state implied fraud on the part of the winner. One wonders how the fraud could be on the part of the contestant when the state controlled the wheel. No one checked the wheel that had magically kicked the ball out of the big prize slot, even if it did so a little slowly.

Casinos, like bookies and lotteries, are also reluctant to pay winners. In 1988 Caesar's Palace refused to pay $1 million dollar slot payoff to Kirk Erickson because he was 19. Despite notification to the hotel that the party had teenagers there was no warning that they could not gamble. Staff repeatedly sold him tokens and no signs were posted in the casino. Apparently, teenagers can play and lose, they just can't play and win.[42] Of course, casinos need all the money they can get because so much cheating goes on. Players attempt card switches, and catwalks behind one way mirrors are a necessary part of casino operations to watch for player and employee fraud. Fraud flows both ways, however.

There are cases of outright fraud and incompetence on the part of state lotteries. In the Midwest, games have been pulled because no winning tickets were printed and at other times because too many winning tickets were printed. The New York Lottery was shut down by Governor Hugh Carey for eleven months, from October 1975 to September 1976, because it was in such disarray due to corruption.[43] Part of the difficulty was that nearly half the winning tickets were not sold, leading to a reduced payoff by the state. In other cases winning tickets were produced in duplicate and triplicate.[44] Cheating by vendors is a common problem, including delayed payments to the state, allowing vendors to collect interest at best, to manipulate audits at worst. The Maine Lottery once had to pay $3 per winning ticket instead of the promised $25 to winners because a Portland store owner discovered that tickets with similar patterns of numbers were run off the presses at the same time. He purchased books with consecutive ID numbers, scraped all boxes on enough tickets to find the pattern (only 3 of 12 spaces were to be scratched) and then scratched winners at the rate of 1 in 20 instead of the expected 1 in 200.[45] Perhaps the largest and saddest case was the Kentucky store clerk who scratched $130,000 worth of tickets with the expectation that he would repay the money from his winnings. Any business, except the lottery business, would be under constant investigation if beset with this much corruption.

Betting in Britain

When gambling proponents want to find support for the legal expansion of gambling they always point to England. England is supposedly the prime example of the benefits of cleanly run gambling. Such citations simply do not tell of the fixed races, the drugged horses and the infiltration of the controlling office by agents of the crooks. All these are ongoing problems in England. Gambling groups which run the casinos have been guilty of buying names of known gamblers from the police as well as paying kickbacks to gamblers who bring other gamblers to the tables.[46] Playboy once lost its license for failing to follow the English rules, which are strict. Directors of the operation may not gamble at the club, credit may not be extended (clubs were accepting checks they knew would bounce if cashed immediately) and licenses were sold to unacceptable owners in an attempt to reduce the control of the gambling commission.[47]

Wherever there is a quick buck to turn, crooks get involved. What is also usually ignored is that England is a smaller place, more easily policed. Further, there is only one jurisdiction, not fifty. England's experience is not really relevant to the argument for expanding gambling in the United States.

The Mob and Legal Gambling

Another argument of proponents is that the impact of the mob is grossly exaggerated. The police and FBI are less optimistic. They suspect that money is laundered through legal gambling. Winnings are stated on tax returns that don't exist. While this makes a tax bill due, it moves money from illegal sources over to the legitimate realm and covers the expensive lifestyle of the hood. The small number of reported cases, which give the impression that there is not much crime, are really the tip of the iceberg. The mob has been forced to move into legitimate business to launder money as well. This move was well underway in the early days of the lottery.

The control of the mob over gambling in Chicago and New York is most widely known, due to a variety of articles and books by former FBI agents. Probably the most popular are the three books that William E. Roemer, Jr. has published; *Roemer: Man Against the Mob, War of the Godfathers* and *The Enforcer*. In these books he details the control of the Chicago mob west of the Mississippi, the New York mob's various attempts to move in and the methods of controling gambling. He indicates that the mob directly controls illegal gambling, takes a "street tax" from criminals engaged in other activities like prostitution, theft and drugs, and controls the skim from the Las Vegas casinos. He estimates that the skim reached a peak in 1983 under the leadership of Tony Spilotro in Las Vegas but declined with Spilotro's fall. After 1990 he suggests that only three casinos appear to be held by fronts for the mob, with the rest clean except for minor violations. He also claims that Atlantic City is free from direct mob influence, due to the $3 to $5 million spent annually on each casino to supervise it for possible corruption. The mob is present, however, through union influence and control of trucking and service contracts. Other sources confirm that gambling money was financing the mob's move into the trucking industry, vending machines, juke boxes, pizzarias and various other enterprises.

The harsh reality is that crime does not slink away when confronted with legal gambling. People introduced to gambling by the lottery move on to other forms, eventually learning about and becoming customers of illegal gambling. The idea of getting money without working makes many easy prey for the bookies' untaxed wins, easy credit and same-day payoffs. The ease of placing a bet over the phone also appeals. First-time lottery players normally do not know a bookie and are initially unattracted by illegal gambling, but time erodes such thinking. Once they begin gambling, lottery players become convinced that the illegality of other forms of betting is artificial. After all, they wonder, how can government go into the same business as the mob and expect to stay clean? Legal gambling is an unsuccessful attempt to take the ugliness of moral debilitation, greed and cheating and make it pretty.

Lest we think that lotteries are the ultimate in state-supported gambling, be aware that a push for casino gambling follows. Atlantic City was just the first place. Federal legislation passed in 1989 allows the 524 Native American tribes to match any gambling on tribal lands that already exists in their state. The tribes have built great bingo halls in Florida and casinos in 21 states including Connecticut, Oklahoma, Minnesota, South Dakota, Iowa and Wisconsin, where casino nights were allowed to charitable organizations. The Indians run theirs every night.

Grand jury indictments provide an occasional glimpse into the world of the casinos' "unlisted" shareholders. Testimony in the 1960s revealed that Meyer Lansky (of New York and Miami), Tony Accardo (of Chicago), Sam Giancana, Felix Alderisio, Israel Alderman, Salvatore Giancana (of Chicago), John Scalish (of Cleveland), Bennie Seigelbaum (of Miami Beach) and Gerardo Catena (of New Jersey) all had interests in Vegas casinos. As the take was counted, large amounts were simply set aside and not recorded in the casino's books. Some of the leading casinos were involved.[48] Infiltration by the mob was easier because while over 1,000 businesses had licenses for slots in Nevada, the top seven casinos took in 35% of the money, and the top 21 took in 70% of the gross.[49] This virtual monopoly meant the mob had to work with only a few casinos to haul in major amounts of money.

Most customers of the mob assume they are in little danger from crooks because some of them seem so respectable. A classic example of this was Alfie Mart of Miami Beach. He ran various gambling operations around Miami Beach for over thirty years, with local officials making only halfhearted attempts to catch him. When he was finally implicated in serious crimes and the police could no longer ignore him, they found that he had ties with the mob in Chicago, Las Vegas, New York and Newark. He had apparently taken over the mob that attempted to move into his territory. This experience alerted Floridians, so when Miami Beach hotel owners sought to open casinos on a 21-mile strip in 1978 they found Governor Askew, the Dade County sheriff and the former mayor all against it, on the basis that it would attract even more organized crime.[50]

An even more unbelievable case is Morris Barney "Moe" Dalitz. Dalitz had organized the Cleveland Mafia in the 1920s with four associates. The mob became known as the Mayfield Road Gang and controlled bootlegging and gambling in Cleveland for decades. With the end of Prohibition, Dalitz expanded his gambling operations into Kentucky, West Virginia and Indiana before the heat from authorities encouraged him to move to Las Vegas in the early 1950s. He built the Desert Inn casino and managed the Stardust and the Fremont for the Chicago mob, becoming the most powerful mob figure in Las Vegas until the arrival of Tony Spilotro in the 1970s. While he was making millions from the casinos, he led the contribution drive to build Guardian Angel Catholic Cathedral in downtown Las Vegas. He helped with fund raising and made major contributions to, or provided financing for the Sunrise Hospital, the Valley Bank Plaza, the Las Vegas Convention Center, the Las Vegas Country Club and several University of Las Vegas buildings. In 1982 *Forbes* listed him as one of the wealthiest men in America. Las Vegas named him "Humanitarian of the Year."[51] Society honored one who became wealthy taking money from little people and causing immense heartache. What irony.

Atlantic City

The mob has been interested in Atlantic City from the beginning, although *Time* reported that the mob declared a two-year moratorium upon direct infiltration of the casinos to give them time to become real money makers.[52] The statewide referendum allowing casinos was financed by a mysterious $1.2 million with tenuous mob ties. The largest donor was Resorts International, which was the first group in line for a license.[53] Religious leaders fought with a limited budget and the prediction that casinos would attract prostitutes, crooks and loan sharks. They were right. City officials, real estate developers and others made money from skyrocketing market values, which jumped 200% during the first months after the referendum passed and 500% by 1982.[54] Many in the middle class lost their homes to increased taxes. Many among the poor and elderly lost their dwelling places because they lived in the older hotels which were purchased and torn down to make way for new casinos. The "Inlet" area was heavily populated by Puerto Ricans, and 3,500 of 6,000 of them were pushed out.[55] The state had to step in, passing a law requiring casinos to allow residents to stay up to two years at the current rent, stay five months free, or receive five months rent if evicted immediately. In all, 3,859 dwelling units were destroyed between 1977 and 1982.[56] From 1960 to 1977 the population declined from 69,000 to 41,000, with unemployment increasing to 17.6%.[57] Even though the Philadelphia mob led by Angelo Bruno controlled prostitution, loan sharking and illegal gambling in Atlantic City before the casinos, it was declared an open city like Vegas, with several mobs moving in.

The area where the casinos desired to build happened to contain many of the largest and oldest homes in the historic district. When owners resisted selling, over 50 per month of these houses burned at the hands of arsonists. Entire blocks were "torched" in multiple "nights of terror."[58] This continued until all the land desired by the casinos was cleared. Other land scams followed. A certain Edmund A. Tiero, chairman of Chris-Mond Corporation, sold $475,000 in unregistered securities in an $85 million recreational development project that did not exist. He operated out of a Philadelphia hotel room with a phone and no employees.[59] Numerous churches also closed.

When the casinos opened, crime and drug use reached epidemic proportions, and the cost of city services soared, wiping out the tax increases the city was receiving.[60] The casinos refused to cooperate with the city in other ways. The state required a minimum of 500 hotel rooms to be built with each casino with the intention of promoting convention traffic as well. The hotels which did not already exist were built with the minimum rooms and no meeting rooms in order to discourage convention traffic. The casinos wanted the nearby day-trippers who would come, drop their money and leave.

Another interesting issue was the gambling licenses. The state intended to be tough. Resorts International, with casinos in the Bahamas, was the first applicant. *Rolling Stone* magazine revealed the ties of the leaders to various East Coast mobsters. Resorts International slapped the magazine with a multimillion dollar defamation suit. Despite this attempted intimidation the state licensing board indicated that a permanent license would be issued only if the officers with mob ties were removed. Resorts International complied and was the first casino to open, doing very well, grossing nearly $600,000 a day and recovering nearly half its total investment in the first year.[61]

The second casino to get a temporary license was Caesar's World. Because of their underworld ties, the chair and vice-chair who owned 18% of the stock took extended leaves in order for that group to get a permanent license. They were connected with Alvin Malnik, lawyer for New York crime boss, Meyer Lansky.[62] Similarly, the chairman of the board of Bally Manufacturing stepped down while hearings were in progress for their permanent license. Yet another resignation was the CEO of The Golden Nugget, who stepped from the board of the New Jersey subsidiary to enable them to get a license. Insider trading of Golden Nugget stock and a grand jury investigation of the land acquisition deal in New Jersey apparently led to The Golden Nugget's difficulties.

The first two casinos were very successful, becoming the busiest in the world. Some 37 million people live within 300 miles of Atlantic City, a very large pool of potential gamblers. The expectation was that this influx of money would rejuvenate the city and provide jobs. Unfortunately, very few locals found work in the casinos. Most found the only jobs available were low paying hotel jobs. As anticipated by the police, assault, larcenies (up 40%), prostitution, auto theft (up 38%), drug dealing, extortion and fraud all exploded, some to over four times the level before the arrival of the casinos. Massive hiring for the police was necessary as the "whiff of the underworld" became strong. As one observer said, "Atlantic City today resembles pictures we sometimes see of Latin American capitals: boarded buildings, vacant lots, and "sheetmetal villages" against a background of ultra-modern office buildings."[63] I. Nelson Rose, lawyer and gambling consultant, echoed the same thought, saying, "Atlantic City used to be a slum by the sea, now it is a slum by the sea with casinos."[64]

Topping everything was the casinos' refusal to pay the city the 2% tax for urban renewal, which was supposed to begin after five years. A negotiated settlement directed the money into projects that would directly benefit the casinos. They still delayed paying. There were other problems. By February 1980, the vice chairman of the Casino Control Commission, Kenneth MacDonald, resigned because of licensing irregularities uncovered during Abscam.[65] The purpose of the regulations was to keep out the mob, which MacDonald had helped to circumvent. Later that year the chair of the commission, Joseph Lordi, also resigned because of influence peddling.[66] Lordi had granted temporary licenses even though state investigators had revealed mob ties. Lordi conducted negotiations without consulting with other commission members. By this time several local politicians were found to have ties with the gaming companies. The casinos eventually became New Jersey's largest private employers, giving them tremendous clout with the legislature, whom they lobbied heavily and whose members speculated in casino stock.[67] The casinos eventually retained every law firm in the state that had former state officials on the letterhead.[68]

The New Jersey attorney general, John Degman, found that the mob from Chicago, New York and northern New Jersey was involved in the purchase of land, pizza parlors, discotheques, night clubs, service contracts for liquor, food services and prostitution, often using front men with clean records in a ". . . mysterious movement of cash and checks through a strange mix of bank accounts and people."[69] One example was Domenico Adamita, who borrowed $350,000 to buy Casanova's Disco from a man who kept his money in a bag in the basement. The police traced the money to a cousin of Carlo Gambino, a New York crime figure. The mob used its money and muscle to deceive politicians, banks, builders and insurance companies.

Some of the mob activity centered around organizing the unions, as it had done in other cities at earlier times. The Teamsters recruited hotel and restaurant employees with the benign approval of Anthony (Tony Pro) Provenzano, who keeps tabs on the unions from semi-retirement in Florida. In a classic case of the fox guarding the henhouse, the allegedly New York mob-affiliated Association of Public and Private Labor Employees (APPLE) organized the private detectives and guard services. Anthony (Big Tuna) Accardo's Chicago mob signed up bartenders through a Cincinnati affiliate. Atlantic City prosecutor Richard Williams predicted that the government would be controlled by the stranglehold of the unions.[70] However, only about one-third of the employees were eventually unionized. These tended to be in the lowest paying jobs. Some analysts say mob influence has been exaggerated by stories planted by the casinos to suppress unionization.[71] Police assumed that since there had been no mob killings, this made Atlantic City officially open. The presence of the Cuban Malagamba gang selling cocaine and hookers seemed to confirm the openness. Public trading does not, of course, assure integrity.

Despite all this, when scholars studied the situation in the mid-1980s they found that the casinos were relatively free from mob influence, saying, ". . .all the casinos of Atlantic City and many of those found in Nevada are owned and operated by publicly traded corporations that have excellent reputations."[72] Even *The Economist* claimed that precautions were strict and that gambling stocks were a good investment.[73] In 1984, however, a *Washington Post* story revealed mob penetration into gambling in New Jersey. Even proponents of the casinos admitted it.[74]

Strict precautions meant that by 1980 New Jersey had to install a full-time commission to replace the old part-time one in an attempt to control the corruption. The corruption reached all the way to Senator Harrison Williams, who was exposed during Abscam. The state also had to stop granting temporary licenses because the casinos were slow to comply with permanent license requirements and sought renewals of the temporary licenses. The governor, Brendan Byrne, sought laws to prevent politicians and their relatives from taking jobs with the casinos for a minimum of two years after leaving office. This was an attempt to slow the buying of public officials and their influence. By 1987 the cost of regulating the casinos was $52 million per year, nearly $4 million per casino.[75] By 1982 Atlantic City had the fifth highest homicide rate in the country, despite having 534 police officers in a town of 40,000, a force big enough for a city ten times its size.[76]

In addition to all the crime control problems, Atlantic City has also reaped a harvest of social welfare problems: prostitution, racketeering, influence peddling, poverty, inadequate housing on a continuing basis and the poverty of visitors who lose everything they have at the tables. The remote location of Las Vegas allowed a city ordinance to prevent airlines from selling one-way tickets to the city. In Atlantic City, where many arrive by train, automobile, and even by hitchhiking, people come, lose their money and have no way home. Juveniles come seeking a future and wind up in homes for runaways. The shelters experienced a 100% increase in homelessness the first year after the casinos opened.[77]

What we know of mob activity in Vegas and Atlantic City is relevant to the expansion of casinos elsewhere. Every brand of gambling has been touched by the mob. Jai alai, for example, has been investigated in two of the four states that have legalized it because of suspicion that hidden rigging enhanced payoffs. The rich profits for gambling's unseen controllers will keep the pressure on all states to consider the expansion of gambling. While only limited exposure of lottery crookedness has been presented, one must realize that lotteries are the relatively clean window dressing for other forms of gambling. All the states' experiences with jai alai, casinos and slot machines prove that it is extremely difficult to keep the mob out of legal gambling, let alone the illegal.

The Future of Gambling and Crime

The real goal of the casino operators is to open the midsection of the country. They have built connections with the Native American casinos, with Las Vegas managing many casinos on behalf of the tribes. Several midsize casino corporations run the many riverboats and are a rapidly growing segment of the casino business. Repeated efforts have been made to introduce casinos to New Orleans, Chicago and Gary, Indiana. They have finally succeeded in all of these places except Chicago. Players International purchased an interest in a Kentucky racetrack in 1993, and two other casino operations have purchased interests in other tracks, in anticipation of approval in that state.

For a time it appeared that sports betting would be the next realm of expansion of gambling, especially after Delaware and Montana joined Nevada in allowing it. The public recognition of vulnerability to the fix of legal sports betting has created surprising resistance to this expansion. Illegal betting on sports could also lead to the fix. Most bookies, however, wish to avoid the fix unless they control it. The fear of two fixes in the opposite direction of the same event keeps criminals away to some extent. No one knows how many events have been fixed. Only the most naive believe that the fix ended after 31 athletes at seven schools were caught in the late 1940s and 1950s.

One of the more widespread forms of sports gambling in the 1950s and 1960s was the football card pool. Bookies handled these in the late 1940s but later got out. The cards were too time-consuming for the amount of return. For factory workers and students who wanted to pick up a little extra money the mob supplied the cards for $5 per hundred, or an enterprising person with access to the Vegas line could print his own. You bought your card from the dealer who paid at 9-to-1 if you picked four out of four games right (the real odds were 16-to-1) to 150-to-1 for picking ten out of ten (the real odds were 1,024-to-1). If you missed any game you were a loser with no payoff. Up to 25 million of the cards were sold each week during the football season.[78] During the summer baseball pools were similarly run.

The more modern form of sports gambling seems to be for the players to gamble and lose big themselves. Denny McClain, the last pitcher to win 30 games in a season (31 in 1968) became involved in bookmaking. Jigs Gazell, a small-time Detroit mobster, offered to cut him in on the action. "Denny the Dupe" wound up paying the winners while the mob pocketed the money of the losers. When he failed to pay off a big winner, Tony Giacalone broke his toes, he lost the last three games of the season and Detroit lost the pennant to Boston.[79] McClain was ultimately caught gambling on baseball games and was suspended for life. He later turned to golf hustling, drug running and finally served time, all the result of his gambling habit.

In 1990 Pete Rose, baseball's all-time hit leader with 4,142 career hits, was also banned for life from baseball and so far is ineligible for the Hall of Fame. His apparent crime was betting tens of thousands on baseball, including his own team. Many pleas on his behalf have centered on the claim that he bet only on his team to win, implying that the games were not thrown. Do you suppose he managed as diligently when he did not have several thousand riding on the game? As with most pathological gamblers, Rose denied the charges, despite betting sheets in his handwriting and two witnesses who ran bets for him.

Football has had similar cases, the most prominent of whom was Art Schlichter. After graduating from Ohio State, Schlichter went on to the Baltimore Colts where he became a successful quarterback.

After his rookie season, overwhelmed by his gambling debts that had reached $389,000, he was discovered.[80] He was banned from the National Football League and wound up playing arena football, where he was again indicted for gambling in July of 1992.

This survey of corruption merely scratches the surface of what is occurring. The mob touches gambling everywhere its wire gambling line reaches. Crime seeks to permeate gambling wherever it occurs. Proposals for new gambling are always outrageous since the proponents know that by asking for too much they usually get some expansion. That means more money for the managers of the games, whether legitimate or illegal. Lotteries will inevitably be followed by proposals for casinos, riverboat gambling, off-track betting, sports gambling and legal bookies. The expansion will continue at the direct expense of our economy, our political system, our morals and eventually our young people, since the target of gambling is ever younger players.

The legalization of gambling has reduced police and judicial corruption only because there are fewer laws to enforce, less public desire for enforcement and no need to bribe the police who aren't enforcing the laws against illegal gambling. Current attempts to expand gambling center around attempting to "influence" legislatures to pass gambling bills. The extent of such lobbying efforts was exposed in Kentucky by the FBI "Boptrot" investigation which resulted in the indictment of 18 Kentucky legislators and the imprisonment of several for the fixing of racing dates and other infractions. Legislatures are a more compact group to corrupt and are often greedy enough to be corruptible.

The only way to stop the mob is to starve it. That means you yourself will have to stop gambling.

Review Questions

1. Why does gambling attract criminals?
2. Are Las Vegas and Atlantic City now clean?
3. How do you contribute to criminal activity by gambling?
4. What are the main kinds of gambling crime today?
5. Why do criminals want expanded casinos?
6. Why would you oppose a casino in your neighborhood?
7. Should Christians care about the growth of casinos?
8. Where does all the money spent on gambling come from?
9. Who gets hurt by excessive gambling?
10. Why is the number of teenage gamblers increasing?

Endnotes

[1] The details of Tony Spilotro's life are told in William F. Roemer, Jr., *The Enforcer: Spilotro: The Chicago Mob's Man Over Las Vegas,* New York: Ballantine Books, 1994.

[2] McKenna, David L., "Gambling: Parasite on Public Morals," *Christianity Today,* 17:5, June 8, 1973.

[3] _____, "History: Circle the Wagons," *Newsweek,* 119:10, May 25, 1992.

[4] Adlow, Elijah, "Gambling: The Legal Vice," *The Nation,* 190:186, February 27, 1960.

[5] _____, "Slot Machines and Pin Ball Games," *Annals of the American Academy of Political and Social Sciences,"* 269:62, May 1950.

[6] *Ibid.,* pp. 63-65.

[7] *Ibid.,* pp. 66-68.

[8] _____, "High Stakes in Miami Beach," *Time,* 111:21, February 20, 1978.

[9] _____, "Numbers' Racket," *Popular Mechanics,* 62:200, August, 1934.

[10] _____, "Lottery Round-Up," *Newsweek,* 11:12, January 10, 1938.

[11] Reuter, Peter, "Police Regulation of Illegal Gambling: Frustration of Symbolic Enforcement," *Annals of the American Academy of Political and Social Sciences,* 474:36, July, 1984.

[12] _____, "Lotteries are Both Wrong and Stupid," *The Christian Century,* 49:1190, October 5, 1932. See also _____, "What Church (if any) Runs Lotteries?" *The Christian Century,* 49:1045, August 31, 1932.

[13] Starkey, Lycurgus M. Jr., "Christians and the Gambling Mania," *The Christian Century,* 80:267, February 27, 1963.

[14] Roemer, William F. Jr., *The Enforcer: Spilotro: The Chicago Mob's Man Over Las Vegas,* New York: Ivy Books, 1994, p. 49, and numerous other locations throughout the book. This is supported by Carl Safakis, *The Encyclopedia of Gambling,* New York: Facts on File, 1990, p. 210.

[15] _____, "Gambling: The Fat Boys," *Time,* 55:15-16, May 8, 1950.

[16] Deland, Paul S., "The Facilitation of Gambling," *The Annals of the American Academy of Political and Social Sciences,* 269:27, May, 1950.

[17] _____, "Gambling: The Bookie Blues," *Newsweek,* 38:30-31, November 12, 1951.

[18] _____, "Gambling: Uncle Syndicate," *Newsweek,* 38:25, December 17, 1951.

[19] _____, "Gambling: The Gloom Lifts," *Newsweek,* 39:33, May 19, 1952, and _____, "The Supreme Court: Protecting Gamblers and Gunmen," *Time,* 91:74, February 9, 1968.

[20] _____, "The Real Thing," *Time,* 62:46, July 27, 1953.

[21] _____, "Mayor's Nest," *Time,* 68:62, July 23, 1956.

22 _____, "Crime: Numbers Doctor," *Newsweek*, 34:20, August 8, 1949.

23 _____, "Ice Money," *Time*, 53:78-79, January 13, 1949.

24 _____, "The Battle of Peoria," *Time*, 52:58, November 1, 1948.

25 _____, "Fourth Estate," *Newsweek*, 14:27, September 4, 1939.

26 _____, "Officials: Gallery Linked to Gambling Hall," *Lexington (KY) Herald-Leader*, p. B2, July 4, 1993.

27 _____, "The Will of the People," *The Nation*, 188:305-306, April 11, 1959.

28 Pierce, Phil, "Press Anti-Vice Drive," *The Christian Century*, 68:1358-1359, November 21, 1951.

29 Adlow, *loc. cit.*

30 _____, "Gambling in Texas," *Time*, 61:74, January 12, 1953.

31 Adlow, *ibid.*

32 Fowell, Myron W., "Catholic-Protestant Cooperation," *The Christian Century*, 76:76, January 21, 1959.

33 _____, "Massachusetts: 'Beneath the Sacred Dome,'" *Time*, 79:23, February 16,1962.

34 _____, "Everybody Wants a Piece of the Action," *Newsweek*, 80:46, April 10, 1972.

35 _____, "The Legal Numbers Racket," *Newsweek*, 86:31, November 3, 1975.

36 Bellico, Russ, "On Lotteries," *The Progressive*, 41:24-25, April, 1977.

37 _____, "Social Issues: The States Muscle in on the Numbers Game," *Business Week*, p.114, May 9, 1977.

38 *Performance Audit Report Kansas Lottery: Reviewing Vendor Contracts and Financial Management and Accounting Procedures,* Legislative Division of Post Audit, State of Kansas, October, 1988 (1988-56/57), p. 1.

39 This summary is based upon numerous reports in the Lexington and Louisville newspapers during the month of July.

40 _____, "Their Lottery Number Was Up," *Newsweek*, 96:30, September 29, 1980, and Mikesell and Zorn, *Public Administration Review, loc. cit.,* p. 313.

41 _____, "Calif. Lottery Moves to Get Back $3.4 Mil. Win by Los Angeles Woman," *Jet*, 76:25, May 22, 1989, and _____, "New Ruling Favors Barnett in Calif. Lottery Battle, *Jet*, 76:36, June 26, 1989.

42 Brogan, David, "Kirk Erickson Will Render Unto Caesar's What is Caesars', But He Says the Jackpot is His," *People Weekly*, 30:87-88, October 17, 1988.

43 _____, *New York's Lottery, 1976-1983,* A Publication of the New York Lottery.

[44] _____, "The Legal Numbers Rackett," *Newsweek*, 86:31, November 3, 1975, and _____, "Gambling: Bad Bets," *The Economist*, 257:74, November 15, 1975.

[45] Smith, Lee, "An Instant Success Story," *Dun's Review*, 108:58, December, 1976.

[46] _____, "Playboy: No Dice," *The Economist*, 281:33, October 10, 1981.

[47] _____, "Troubles in Bunnyland," *Time*, 118:79, October 19, 1981.

[48] _____, "The Game is Skimming," *Newsweek*, 68:18-19, August 29, 1966.

[49] Zubrow, Reuben A. and Robert L. Decker, "The Taxation of Legalized Gambling in Nevada," *National Tax Journal*, 15:73 and 79, March, 1962.

[50] _____, "High Stakes in Miami Beach," *Time*, 111:21, February 20, 1978.

[51] Nash, Jay Robert, *World Encyclopedia of Organized Crime*, New York: Da Capo Press, 1992, p. 127, and Roemer, *The Enforcer, op. cit.*, pp. 69, 208-211.

[52] _____, "Betting on the Boardwalk," *Time*, 111:26, May 29, 1978.

[53] _____, "Atlantic City: Rules of the Game," *The Economist*, 261:55, December 4, 1976.

[54] _____, "Gambling Goes Legit," *Time*, 108:65, December 6, 1976, and Alnor, William M., "Atlantic City: The Gamble That Lost," *Eternity*, 36:26, April, 1985.

[55] Ward, Hiley H., "Special Report: Gambling Comes to Atlantic City," *The Christian Century*, 96:81, January 24,1979.

[56] *Eternity, loc. cit.*

[57] _____, "Trouble in Las Vegas East," *Time*, 111:14-15, January 16, 1978.

[58] *Eternity, op. cit.*

[59] _____, "Render Therefore Unto Caesars?" *The Economist*, 277:105, November 22, 1980.

[60] _____, "Atlantic City: Pot of Gold?" *The Economist*, 276:29, September 20, 1980.

[61] Ward, *loc cit.*

[62] *The Economist*, 277:105, November 22, 1980 and 277:84, November 1, 1980.

[63] Wisz, Gerald, "All That Glitters Is Not Gold," *World*, p. 13, August 14, 1993.

[64] _____, "America's Gambling Craze," *U.S. News and World Report*, 116:46, March 14, 1994.

[65] Greene, Robert W., *The Sting Man: Inside Abscam*, New York: E.P. Dutton, 1981, p. 155.

[66] _____, "New Jersey: The Stakes are High," *The Economist*, 275:41 and 43, May 24, 1980.

67 _____, "Atlantic City: Organized Crime Barrier Develops Major Fissures," *The Washington Post*, p. 2, January 16, 1984.

68 _____, "New Jersey: Corruption Jackpot," *The Economist*, 274:24, February 16, 1980.

69 _____, "Troubles in Las Vegas East," *Time*, 111:14–15, January 16, 1978.

70 *Time, loc. cit.*

71 Lee, Barbara A. and James Chelius, "Government Regulation of Labor Management Corruption," *Industrial and Labor Relations Review*, 42:538, July 1989.

72 *Annals, op. cit.*, p. 9, 1985.

73 _____, "Gambling: Odds On, Odds Against," *The Economist*, 268:35, July 22, 1978.

74 *The Washington Post, loc. cit.*

75 Lee and Chelius, *op cit.*, p. 541.

76 *Eternity, op. cit.*, p. 26

77 Ward, *op. cit.*, p. 82.

78 _____, "Football: The Gambling Game," *Newsweek*, 52:75, November 24, 1958.

79 _____, "Denny the Dupe," *Time*, 95:51, March 2, 1970.

80 Hammer, Signe, "Gambling Better Than Sex," *Science Digest*, 92:24, June, 1984.

Chapter 8

The Loss
of Law

Kate had a secret life. After her husband Steve went to work and the children left for school, she slipped away to the Casino Queen riverboat to gamble. This went on for two or three years before Steve found out. As the family's debt swelled, Kate's depression grew. By the time she shot herself in the head in a mall parking lot, she had not made 17 payments on the house. It had been foreclosed, and they were to be evicted the morning she committed suicide. She had spent $8,000 in savings, a $5,000 tax refund, had not paid utility bills for months and had pawned their wedding rings.[1]

We have seen that changing American attitudes led to a great increase in gambling. We have also investigated some of the economic, social and moral impacts of these changes. Now we must look at the consequences of detaching our legal system from its biblical roots and basing it upon the changing social structure of our society.

The basic myth that prevails in our society is that "you cannot legislate morality." Many people quote this incredible lie even though legislating morality is what any legal system involves. If we did not legislate against murder and penalize it, killing would happen much more often than it does. For centuries murder was regarded as immoral, until recent decades when it is no longer considered murder to kill the unborn and the aged. This latter change is based on social attitudinal change, not upon any moral code. The remaining restraints may also erode and "justifiable homicide" may become punishment-free in the years ahead. In all these cases, the law reflects the moral code of the society. We indeed legislate morality at every point. The only question is whose morality is legislated.

The proponents of gambling—those who make money from it—simply do not want laws against gambling. To shame society into letting down its guard, they claim that a society cannot legislate morality. Note that their claim implicitly indicates that gambling is immoral. If any immorality is connected with gambling, such as oppression of the poor, encouragement of criminal activity, devastation of families and children, then the failure to legislate against gambling is legislation of immorality. We are clearly being asked to legislate immorality by opening our states to expanded gambling. In the light of the damage that comes to the pathological gambler, it is impossible to argue that gambling is a harmless, moral recreation, even if that were true for some small percentage of middle class players. The recreational gambler simply cannot claim a "right" to gamble when it is at the expense of great harm to people and society.

In this chapter we explore the evolution of American law governing gambling. The story is one in which the continuous erosion of laws against gambling has shaped the future in socially and economically destructive ways.

Gambling and Legislation

Legalization lends state approval to lotteries and gambling. If economic, social and moral damage is associated with gambling, legalizing it will not make the evils go away. The lessons of the history of gambling are not simple. The evidence, however, seems to point to the fact that bookmaking was neither significant in scope nor heavily involved in organized crime until pari-mutuel betting was made legal. We find that all legalizing of gambling tends to expand it to the detriment of society. This was known as long ago as 1950 when Paul S. Deland stated, "The history of gambling in the United States proves that its legalization has invariably increased gambling with all its attendant criminal evils."[2] This truth is even more apparent today.

As we noted previously, the lottery was born during the Renaissance. Its development became possible as scholastic thought and the medieval church loosened their grip upon intellectual life. Florence, Italy, ran a municipal lottery as early as 1530, just thirteen years after the beginning of the Reformation, and just thirty-eight years after Columbus discovered the New World. With the lotteries came immediate corruption. The lottery was imported from Italy to France in 1533. The first recorded bribe of a public official in order to obtain official approval came when the king was awarded a prize in the lottery even though he did not purchase a ticket. On August 23, 1567, Queen Elizabeth proclaimed the first English lottery.[3] The organizers had to be coerced to award the prizes. They simply wished to keep all the money collected for themselves.

In England gambling became so corrupt that by 1776 private lotteries were suppressed and only municipal and public ones remained. By 1826 the public ones were also disbanded because of continuing corruption on the part of the managers. The English lotteries were not so much more corrupt than those in other countries, for Belgium followed suit and outlawed lotteries in 1833, Sweden in 1841 and Switzerland in 1865.[4] In a change of heart that again reflected public attitudes, England reinstituted small charitable lotteries in 1844 and public lotteries in 1956.[5]

As we have also noted, lotteries were a part of American life from very near the beginning—from 1612 until the middle of the 1800s. Most histories mention the financial problems the Virginia Company had in raising the money to send relief to the colony they attempted to plant in Virginia. The relief expedition sent in 1612 was in part financed by a lottery. As noted in a previous chapter, numerous colleges attempted to raise building funds from drawings that awarded prizes, a form of lottery. All thirteen colonies at one time or another used lotteries to attempt to finance roads, canals and bridges. Experience demonstrated, however, that tolls proved a more enduring and stable means of financing and maintaining the roads. Under crown rule some cases of corruption came to the attention of the law. As early as 1719 the Massachusetts legislature denounced lotteries for tempting the lower classes to waste money in vain and foolish hopes. Shortly thereafter a law was passed forbidding public and private lotteries as a public nuisance. This did not end lotteries in Massachusetts, for they continued to run illegally, but it did stop advertising of lotteries. New York and Connecticut joined Massachusetts in prohibiting all lotteries that did not have the approval of a special act of the legislature. In 1733 Rhode Island banned all private lotteries. Pennsylvania followed suit in 1762.

As noted earlier, the Continental Congress attempted to finance the Army by means of a $10 million lottery. The Congress intended to clear $1 million, but only a few tickets sold, and the lottery was quietly withdrawn.[6] George Washington bought the first ticket with great ceremony, but that was insufficient to boost sales. Washington was somewhat inconsistent in his personal attitude toward gambling. While he said, "Gambling is the child of avarice, the brother of iniquity, and the father of mischief . . . ," he kept a diary of his wins and losses at cards, raffles and lotteries. His big win was 16 pounds in the 1766 New York Lottery.[7]

Lottery fever increased after the Revolution. From 1790 until 1860 the nation grew from 13 colonies to 36 states. During that period of time, 24 of the 36 allowed state-approved lotteries at one time or another. The sales for all these tended to be concentrated in the cities. Gambling has always been stronger in cities than in rural areas, even to the present. In the early days irregular mail service contributed to the concentration of gambling in urban areas. Municipal and private lotteries proliferated alongside state-approved lotteries, reaching a peak between 1800 and 1830. In Philadelphia alone there were over 200 lottery shops and over $50 million in prizes were distributed, worth more than $600 million today.[8] Since the percentage for the house varied widely, it is difficult to estimate how much was spent on lotteries. There is no doubt that much of the poverty of the period centered around the waste of resources that funneled into lotteries. Not until the lotteries began to be suppressed did American ingenuity and enterprise begin to develop the resources of the continent.

As lotteries grew, so did corruption. Pennsylvania joined Massachusetts in suppressing lotteries in 1833 as a result.[9] Other states gradually followed, ending the dominance of state lotteries and outlawing the private lotteries. Over 30 states eventually wrote clauses into their constitutions prohibiting the institution of lotteries by the legislatures.

The continuation of the Louisiana Lottery and the existence of illegal lotteries that frequently escaped from one state jurisdiction to another led to pressure for national legislation against lotteries. In 1880 the Supreme Court sought, through a decision, to encourage Congress to take action by declaring that lotteries were demoralizing and wrong in their influence upon the people. The experience of the last thirty years is merely an echo on the grand scale of that earlier finding. They discovered gambling's demoralizing influence without the benefit of the formal studies and better records to which we have access today.[10]

The Louisiana Lottery

The last gasp of nineteenth-century major lotteries was the Louisiana Lottery, which provided the final impetus to the suppression of all lotteries. We have already surveyed the Louisiana Lottery in general terms in the first chapter. We will not repeat all that data here but will primarily look at the legal consequences of that lottery. As noted previously, the Louisiana Lottery was chartered on August 11, 1869. The charter was granted after heavy lobbying and more than a little bribery. Later affidavits in court cases revealed that $50,000 was spent to bribe legislators that first year and $300,000 in the first seven years.[11] Under the terms of the charter, the lottery was to make a contribution of the then-handsome sum of $40,000, which was directed to the financing of the Charity Hospital of New Orleans, a hospital for indigents.[12] This was presented and widely regarded as a marvelous boon to the state's finances. The public had no way of knowing that the gross income from the lottery would eventually reach $30 million per year.[13]

The lottery corporation bribed legislators, judges and the press, spending much more than it contributed to the state. The bribes were intended to stifle any motions to repeal the charter. During the first six years estimates of bribes were more modest, just $60,000 per year, but this was still more than was contributed to the hospital. The corruption of the court system meant that there was little harassment of vendors in the city of New Orleans.

Drawings were held daily, monthly and twice annually, with larger prizes in the less frequent drawings. Tickets were sold whole and in parts, the poor being able to purchase as little as an eighth of a ticket for a few cents. The lottery was truly democratic, allowing even the poorest people to lose their money.

John A. Morris, the chief entrepreneur, brought the charter up for renewal in 1889. At first, it appeared that the charter renewal would fail. Strong opposition had developed among the clergy and various leading citizens, along with some lawyers and judges who were tired of the corruption of the legal system. With their gross receipts exposed, the lottery directors raised their offer to the state over ten times to $500,000. This was still only 2% of their gross income. Some estimated that the promoters were pocketing nearly half of the gross personally, while more conservative and probably more accurate estimates suggested they made up to $5 million per year. This compares with the average of about 37% of the gross receipts of the lotteries that the states receive today. When it became apparent that the lottery charter was in danger, the promoters raised their donation to the state to $1.25 million, which was about 4.5% of their gross. The charter moved through the legislature, although the governor vetoed it. The charter was repassed by the House, but when it fell one vote short in the Senate, the Senators decided they had passed the bill before the veto and did not need to take another vote. The Supreme Court hastily certified it to be forwarded to the people for a vote.[14]

Instead of disappearing after this legislative approval, resistance to the lottery continued. Earlier in the early 1880s Anthony Comstock had initiated an effort to repeal the charter. Knowing that he had little chance in Louisiana, he had also begun efforts to get federal legislation barring lottery ads and tickets from the mails. This would have restricted the interstate sales of the tickets. This struck at the virtual legal monopoly that the Louisiana Lottery had on nationwide lotteries.

News coverage of the lottery's ill economic and social effects began to dampen public support. In New Orleans, vendors were located on every commercial street. The vendors had to pay for the tickets in advance, although a few wholesalers extended credit to certain reliable vendors. They could sell all the tickets and make a few cents. What happened was that most of them sold only enough tickets to buy the next batch and held the rest in the vain hope of striking it rich. The result was incredible hardship among the vendors and, since they sold largely to the poor, hardship in the city as a whole. Visitors commented upon the increasing squalor of the city and the desperateness of the vendors in attempting to sell the tickets. The situation served only to increase resistance to the lottery. When the time to vote on the issue finally came in 1892, the voters rejected the new charter.

The lottery owners tried again in 1893, with the legislature cooperating in passing the charter. The governor refused to sign the bill, however, and on January 1, 1894, the Louisiana Lottery joined all the other illegal lotteries of the country.

Lottery officials moved the lottery to the Dominican Republic, expecting only minor revenue losses since tickets could still be sold in most states and shipped anywhere. That plan was seriously damaged during 1894 when federal legislation was passed making it illegal to ship advertising materials or tickets through the federal mail system. This cut off the distribution system, since it was impossible to maintain it prior to the coming of the mob in the 1930s. Newspapers delivered the final blow by refusing to accept advertising, since they feared that the Post Office would refuse to deliver their newspaper. This effectively killed the lottery.

Twentieth-Century Developments

From 1894 until the 1940s, the U. S. Penal Code described lotteries as an unlawful public nuisance. This stance began to weaken in the 1930s when Postmaster General James A. Farley announced that the Post Office would enforce the law more loosely in an effort to aid charitable lotteries during the hard times of the Great Depression.

The Depression brought a number of changes in attitude which were followed by legal changes. Crime became "organized" during the 1920s in the war with the state governments over illegal alcohol. With the repeal of the Prohibition Amendment in 1933, the market for illegal alcohol declined. The mob expanded its efforts in prostitution and gambling to make up for its losses. A further change came during the Depression as a result of the inability of the charitable system to keep up with the demand for food as unemployment soared to 30%. After bingo was invented in 1934, numerous municipalities, churches and charitable organizations turned to the new game to raise money. They operated illegal games and discouraged enforcement of the law in many places. Ironically, churches often led the fight to legalize gambling, not realizing the potential disaster when it eventually fell into the hands of the mob. Bingo is a form of lottery or numbers game, creating an audience primed for the mob-run numbers game.

The legal community faced a dilemma. While many lawyers were willing for the law to reflect the mores and attitudes of society, that is, they were relativistic about the law, they were still ambivalent about legalizing a system that most believed historically had exploited human weakness, avarice and cupidity. The social and economic effects upon individual families were also recognized. Other lawyers expressed concern over the issue of "chance" as a source of legal difficulty, questioning the rightness of hazarding resources with little opportunity for gain. While this was essentially a moral issue, many felt that there would be legal complications stemming from it, although they were vague about what they might be. Whatever their legal scruples, most lawyers, if paid, joined in the drafting and evaluation of legalizing legislation.

Lotteries began their legal comeback in 1934 when Blanton Winship, the governor of Puerto Rico, reinstated a government lottery on the basis that it would undercut the smuggling of illegal lottery tickets into Puerto Rico. Winship stopped a small problem by creating a large one. With striking official indifference, it was possible for ". . . lottery officials [to] estimate that impoverished natives will find at least $500,000 to gamble with this year."[15] This first lottery clearly intended to take money from the poor regardless of the consequences, all for the magnificent purpose of stopping a minor crime. This mentality of stopping a minor crime with major social and economic disaster has been with us ever since. Half the money from the lottery was designated to fight TB and improve health (half a million in food might have done even more for the health of the island). The other half went to administration and prizes.

During the Depression, the states continued to look longingly at France's income from the lottery. The $56 million that France took in during one of the Depression years looked like a bonanza. By ignoring those pushed over the edge into poverty and despair, the electrification of the railroads in Italy under Mussolini looked like a magnificent achievement. During this time Sweden turned to a lottery to support the arts, for which there was simply no discretionary money available. Ironically, actors and artists endured some of the most abject poverty during the Depression.

Touting these European examples, in June of 1933, Representative Kenney, a Democrat from New Jersey, proposed a national lottery to aid the Veterans Administration. The bill was introduced for three consecutive years but was buried in the Ways and Means Committee each time.[16] In 1934, New York sought to establish a lottery by misdirection. The New York Relief Plan was a lottery in everything but name. Everyone who bought a ticket was eligible for a limited number of high paying jobs with no duties. The employed were to be selected by chance.[17] The year 1934, following on the heels of the worst year of the Depression, saw a number of other bills floated in Maine, Maryland and New York. All sought to establish lotteries for relief purposes. Support for these came from one surprising source. Many stock market managers jumped on the bandwagon, believing that the lottery would draw "undesirables" away from the market. The undesirables were little investors who bought highly speculative stock, hoping to turn a quick buck, lost their money and then complained to the marketers, their congressman and anyone else who would listen. The threat to the stock brokers was that the government would step in and regulate the market, curbing their profits.

Immediately upon the heels of the Great Depression came World War II, which we have already noted was a major factor in changing attitudes among males toward gambling. After Pearl Harbor many lottery bills were proposed: in 1941 by Senator Tomas, a Democrat from Oklahoma, and in February 1942 by Representative Knutson, a Republican from Minnesota, for the purpose of increasing pensions, and the following month by Representative A. J. Sabath, a Democrat from Illinois. The latter proposal was supposed to raise billions and keep people from spending, which was causing inflation in the prices of wartime restricted goods. In other words, the government wanted to bilk the people of their money to promote the noble goals of suppressing inflation and the black market. Other representatives accused Sabath of wanting to put the government in the business of cheating the people. He was just a couple of decades before his time.[18]

Following the war, as expected, there was a further softening of legal and legislative opinion, primarily on the false basis that legal gambling would make illegal gambling go away. Representative Sabath revived his bill in 1946. He scaled down the potential income from billions to millions in the light of the fact that $1 billion in income represented 20 tickets for every man, woman and child in the entire country. At that time moral resistance was so strong that such broad participation was unrealistic. The payoff would be in war bonds, as his first proposal had suggested. His purpose remained the same: to prevent people from spending while things were still scarce, until the transition to the peacetime economy was completed, which would, in his opinion, suppress inflation. In 1949 Representative Clemente, a Democrat from New York, proposed yet another lottery to aid veterans.[19]

Enforcement of the Law

During this period there was much "soft" enforcement of existing laws against gambling. Since a sizable majority still opposed legal gambling, there were occasional raids in the cities to satisfy the public need for something to be done about the obviously available illegal gambling. These came to be called "showcase" raids.

The raids often netted a little equipment, only occasionally an arrest or two and practically no convictions. The few convictions carried light fines which the bookies and slot operators regarded as nuisances that were part of the price of doing business. Judges were especially lenient on first-time offenders. If the cops were on the take, the arrangement was for some minor functionary with a clean rap to take the fall for the mob. The raids were especially ineffective if a major local well-known figure was accidentally netted. The vigorous defense, and the community sympathy for the figure having some innocent fun, often caused repercussions for the police and a period of lessened enforcement activity.

Raids were often leaked to the criminals involved. That was of course the reason for the mob payoff in the first place and the reason why gambling payoffs became the principal source of police corruption during the postwar period. If the cops were on the take but a judge wasn't, then the arrests were made in a fashion that violated the person's rights, and the judge would be forced to release them on a technicality. Numerous grand juries were empaneled to investigate gambling enforcement. They found evidence over and over of payoffs to police and judges but were largely unable to do anything effective to shut down the system.

The leniency of law enforcement led to various movements across the country to pass harsher laws against gambling, both for participants and for the operators. In some localities these succeeded in passage, but not in practice. These laws did not decrease gambling, but they clearly did decrease convictions. The police became even more reluctant to make arrests and judges more reluctant to convict.

The main federal barriers to gambling come from Title 18, United States Code, Sections 659, 1301 and 1082. The first prevented games of chance that caused the exchange of money on public carriers. The second prevented the owning of gambling ships under U. S. registry. The third prevented the transportation of lottery tickets, certificates or shares, gifts, advertising or prize lists across state lines.[20] All of these were difficult to enforce and were widely broken, especially in the shipping of slot machines. The gambling ships were operated by placing them under foreign registry.

By 1950 when Kefauver focused national attention on the problem of the mob and its ties to gambling, accompanied by the corruption of public officials, there was widespread desire for stronger laws. Among the leaders in this movement were the American

Municipal Association, the crime commissions of Chicago and California, and the mayors of Los Angeles, New Orleans, Portland and many other cities.[21]
Some efforts to curb gambling seemed to work. Idaho was surrounded in the late 1940s by states that allowed slot machines: legal ones in Nevada to the south and Washington to the west (until 1952), and illegal but unsuppressed ones in Wyoming and Montana. As a result Idaho legalized slots on a local-option basis in 1947. While many communities and the state benefited from tax revenues, "Doctors and dentists began having trouble collecting their bills. Restaurant owners said that slot clubs were luring away their customers with 19-cent steaks, and luring away the customers' money afterward." As a result, the larger cities gradually banned them, and the state eliminated them in 1953.[22]

The next pressure to liberalize the gambling laws was brought by all the oil company and grocery store giveaways of the 1950s. These resulted in some increased clarity about what constituted a lottery. Legally, the three components of a lottery were recognized to be a prize, the element of chance and a "consideration." The consideration was the thing of value that the customer gave up in order to participate in the game. The state of Florida added a fourth element, called "widespread effect." It was the only state to do so.[23] A variety of cases in a number of states established that these games had the elements of prize and chance, but the primary focus was the consideration. The companies had to modify rules in order to keep the games legal so that no purchase was necessary to participate. This left the muddy area of whether attendance at the place of business that took time or effort was a consideration. The loose attitudes toward gambling at the time led to a strict interpretation in most states that money had to change hands for it to be gambling. Thus, millions of people were lured into gambling, trying to get something for nothing, providing the seedbed for the next stage.

The approach that finally was successful in breaking down resistance to gambling was the concept of controlled extension. Controlled extension was the idea that states ought to gradually move into enlarged gambling for the sake of revenues and for the reduction of crime. In the 1950s and 1960s there was no wholesale movement into gambling as there was later, but there was an eroding of resistance. After gambling was introduced in any fashion, there was little moral ground to prevent some forms of gambling while allowing others. The moral will was weakened as well.

Gamblers promoting legal gambling lured the states into seeking a monopoly on gambling that simply never materialized because illegal gambling grew alongside the legal games. The result of this erosion were laws such as the 1953 New Jersey act that legalized bingo, lotteries and raffles for educational, charitable, patriotic and religious bodies. This move prompted a number of similar acts in other states.[24]

The legal framework changed in 1964 when New Hampshire started the first lottery. The lottery has come to be seen as a "gateway" form of gambling. It attracts the amateur into gambling and often leads him on to other forms, legal and illegal. It serves as a gateway in another sense, in that it is always the forerunner of requests for other forms of legal gambling. Casino requests, riverboats and expanded off-track betting follow lotteries in the urban areas.

The Final Collapse

Only a few national figures attempted to slow the tide of gambling in the 1960s and 1970s. Wright Pittman of Texas, a member of the House Banking Committee, managed to push through legislation making it illegal to sell tickets in a federally insured bank. That remains true to the present. For ten years after the opening of the New Hampshire Lottery, opponents succeeded in keeping lottery advertising and tickets out of the U. S. Mail system. In 1974 the House Judiciary Committee reported out a bill that later became law which exempted state lotteries from gambling laws.[25] When President Ford signed public law 93-583, which allowed use of the mails, TV and radio for the announcement of prizes and for advertisements within state boundaries, legislation was immediately introduced to allow the same across state lines.[26] The advertising battle was lost in 1976 and has never been revived as three-fourths of the states now have lotteries.

The media also were co-opted. Television became enthusiastic to carry gambling advertising. The programs announcing winning numbers often held the largest market share during their time slot. The newspapers usually have an open policy toward advertisers even if they oppose the product. Only a few newspapers have been outspoken opponents of the gambling growth. The most notable is the Knight-Ridder chain, which has an editorial stance against gambling, but like all other papers carries the wire service stories which glamorize and laud big winners. The main bias of the media is that they are slow to report the dark side of gambling, and local reporters frequently do not accept that there are economic and social consequences.

The duplicity of politicians is probably the most reprehensible of all. In the face of what limited moral outcry there has been over putting the government directly into the role of bilking people through gambling, states have often created "independent" lottery corporations. What the state gains from this is hard to determine, but the corporation gains a great deal of freedom from state regulation. The most obvious advantage is escape from the Civil Service Laws, which allows the positions at the lottery corporation to serve as patronage. In a few states the lottery is a direct creature of the executive branch with little control by the legislature. In 1972 the state of Massachusetts passed a lottery with a great deal of vote-switching over Governor Francis W. Sargent's veto. The governor vetoed the bill, not because he opposed the lottery, but because he disapproved of the control of the patronage.

One of the most unfortunate aspects of the lottery corporations is that, unlike other branches of state government which may have media consultants, the lottery has a whole publicity and advertising department. The image is not subject to regulation or honesty. Otherwise the lotteries would be required to prominently display the odds against winning on the ticket, in the vending location and in advertising. Further, they ought to be required to state the prizes in current value (roughly 60%) of prizes distributed over long periods of time. This kind of integrity would be expected of any other business operation regulated by the government.

The primary beneficiaries of lotteries, other than the tiny number of big winners, are the managers, the advertising companies, some of the merchants who sell the tickets and the banks who hold the money. All of these groups lobby for the expansion of gambling, although some bankers have backed away as the effect upon the economy has become more clear. The merchants who sell great numbers of tickets benefit, but their customers are often annoyed by having to wait while others buy tickets. As noted previously, many grocery stores actually lose sales to the lottery, so it is difficult to see why they continue to sell them.

The public has accepted the idea that it is socially (morally) unacceptable to restrict the sales or advertising of lotteries. In 1984, for example, lotteries were approved in California, Missouri, Oregon and West Virginia. In only 10 of 274 counties did the majority oppose the lottery.[27] Too bad those ten counties did not have the right to keep the lottery out so they would not have to suffer the consequences. The consequences of such gambling growth is a locally declining economy, an increasing pool of pathological gamblers, an increase in demand for social services and a moral decline which causes one to focus only on oneself and consider no responsibility for the well-being of others.

As a society we must look beyond what has become legal to the effects caused. If the effects are detrimental, it is time to curb gambling through legal means. Restrictions on advertising are appropriate. Rejection of expanded forms of gambling is appropriate. Stating the moral issues is appropriate. Some claim that moral issues really should not be discussed in public debate. This is a serious restriction of First Amendment rights. The future is shaped by what is legislated now.

As we noted in Chapter 6, gambling is immoral on two counts: the managers exploit the players, and it is covetous on the part of the players. Without remorse the casino owners target depressed areas like Atlantic City; Gary, Indiana; and Tunica, Mississippi, with promises of economic development. The operators are crassly targeting poor and black people. The vain attempt of states to annul, disguise or avoid these moral issues by devoting part of the tax receipts to "good ends" must be recognized for what it is—hypocrisy. The representatives we elect are to protect the well-being of citizens, even when the majority of citizens are wrong. We have an ongoing responsibility to present the moral issues that the gambling interests ignore.

Probably the very worst argument for gambling is that since the government has been unable to suppress illegal gambling it ought to legalize it all. First of all, the number of people who will gamble if it is legal is larger than the number who will gamble if it is illegal. Such logic could also be applied to any moral issue. Perhaps since stealing has not been suppressed we should legalize stealing for a good cause, say, paying your taxes, or paying your hospital bill. The outcry against such a proposal would be overwhelming. Why have we allowed the lottery to steal from us without a whimper?

Merely citing the early use of lotteries in American history misses the very point of that history. Our forefathers abandoned lotteries, not because they all agreed that the moral issue of gambling was paramount. They agreed that the social, economic *and* moral ill effects outweighed the benefits of lotteries. That is the lesson that we must learn all over again. The mere legality of gambling does not make it moral, purposeful, helpful or worthy of approbation.

Review Questions

1. Is the claim that "you cannot legislate morality" logical? Why or why not?
2. Why did so many states use lotteries to try to finance public works in the early days of our country?
3. How did the Depression cause changes in attitudes toward gambling?
4. Who suffered the most from legalized gambling in the nineteenth century?
5. When the lotteries were suppressed, what happened to entrepreneurship in America?
6. Why are lotteries the "gateway" form of gambling for both individuals and states?
7. What was "symbolic enforcement" and why was it common in the 1940s and 1950s?
8. What was "controlled extension," and what was its result?
9. Why do you think so few national figures oppose gambling?
10. Can we equate the concepts of *legal* and *moral*? Why or why not?

Endnotes

[1] Bosworth, Charles, Jr., "Tragedy Leads Husband to Wife's Secret," *Saint Louis Post-Dispatch,* February 23, 1995, pp. 1 and 6.

[2] Deland, Paul S., "The Facilitation of Gambling," *The Annals of the American Association of Political and Social Sciences,* 269:23, May, 1950.

[3] Drzazga, John, *Wheels of Fortune,* Springfield, IL.: Charles C. Thomas, Publisher, 1963, p. 252.

[4] *Ibid.*

[5] _____, "Lotteries Relegalised," *The Economist,* 263:25, April 30, 1977.

[6] Drzazga, *op. cit.,* p. 254.

[7] Watson, Tom Jr., *Don't Bet On It,* Ventura, CA: Regal Books, 1987, p. 62.

[8] Sullivan, George, *By Chance a Winner: The History of Lotteries,* New York: Dodd, Mead, pp. 43 and 46.

[9] Drzazga, *op. cit.,* p. 254. See also, E. E. Blanche, "Lotteries Yesterday, Today, and Tomorrow," *Annals of the American Academy of Political and Social Sciences,* 260:73, May, 1950.

[10] Bellico, Russ, "On Lotteries," *The Progressive*, 41:25, April, 1977.

[11] Buel, C.C., "Degradation of a State: or the Charitable Career of the Louisiana Lottery," *Century Magazine*, 43 (ns21): 623, February, 1892.

[12] Peterson, Virgil W., "A Look at Legalized Gambling," *The Christian Century*, 82:675, May 26, 1965.

[13] Robbins, Peggy, "Louisiana Lottery Was so Big it Didn't Have to be Rigged," *Smithsonian*, 10:114, June, 1980.

[14] Buel, *op. cit.*, pp. 629-630.

[15] _____, "Puerto Rico: Gov. Winship Legalizes National Lottery," *Newsweek*, 3:13, May 26, 1934.

[16] Blanche, *op. cit.*, p. 75.

[17] _____, "Lotteries: N.Y. Relief Plan Called Ill-Advised, Immoral," *Newsweek*, 4:9, September 29, 1934.

[18] Blanche, *loc. cit.*

[19] Blanche, *ibid.*, p. 70.

[20] Deland, *ibid.*, p. 21.

[21] *Ibid.*, p. 22.

[22] _____, "Idaho: Out Damned Slot," *Time*, 61:17, March 2, 1953.

[23] Gaines, Robert P., "Criminal Law: Florida's Legal Lotteries," *University of Florida Law Review*, 9:93-95, Spring, 1956.

[24] Ludwig, Frederick J. and Dominic Hughes, "Bingo, Morality and the Criminal Law," *The Catholic Lawyer*, 1:8, January, 1955.

[25] Wall, James M., "Why Isn't the Church Fighting Lotteries?" *The Christian Century*, 91:1163, December 11, 1974.

[26] Powers, Edward J., "The Prospects for Legalized Wagering," *The Futurist*, 10:153, June, 1976.

[27] Mikesell, John L. and C. Kurt Zorn, "State Lotteries and Fiscal Savior or Fiscal Fraud: A Look at the Evidence," *Public Administration Review*, 46:311, July/August, 1986.

Chapter 9

Weak Leadership from the Churches

This is a disappointing chapter in the history of gambling. The churches should provide moral leadership, but they have been ambivalent. They have not taken a clear stand against the economic unfairness, the social disintegration and the moral deterioration caused by gambling. Despite gambling's devastating effects on the poor, despite its clear linkage to crime, despite the ten million souls who have fallen into pathological gambling, the church does not seem sure there is a moral issue. One wonders how those who believe in Lady Luck, following hunches, taking a chance and superstition can also believe the tenets of the church. It is as hard to approve of a little gambling as it would be a little murder or a little incest.

Churches have not taken a stand against gambling for many reasons. Three of four church members gamble at least occasionally, and some church board members gamble regularly. There are even members of churches who are pathological gamblers. Nearly every pastor I have talked with has a gambling-related horror story from a previous parish, although most will not discuss current situations. As we have noted, many churches run bingo games to supplement the financing of their schools or church. Few church leaders in our day are willing to risk their reputations to say, as United

Methodist Bishop James K. Mathews did years ago, that the chief fruit of gambling is social evil and fraud.[1]

We noted in chapter six the biblical injunctions in the Ten Commandments against theft and covetousness. No set of moral injunctions have had a more powerful impact upon the history of humanity than these. They have also been roundly observed in their breaking as well. Many scholars and historians recognize that the moral fiber of the "good" people of a community are what hold society together and allow its survival. Expecting something for nothing and the desire for a million dollars are both evidence of coveting, whether or not we wish to admit it.

The Church's Changing Stance

In the third century the Christian theologian Tertullian condemned playing at dice for money.[2] At that time gambling was not a general problem in the church. Another church father, St. Cyprian commented, "A common Gamester or Dice-player may call himself a Christian, but indeed he is not." Similarly, Chrysostom said, "Not God but the Devil found out play."[3] During the medieval period as the clergy became more wealthy, and as the papacy sometimes became a pawn of the ruling class, gambling became a greater problem. By 1215 it was severe enough that the Fourth Lateran Council specifically forbade the clergy to gamble.[4] Another church council specifically indicated that "A Christian playing at Dice or tables is not to be admitted to the Holy Communion, but after a year's penance and abstention, and his total amendment."[5] Despite this legal formulation, the attitude gradually developed within the Catholic Church that gambling itself was not intrinsically sinful. Gambling in excess, especially when it affected the well being of others, was still regarded as sinful. Gambling with the money of others (borrowed) was consistently reproached. By the time of the Crusades, gambling was so common among the laity that Richard I laid down strict rules governing the gambling behavior of his soldiers. Some Catholic theologians continue to regard gambling as evil, but Catholic practice is a different matter.

With the coming of the Renaissance, various forms of decadence characterized court life. Gambling became a staple of that class, a "ruling passion" for some, especially in the seventeenth and eighteenth centuries. The popularity of gambling caused certain problems to come to the attention of the mathematicians. Benvenuto d' Imola considered the probabilities of throwing dice in a commentary upon Dante's *Divina Comedia* in 1477. In 1494, Pacioli posed a question of the division of stakes in a game that ended before a winner was declared. The same problem appeared in the works of Jerome Cardan (1501–1576) in 1539 and in the works of Tartaglia in 1556. In 1654 Blaise Pascal and Pierre Fermat carried on a correspondence concerning the same problem. They agreed upon the solution and in the process founded the modern science of probability, the branch of mathematics that studies situations that arise in gambling, as well as the analysis of other types of data.

As noted earlier, Cotton Mather, the Puritan New England minister, spoke out against lotteries. Perhaps due to his influence, in 1699 the Congregational ministers, meeting in Boston, condemned lotteries as ". . . a plain cheat upon the people."[6] Pennsylvania, under the influence of the Quakers who opposed all gambling, passed a law against cards, dice and lotteries with a penalty of five shillings or five days in jail. William and Mary nullified the act in 1693. The act was passed again in 1693, 1700 and 1705, followed by nullification by the Crown each time.

We have noted that the politicians, media and churches allied to bring about the reduction and the eventual disappearance of legal lotteries in the nineteenth century. Most gambling that occurred in this century was done in private clubs or more informally. Dice and card games were the most common.

Then we come to the twentieth century, when the evils of gambling have expanded so radically, and when the church was most needed. Instead the church has often contributed to the problem. Bingo was invented in 1934 as an adult variation of the children's lotto game. Lotto was used to teach children to count. The game was quickly adopted by the Roman Catholic Church as a moneymaker during the Depression. By 1938 more people were gambling at church bingo and raffles than all other forms of illegal gambling combined, according to a Gallup poll.[7] By 1939 fewer than a dozen out of 200 Catholic and Episcopal bishops prevented the use of bingo as a fund raiser.[8] Most of the games were illegal but were ignored by the police.[9]

Large numbers of people were introduced to gambling through church bingo games. They then moved on to the daily numbers game, and, if wealthy enough, to gambling through a bookie. Such activities ought to be unconscionable for the church. By 1950 over 26 million Americans played bingo for money, approximately one-fourth the adult population. In New York, by 1955 over 85% of the

Catholic churches were running bingo operations. Most games remained illegal, since the push for legalization did not come until the 1970s. Churches in 1957 reaped only 14 cents on the dollar in their games of chance.[10]

On the other hand, a few individual Catholics have spoken out strongly against gambling. In the 1950s one outspoken critic of gambling was Archbishop Stritch of Milwaukee. Another was Richard Cardinal Cushing, onetime archbishop of Boston, who argued that ". . . it does not create new sources of revenue, but rather draws from those which already exist in ways which tend to disturb the normal and healthy process by which economic prosperity is promoted." He also said, ". . . it creates serious temptations to theft in those who handle money which does not belong to them, and because it stands in the way of prompt and systematic payment of debts and other obligations of justice. . . ."[11] Despite his viewpoint, gambling continued under his jurisdiction.

Where the United States is today, with $1 trillion gambled annually, was unthinkable to church leaders just 40 years ago. In 1959 Alson J. Smith wrote,

> The answer [about the future of gambling] seems to be that while there will be some relaxation of the laws governing minor forms of gambling like bingo, lotteries and raffles in certain states containing a high proportion of Roman Catholics (e.g. Connecticut) there will be no general repeal of the antigambling statutes. There is not likely to be any legalization of off-track betting in spite of the anguished cries for new sources of revenue by mayors and other public officials. There will be no gambling casinos. No more Nevadas, no national or state or municipal lotteries.[12]

Smith was an expert in 1959, but he missed the mark because the churches were a paper tiger with no will to battle gambling.

The Church's Confused Position

All churches are not the same. Some still oppose lotteries and gambling. What opposition to expanded gambling has existed has come from ministers and church members who are usually Protestant and most commonly Baptist or Methodist. As late as 1977, Dr. Dan M. Potter, executive director of the Council of Churches of New York City said, "Trying to get something for nothing is one of the greatest moral sicknesses of our times."[13] He also said that bank robbing, shooting craps and spending the milk money on lotteries are all the same sin: greed. In the rush to gain material things only a few take morality seriously. Those who have spoken out against this naked greed have been drowned by the sound of cash registers: money over morality.

Today the situation is as muddied as it was in the medieval period. The Roman Catholic Church in general does not oppose gambling in moderation. Many Catholics have supported legal gambling enterprises and are employed by them. If the stories in the media are accurate, many of those involved in illegal gambling are also Roman Catholic. Many Catholic churches still sponsor bingo games, now mostly legal, especially for the support of their private schools. Catholics have been accused by their harshest critics of using "Tetzel techniques" for raising money, named after the seller of "indulgences" whose abuses contributed to Luther's ire and the beginning of the Reformation.[14] Many of us have received coupons from the Pallotine Sweepstakes (a Roman Catholic missionary order) conducted since 1965. Perhaps the largest Catholic lottery is the Pot o' Gold conducted three times a week from Sault Ste. Marie, Ontario.[15]

Protestants seem as confused as the Catholics. Some years ago a survey revealed that 77% of the Presbyterians and Episcopalians gambled at least occasionally. Sixty-three percent of the Methodists, 43% of the Baptists and 35% of the nondenominational congregations took at least an occasional plunge into gambling.[16] This fits the perception that the more theologically conservative churches are more likely to oppose gambling. The strongest recent efforts against the expansion of gambling have come from the Southern Baptist Convention and other Baptist groups. These opponents of gambling have received abuse in the media, as well as tire slashings in Kentucky and obscene and threatening phone calls. The most common press description of gambling opponents is "prudish." Nevertheless, many opponents of gambling would rather be right about gambling despite the harassment. Typical of the gentle gibes toward Christian opponents of gambling is that of Heywood Broun who said, "The urge to gamble is so universal and its practice so pleasurable that I assume it must be evil."[17] He did not have the opportunity to observe the pleasure of grand-scale gambling depression as we now can. When the president of Holiday Inns, Lem Clymer, resigned in 1980 because his board decided to build a casino in Atlantic City, many of his Christian friends chided him, saying that people would gamble whether he built a casino or not.[18]

Rather, they should have admired his refusal to participate in the fleecing of his patrons.

While the more conservative churches are leading the battle against gambling, the more liberal churches have traditionally also opposed gambling. The journal *The Christian Century* has long opposed lotteries on the basis that they negatively affect the personality of the individual. They also frequently argue that gambling undermines the concept of worthwhile and productive work, self-discipline and achievement in the areas of life most worthy of reward. Gambling epitomizes the effort to get something for nothing. The United Methodist Church's "Social Principles" state that ". . . gambling is a menace to society, deadly to the best interests of moral, social, economic and spiritual life, and destructive of good government. As an act of faith and love, Christians should abstain from gambling and should strive to minister to those victimized by the practice."[19] That statement is still in effect.

Despite the official stand of some churches and the clear moral case against gambling outlined in Chapter 6, many Protestants exhibit superstitious thinking about gambling. They simply weave God into their magic thinking, concluding that God will somehow bless their gambling because they are "Christian." This is not the only inconsistency. Many Christians look down on dog tracks and jai alai frontons as somehow reprehensible, yet they will freely visit a horse track without thought and gamble "recreationally" while there. While some Christians frequently criticize police and judicial corruption, other Christians patronize the bookie system and thus the mob which is responsible for it. Many churches are officially opposed to gambling while their members participate in it without correction. Gambling is seldom mentioned from the pulpit. When it is, the sermon is frequently followed by criticisms and even obscene or threatening phone calls. Christians who ignore the connection with crime when they gamble are simply rationalizing beyond reason.

Most followers of Judaism believe that moderate gambling is not a moral problem. Many of those outside the Orthodox community seem unaware that in addition to the Ten Commandments there is a Talmudic dictum urging them to shun the dice player. Sixty years ago, during the Depression, this was sufficient to give many a synagogue pause before participating in gambling games. Anguished debates took place when they considered using bingo games to raise money during those hard times. More often than not, however, the bingo games won.

Unfortunately, the churches, along with fraternal and veterans' organizations, provided much of the initial impetus toward legalization of gambling by pressing for legal bingo and Bean-O games. In several northeastern states, churches even pressed for nonenforcement of the law while they were running illegal games. They were on the same side as the bookies! This hardly fits the biblical injunction of obeying civil authorities who are ordained by God. During those hard economic times, fervor and faith were partially replaced by bingo and raffles as the means of keeping the institutional church afloat.

Cheating has often been found at the church games, but not necessarily by the churches. Church bingo games are usually managed and eventually consolidated into a central location. The bigger the game and the prizes, the more tempting the fix. One very common technique was for the caller to memorize the numbers on a confederate's card, giving him an edge toward winning. Some contractors withheld numbers so that no one won, giving them their percentage without having to award prizes. Also, various schemes have appeared for altering cards.[20]

Clearly then, the churches have settled for expediency and compromised their right to speak with moral authority about gambling. Denunciation without action is also worthless. Long ago Cotton Mather railed against gambling. We still should be, but with some effort behind the talk as well. In 1817 Francis Scott Key, an Episcopal layman and author of our national anthem, introduced a resolution condemning gambling as ". . . inconsistent with Christian sobriety, dangerous to the morals of members of the church, and peculiarly unbecoming the character of communicants." The resolution failed in that church body, but the message is even more clearly true today.[21] In the nineteenth century the Methodists and Baptists led the battle that ended in victory over lotteries. However, they appear too weak and divided to do it again.

While only a few national organizations oppose gambling, the antigambling movement is gaining strength. One of these organizations is the American Council on Alcohol Problems, which has 33 associated state Temperance Leagues of varying strength. While alcoholism has been their traditional interest, they have extended their efforts to other addictive behaviors, especially gambling, since it is so frequently allied with alcohol. Another major organization is the National Council on Problem Gambling, which has over twenty state affiliates. This is primarily an educational effort. These organizations have publications that provide information to those who wish to oppose legislation for the expansion of gambling. The Commission on Christian Life within the Southern Baptist Convention in Nashville has provided leadership in that denomination and in statewide efforts. The General Board of Church and Society of the United Methodist Church can provide leadership and information. The National Coalition Against Legalized Gambling, while only a few years old, has been growing rapidly and has had a major impact upon both local and statewide elections since 1994. About twenty-five state organizations are associated with this coalition.

The bottom line is that the churches have not been persistent enough in battling this major social, economic and moral issue. The pressure from the gambling interests is persistent and well-financed. The pressure will be continuous, and forming temporary crisis-oriented committees against lotteries or casino gambling is not the final answer. A well-financed, sustained effort to educate the public is necessary. Gambling is the addiction of choice in the 1990s, a major player in the economic demise of our nation. There is an ethical problem when the state lures its citizens into gambling by means of advertising a false hope. There is a further ethical problem when the church fails to warn and discipline its members who gamble and fails to warn society of the magnitude of the social and moral issues.

Sin is not defined by the law of the land, nor ethics by the whim of society. The condition of our heart and our will matters in this issue. Just because gambling is legal does not make it ethical to rob the poor. Legal gambling is poor stewardship of the resources the Christian is supposed to believe were provided by, and belong to, God. The state has defined its own morality and sense of social justice, but that morality is destroying people, and the churches must sound an alarm. If stealing from the poor is appropriate, then just a little embezzlement, just a little appliance theft, just a little murder ought to be okay as well. Just don't do it to excess. In reality, however, quantity is really not the issue, it is the quality of the action. Belief in luck and belief in God are contrary.

Churches that run games of chance simply cannot justify gaining wealth regardless of who suffers or who is led into a life of gambling. The church that is indifferent to gambling cares little about the virtues of thrift, industry and service to God and man. Society is in distress, and the church has lost its voice. As a secular reporter once complained after a Catholic priest had defended gambling, "Apparently it is left for mass communications, and those reporters who serve it best, and playwrights, to awaken the public conscience."[22] Our faith in God is much more important than finding an easy way to meet the financial needs of the church.

By glorifying chance, gambling directly challenges the view of God and the structure of his creation that the church is called to uphold. A top official in the Church of England helped form the Union of Bookmakers' Employees. Is that the church's best answer?

Review Questions

1. Describe some of the variations in Roman Catholic thought about gambling.
2. How did churches contribute to the modern gambling boom?
3. What does "materialism has drowned morality" mean?
4. Why do Protestant and Catholic views of gambling differ?
5. What main groups oppose expanded gambling?
6. Which are more important reasons for opposing gambling: economic or religious reasons?
7. Why is gambling one issue upon which conservative and liberal Christians generally agree?
8. What is your church's position on gambling?
9. Should the church be concerned about gambling as a social issue?
10. What can the church do to speak out more effectively about gambling?

Endnotes

[1] _____, "Needed: Counteraction Against Lottery," *The Christian Century*, 80:668, May 22, 1963.

[2] *Spectaculis xvi*, cited in Alson J. Smith, "The Church and Gambling," *The Christian Century*, 76:512, April 29, 1959.

[3] Perkins, E. Benson, "Jeremy Taylor on Gambling," *London Quarterly and Holborn Review*, 184:141, April, 1959.

[4] Smith, *loc. cit.*

[5] *Ibid.*

[6] Sullivan, George, *By Chance a Winner: The History of Lotteries*, New York: Dodd, Mead, 1972, p.19.

[7] _____, "Cincinnati Churches Differ About the Ethics of Gambling," *The Christian Century*, 55:1486, December 7, 1938.

8 _____, "Reformer," *Time*, 33:71, April 24, 1939.

9 _____, "LaGuardia Blasts Church Gambling Monopoly," *The Christian Century*, 59:1548-1549, December 16, 1942.

10 Bodey, Richard Allen, "Gambling: A Bag With Holes," *Christianity Today*, 2:25, December 23, 1957.

11 Fowell, Myron W., "Catholic-Protestant Cooperation," *The Christian Century*, 76:77, January 21, 1959.

12 Smith, *op. cit.*, p. 513.

13 _____, "The States Muscle in on the Numbers Game," *Business Week*, p. 113, May 9, 1977.

14 _____, "The Aleatory Urge," *Newsweek*, 45:82, January 31, 1955.

15 Miller, Robert, "Those Crazy Lotteries," *Maclean's*, 97:14, January 23, 1984.

16 Watson, Tom Jr., "Playing the Lottery is Idolatry," *Christianity Today*, 33:8, November 3, 1989.

17 *Newsweek, loc. cit.*

18 Petersen, William J., "The False and Capricious Lady Luck," *Moody Monthly*, 81:37, October, 1980.

19 Witt, J. Robin, "Compulsive Gamblers: Reno's Lost Souls," *The Christian Century*, 91:1012, October 30, 1974.

20 Drzazga, John, *Wheels of Fortune*, Springfield, IL.: Charles C. Thomas, Publishers, 1963, p. 257.

21 Kantzer, Kenneth S., "Gambling: Everyone's a Loser," *Christianity Today*, 27:12, November 25, 1983.

22 Starkey, Lycurgus M. Jr., "Christians and the Gambling Mania," *The Christian Century*, 80:269, February 27, 1963.

Chapter 10

Solutions: What Can We Do About Gambling?

rancis de Sales said in his *Spiritual Maxims*, "The business of finding fault is very easy, and that of doing better very difficult." When confronted by a trillion dollar industry that has given us legalized gambling in every state except Utah and Hawaii and has spent millions to convince the public that gambling is harmless, the description of the problem is much easier than the solution. The rise of gambling is alarming. The size of gambling is appalling. However, none of this should deter us from doing something. The myth that we can do nothing is false, for we can do many things to curtail gambling.

In the past, churches have directed their efforts toward the supply of gambling, paying little attention to the demand for gambling. We must address both sides of the problem. Similarly, we need sustained individual and corporate attempts to stop gambling.

Begin with You!

STOP YOUR LEGAL GAMBLING. Legality does not create morality. You can't blame the poor for succumbing to the lottery when you keep it alive by occasionally playing it. Do not support this agency of the government that feeds on the dreams of the poor, taxes them exorbitantly, destroys the economy of the state and increases welfare and crime costs. Give up the races. They may be great entertainment and a good spectacle, but there are other entertainments and morally acceptable spectacles. Don't support the wealthy who run the tracks with your resources. Give up your semiannual trip to Las Vegas or Atlantic City. There are certainly more pleasant vacation spots. Cut off this direct pipeline of cash to the underworld of America.

STOP YOUR ILLEGAL GAMBLING. No bookie is harmless. They cannot safely operate without the information on the line and the banking privileges of the layoff that the mob provides. Without mob connections, they could not long survive. The mob is always there for their protection, but not yours. If you wish to reduce crime in your city, stop patronizing those who finance it. If just the church members would stop their illegal gambling, some of the bookies would go out of business.

STOP ALL YOUR GAMBLING ALL THE TIME. Even if the only gambling you do is to spend a stamp on the magazine sweepstakes, understand that doing so is an even more futile effort than buying a lottery ticket. Such action implies you really do not wish to depend upon hard work for your material well-being. If Christians would stop gambling, most gambling enterprises would be in immediate difficulty.

The Second Step—Family and Friends

ENCOURAGE ALL FAMILY MEMBERS TO STOP GAMBLING. Once you have cleaned up your own act, work with those closest to you. Present the clear-cut case against gambling. Lead your family toward a lifestyle based on dependence upon God, hard work and good judgment.

You or a family member may be among the 10 to 12 million addicted or pathological gamblers. You may be aware of the sense of loss in giving up the false dream of millions from the magazine sweepstakes or the lottery. You may be in bondage to the feeling that if you do not play your "lucky" lottery numbers this week, this will be the week those numbers win. These low-level entrapments you have experienced are a mere string compared to the chains of pathological commitment to the action, the chase, the high of steady gambling. If you or a family member is entrapped by gambling, *get help.* The most widely available help is Gamblers Anonymous, which has over 1,000 chapters in the United States. This is a twelve-step program like Alcoholics Anonymous that requires honesty and dependence upon a Higher Power. *A SECOND SOURCE OF HELP* may be a gambling treatment center. Following the American Psychiatric Association's 1980 recognition of gambling as a disorder of impulse control, state governments have begun to take the problem more seriously. Maryland, New York, Connecticut and New Jersey have treatment centers for pathological gamblers. At least forty private treatment centers specialize in gambling. If you are a veteran, the VA has eight centers that treat gambling addiction, one in California, three in Florida, two in New Jersey, one in New York and one in Ohio. Many counselors now specialize in gambling and alcohol abuse, since these so often go together. Notice that most treatment programs emphasize total abstinence. If you could not control the attraction before, you will not be able to do so after treatment, if you continue to give the false dream any foothold in your life. Most of the programs also emphasize restitution, that is, the return of all money stolen or borrowed. This sometimes takes a lifetime.

THE MOST RELIABLE SOURCE OF HELP IS GOD through acceptance of Christ as Savior and Lord of your life. The most frightening aspect of gambling addiction is that so few recover without Christian commitment. The temptations are so ever-present. A great effort of the will is usually not enough. A spiritual change of mind, allied with continuous dependence upon God for strength, is the only really viable solution.

Within your family, if you are married or attached to a pathological gambler, you must *stop enabling his or her gambling.* You must not give this person money under any circumstances. You must receive the gambler's check if he or she is working and pay the bills. Go shopping with the gambler and pay for the purchases. You must warn friends and relatives not to lend money to the gambler. Discreetly warn employers not to advance money under any conditions without your involvement. If the gambler is a male, as most pathological gamblers are, this will bring charges of emasculation and treatment of an adult as a child. Either regard these charges as the manipulative statements they are or resign your family to poverty, divorce and despair.

DO NOT PAY OFF THE PATHOLOGICAL GAMBLER'S DEBTS. Doing so merely allows a new round of borrowing and provides a new stake for more gambling. You are as irresponsible as the gambler if you pay gambling debts. If the debt is owed to a bookie and you fear the bookie may resort to violence to collect, address the problem directly. You will pay them in weekly installments if they turn off the loan-shark interest meter. They are to take no more bets from the gambler, or you will not pay. Should any physical harm come to you or the gambler explain that you have made arrangements for the police to receive full information about the times and places when bets were placed, amounts, the interest charged and all the names you can provide of others using that bookie. If you are married to a recovering pathological gambler and a relapse occurs, seek control of all assets and a legal separation until such time as the gambler quits.

REASON WITH YOUR CHILDREN ABOUT THE DANGERS OF GAMBLING. Most pathological gamblers begin before they are fourteen years of age. The pathology of gambling is progressive. The earlier you start gambling, the sooner you get into difficulty. Do not take guarding your children lightly, for their chances for recovery from drug addiction are greater than from gambling addiction, except in the case of spiritual conversion.

Once your related gambler is in treatment, *get help yourself.* Attend Gam-Anon, the dependents' support group or a church-related group that is knowledgeable about gambling. Weekly group meetings provide sympathy, sharing and support. They cut through self-pity, denial, projection and other behaviors that slow the recovery process. Such groups demand honesty and self-responsibility.

DO NOT EXPECT SMOOTH SAILING. With gambling, the relapse rate is as high as or higher than any other addiction. The temptation is even more constant than for other addictions. As our society has moved rapidly to make more forms of gambling easily accessible, it is much more difficult to isolate oneself from the temptation. In days past, the addicted horseplayer could stay away from the track much more easily than today's lottery or bingo player can stay away from the store, the gas station or the church—gambling is everywhere because society does not take gambling seriously as an addiction.

BE PREPARED FOR SOME DIFFICULTY WITH COUNSELING. Because of the length of the procedure to get to the roots of the problem and address them, financing the counseling can be difficult. Debt is usually what precipitated the recognition of the problem in the first place, and the debt frequently puts help out of reach. Gamblers are also notorious for presenting causes other than gambling for their depression. Even the experienced gambling counselor may struggle to peer through the smoke screens. Gamblers lie. Hospitalization becomes necessary if the gambler becomes suicidal or if gambling *is* a part of another serious emotional disorder.

You should be aware that gamblers go through withdrawal with symptoms similar to drug and alcohol addiction. They have headaches, abdominal pain, diarrhea, cold sweats, tremors and nightmares. These may continue for several days until they gradually begin to subside. Those who genuinely wish to be cured respond well to sleep, rigid routines, proper diet and exercise, the venting of feelings and immense amounts of reassurance that they are valued even if they do not win in competition.

ENCOURAGE YOUR FRIENDS TO STOP GAMBLING. Inform them about the economic, social and moral problems associated with gambling. Encourage them to follow the same steps you and your family are taking. Offer ongoing encouragement to make the necessary lifestyle changes. Share your faith as the only sure way to find the motivation to change.

Perhaps the greatest barrier in the mind of the gambler to recovery is the lingering hope for a quick-money cure to all the problems caused by the gambling. That thought does not die easily. The longing for it continues. Society encourages such thinking, for how often do we say, "When my ship comes in . . ." A second great barrier is the adjustment to finding stimulation in life from relationships and activities other than gambling. Gambling's artificial stimulation, which is largely based on anxiety, is equated by the gambler with recreation. The idea that gambling is recreation dies hard.

The final barrier for many is the magnitude of the restitution. This step is necessary to recapture the joy of finding personal worth in work. It is also a necessary step in breaking down the "something for nothing" attitude. Restitution clearly shows gamblers that they got nothing for everything they had financially—they received nothing for something.

The Third Step—Be Proactive!

EDUCATE YOURSELF ABOUT GAMBLING AND ITS CONSEQUENCES. With this step we move away from focus upon self to focus upon society. The first two steps relate to drying up the demand for gambling. We now add attempts to reduce the supply. If you are to persuade your friends and your church of the dangers of gambling, you have to be equipped with the facts. This may take some work, but reading your daily newspaper is the place to start.

There are many other sources of information. The Public Gaming Research Institute provides information about gambling from a pro-gambling stance with the emphasis upon gambling as a source of revenue. The information is essentially statistical, but it does include news about what states are planning. *Public Wagering and Gaming Business Magazine* is a gambling promotional publication. This magazine focuses only on the positive aspects of gambling and efforts to expand it, and it belittles all opposition. More balanced is the *Journal of Gambling Studies* (available by calling 1-800-221-9369), which is sponsored by the National Council on Problem Gambling and the Institute for the Study of Gambling and Commercial Gaming. Such journals as these need to be read to be aware of what is coming in the months ahead. The NCPG (1-212-765-3833) also produces booklets, posters and videos about gambling problems. The NCPG has fifteen state affiliates. For antigambling information see the *NCALG Newsletter*, a publication of the National Coalition Against Legalized Gambling (1-800-664-2680). This organization has a representative who can assist with political organization to oppose gambling and place you in touch with organizations in your state that are already actively opposing the growth of gambling.

Popular opinion is largely formed by the news media and various weekly and monthly magazines. Most publications have essentially bought the revenue issue as the only one of importance and are favorable toward gambling. They spend little time exploring the negative side. Some journals are of special interest, such as *Jet*, the African-American-oriented magazine. This journal enthusiastically follows the fortunes of winners and glamorizes gambling. I have yet to enter a bookstore where the clerks could find a book about the dangers of gambling, but there are popular magazines and books that purport to tell you how to win. Most of the tips are time- and money-consuming, and they only marginally improve your chances of winning. Every bookstore has a dozen or more books telling you how to win at casino games. These sell well despite the strange fact that there are no consistent winners at the casinos, or they would have shut down.

The main merit of the gambling promotion books is that they do urge their readers to move away from high-loss games like the lottery to better-odds games involving skill. They suggest chances are always better in local games than national ones. The best game, however, is the one not entered. The best throw of the dice, as has been said, is to throw them away.

The Fight in the Community

BEGIN WITH YOUR LOCAL NEWSPAPER. When you spot one-sided presentations, the ignoring of crime or the claim that there is no moral issue associated with gambling, it is time to write. You may have to band together with three or four others, since most papers have limits on how frequently they will publish your letters. The papers have word limits. Do not make personal attacks on individuals. Present the facts evenhandedly but firmly. Encourage a look at losers as well as winners, opponents as well as proponents, and the economic, social and moral impact of gambling. Encourage the paper to investigate the appointments to the lottery board, the perks they receive, the security system that supposedly prevents skimming, advertising expenditures, advertising targeting the poor and the need for stronger governance of the lottery or other gambling. These are the frequently neglected issues, primarily because lotteries are assumed to be clean.

ENCOURAGE YOUR NEWSPAPER TO REFUSE GAMBLING ADVERTISING. Expose any cozy arrangements between paper owners and gambling interests. One major example is the Southam Group of Canadian newspapers whose wholly owned subsidiary, Dittler Brothers of Atlanta, Georgia, prints about 80% of all the instant-win lottery tickets in this country. The Southam Group is not noted for its stance against gambling. On the other hand, encourage your editor, if he or she is a member of a chain like the Knight-Ridder papers that have an editorial stance against gambling. Look for connections between horse and dog owners, track owners and the owners of the newspaper. Gambling involvement shades editorial opinion.

THE SECOND PHASE of a meaningful effort to influence the availability of gambling is to contact your state representative and senator. The hottest issues around the nation at present are the expansion of Native American, casino, sports and interactive electronic gambling from your own home. Plead with your representatives to oppose expansion in these areas.

The Native American tribes (524 of them) are seeking to have any land owned by Indians declared tribal land, not just the traditional reservations. If they succeed, they will be able to put any type of gambling that your state allows anywhere in the state under special privileges granted in federal legislation passed in 1988.

The casino issue is hot. Twenty-three states now have some form of casino gambling. Saturation seems to have been reached in Las Vegas and Atlantic City, since some attrition is taking place and not all casinos are making money. The gamblers have been looking at the great midsection of America for a place to tap the gambling fever in that region. They have failed in Florida and Chicago, but they have succeeded with Native American casinos and riverboats, so the battle continues. Some cities have recognized the danger and quickly organized to combat it, but most seem unaware and open.

The largest portion of illegal betting is devoted to sports betting. We have already indicated that on-the-level games help the bookies use the spread to make money. The danger of the local fix is always there. The cry is currently being raised again that legalizing sports betting will cut into the illegal empire of the mob. This is false. The mob will continue to give better odds, credit and untaxed income, all of which will allow them to prosper alongside any legalized betting. The state security system will never be free from potential bribes, so the mob will eventually penetrate legal gambling as well, as they have occasionally done with the lotteries. Because of these dangers more people (36%) oppose sports betting than any other kind. Seek to build on this sentiment and expand opposition to sports betting. There are two specific efforts you can undertake. The first is to get the point spreads out of your local newspaper, since they only serve to encourage gambling. The second is to get the betting channel off your local cable system.

In addition to opposing areas where gamblers are seeking to expand gambling, address the advertising of already existing gambling. Most ads are geared to the poor and are the least defensible aspect of lotteries. The most notorious case involved the Illinois lottery billboards placed in the Chicago ghetto showing a lottery ticket and the words, "This may be your ticket out of here!" Most other advertising is selling an impossible dream. Protest this. If the urge to gamble is so universal, players don't need to be lured with such ads. If it isn't a natural urge to give your money to a stranger, then the state is clearly immoral to promote the lottery. The ubiquitous presence of gambling outlets is sufficient to inform gamblers of their "right" to gamble. Protests that the lottery will not produce as much revenue as anticipated provide opportunity to educate others about the negative effects on the state economy and the expensive social results of gambling.

APPEAL TO THE CONSCIENCE OF YOUR LEGISLATOR. He or she should not be in the business of promoting a vice. Do not fail to express your opinion to your federal legislators as well. They are more remote, insulated and not as frequently assailed with attempts to promote gambling. The casino interests set up a Washington lobbying office in 1995 with a budget of $3 million to influence your representatives. Federal legislation against gambling is more effective, but in the light of the wealthy opposition, extremely difficult to obtain.

Success against the gambling interests is possible. For twenty successive years the churches of California beat the lottery initiatives. They were finally overwhelmed by large amounts of outside money. Texas rejected horse racing and the lottery from 1978 until 1992. They also were overwhelmed by big money. In the defeats, do not lose sight of the many victories and those saved from a life of poverty. Numerous locales have defeated the expansion of casino gambling, and many more will have to fight this battle. There is no benefit to the community in terms of redevelopment when casinos move in. Industry flees and crime increases. The gamblers' tactic of always asking for more than they want can be turned around. Ask for much more reduction than you think you can get and get at least some reduction.

ORGANIZE WITH THOSE WHO ARE LIKE-MINDED, and do business with outlets that do not sell lottery tickets. Inform them why you are shopping there, and inform your previous outlet why you are no longer shopping there. Recruit others to join you in boycotting your neighborhood gas station until it stops selling lottery tickets. This is an especially appropriate strategy if they have been selling tickets to underage gamblers. Many people will join you in an effort to protect children from exploitation. Grocery stores are willing to stop selling tickets, but they are afraid they will lose even more business. Grocers are aware that lottery sales are directly taken from grocery sales. An organized effort can encourage a grocery to stop the sale.

Find out what the gambling ordinances in your community are and encourage strict enforcement. The presence of illegal gambling entices young people into participation. They do not exercise even the minimal restraint that adults do. Enforcement sets an honest example for young people. Lack of enforcement encourages the youthful cynicism about government that is so endemic at present.

The introduction of state-wide local option legislation is one of the most promising approaches to control already existing gambling. There is a grave danger, however, that it could backfire into legislation on a local option basis to introduce new gambling that does not presently exist. Use this approach only if you already have casinos, lotteries and tracks of all sorts. As the addictive nature of gambling and the extreme difficulty in curing it has become clear, there is strong reason for citizens to have the right to exclude it from their city, county or state. The economic and social consequences reinforce the addictive issue and can build support for eliminating gambling on a local level. Stipulations that lottery outlets cannot be within 300 feet of churches and schools are appropriate. Sure, some will go elsewhere to gamble, but the additional effort required will serve to reduce some of the gambling. The parallel to local option regarding alcohol consumption is a valid one. The first state lottery in New Hampshire had local option, but proponents of gambling suppressed it in subsequent states. With a clearer picture of addiction, it is time to revive the procedure.

If your state is one of the fortunate few without a lottery, make sure every legislator in your state knows that it is a sure way to depress the economy. Kentucky, which began the lottery in 1989 and had to pass the largest tax increase in state history the following year and suffered a decline for the next six years, is not unique. Increased taxation invariably depresses an economy. The lottery removes money the same way taxes do and has the same effect. The remaining smaller states without lotteries will be unable to build large lotteries that produce great amounts of revenue. These states are better off financially to lose some millions externally than many millions internally. There will be more Montanas, with only $4 million incomes and larger social service bills, if the remaining states move toward the lottery.

Enlist the business community and the educational system to oppose gambling. They do not have to do it on moral grounds. There are plenty of economic and social reasons. They opposed gambling in the past. Following World War II there were strenuous efforts to rid manufacturing plants of gambling on site because it depressed productivity. This lesson has been forgotten and needs to be revived. The Greater Miami Chamber of Commerce was one of the leaders in defeating the Florida Casino Bill. They argued that ". . . casinos will stop new banking and industry from coming, because they don't like the kind of environment that gambling breeds."[1] Businessmen are needed to help finance the effort as well. Over $1 million had to be raised in Florida to defeat the $17 million outside gambling interests poured into the state.

The schools and their unions once opposed gambling. The evidence is so much more overwhelming today that these groups should join the effort again. The gambling message is anti-education. Gambling also affects the well-being of children in the classroom if they are poorly fed, poorly clothed and subject to constant pressure because of gambling in the home. The will to work in school is undermined by the constant enticement of the dream of winning millions. Over the years I have surveyed over 300 seventh graders, and despite careful explanation of the meaning of the odds, fully two-thirds expect to overcome those odds. Some freely say they don't need to work in school because their moms won a few hundred last week. This seems an immense amount to them.

FINALLY, ADDRESS THE ISSUE IN YOUR CHURCH. The church is the only hope for meaningful opposition to gambling expansion. Whenever you hear of something being awarded on the basis of chance in your church, protest about the unbiblical nature of such activities. Plead for the congregation to tithe honestly to support the church. If the church is not worthy of that measure of support, you and others need to pray for a change.

Defeat and reduction of gambling will take years of continuous effort. Too often in the past, opposition has been temporary and crisis-oriented. A continuous and sustained effort is necessary to make an impact. Those making money from gambling have every reason to keep the pressure on for the expansion of their "business." We have to be as persistent as they are. The public is unaware of the economic and social damage done by gambling. They must be educated. Since only one-third of Americans gamble regularly, the other two-thirds could change things if we recognize the problem and unite.

What Is Next?

Gambling will continue to grow for several more years. The gradual decline and potential collapse of our economy may eventually be traced to gambling, and major efforts to control it may begin. Such efforts may come too late. Concerned persons need to act now.

We can expect the gambling addiction problem to exceed the problems of alcohol and drug addiction by the year 2000 because the latter two are recognized as serious problems while gambling addiction is not. We may expect the continued growth of treatment centers, counselors and Gamblers Anonymous. While the effectiveness of treatment can be expected to improve, the availability will continue to lag far behind the need. This is true even though Gamblers Anonymous has grown from one chapter in 1957 to 16 in 1959, to 130 in 1970, to 524 in 1980 and to over 1,000 chapters in 1990. State-funded treatment centers will expand, even if health funds are cut, simply because of the great need. Insurance companies may eventually be forced to treat gambling addiction the same way they do other mental disorders and addiction to alcohol and drugs.

As the oppression of the poor by gambling becomes ever more clear, we can only pray that the conscience of Christians will be aroused to a new effort to aid those ruined by gambling addiction. Christians are also the only likely source of moral leadership to seek legislation to control gambling. With God's help the church can begin to push back the tide of immorality and pain that comes from gambling.

More research about gambling is desperately needed. Economists have tended to study microeconomic issues like gamblers' understanding of the odds and how choice or preference for games can be influenced. The studies of John Warren Kindt, Earl Grinols, both of the University of Illinois, and Robert Goodman of the Hampshire College are strong recent efforts on a wider basis. The information that is available points to economic decline and declining state revenues as the lotteries grow. Sociologists have also been hesitant to study the large-scale impact of gambling. There are no well-known studies of the impact of gambling upon divorce, individual crime or suicide. Since money issues are known to be the leading cause of divorce, it seems worthwhile to find out what percentage of those money problems are caused by gambling. Gambling has long since outgrown harmless recreation, but insufficient scholarly study has been devoted to the problem.

Americans have begun to battle drunken driving as the death toll has mounted. We have begun to educate about drugs and so-called safe sex as the social problems became clear. How can we continue to ignore the dangerous economic and social consequences of gambling? Gambling is an insidious threat to the well-being of our nation as well as to personal ambition and character.

The reformer John Knox once said, "Give the devil entry with his finger, and straightway he will shoot forth his whole arm." We are well past the arm stage with gambling.

Those convinced of the significance of this issue must unite in both political and spiritual efforts. We cannot just politically limit gambling without delivering the necessary spiritual message that true peace and satisfaction come from a personal relationship with Christ that needs no shoring up with the thrill of gambling or great wealth. Gambling is no panacea for the economic woes of our society. It is a predator that pillages the people spiritually, emotionally and economically.

Review Questions

1. Which of the suggested steps is most difficult for you to take?
2. How do you balance compassion with withholding money from a desperate gambler?
3. Why is total abstinence so important for both the gambling-addicted and Christians?
4. How can you present the issues to a family member without appearing to be a fanatic?
5. What happens in Christian conversion that enables people to overcome a gambling addiction?
6. How would you begin to educate children about the dangers of gambling?
7. Why and how should you interact with your local newspaper?
8. What is the connection between gambling advertising and the editorial policy of your local newspaper?
9. Which is more important in your state: Making gambling less available, or reducing demand for it?
10. Does your state have an organization opposing gambling?

Endnotes

[1]   _____, "Florida's Casino Vote Carries High Stakes," *Business Week*, p. 87, October 23, 1978.

Index